The Third Realm of Luxury

The Third Realm of Luxury

Connecting Real Places and Imaginary Spaces

Edited by
Joanne Roberts and John Armitage

BLOOMSBURY VISUAL ARTS
LONDON • NEW YORK • OXFORD • NEW DELHI • SYDNEY

BLOOMSBURY VISUAL ARTS
Bloomsbury Publishing Plc
50 Bedford Square, London, WC1B 3DP, UK
1385 Broadway, New York, NY 10018, USA
29 Earlsfort Terrace, Dublin 2, Ireland

BLOOMSBURY, BLOOMSBURY VISUAL ARTS and the Diana logo are trademarks of
Bloomsbury Publishing Plc

First published in Great Britain 2020
This paperback edition published in 2021

Selection, editorial matter, Chapter 1 © Joanne Roberts and John Armitage, 2020
Individual chapters © Their Authors, 2020

Joanne Roberts and John Armitage have asserted their right under the Copyright,
Designs and Patents Act, 1988, to be identified as Editors of this work.

For legal purposes the Acknowledgments on p. viii constitute an extension
of this copyright page.

Cover design by Adriana Brioso
Cover image: Colonnade and long pool of the Getty Villa Malibu Villa of the J. Paul Getty
Museum in Los Angeles, California. (© Joseph Sohm/Alamy Stock Photo)

A catalogue record for this book is available from the British Library.

A catalog record for this book is available from the Library of Congress.

ISBN: HB: 978-1-3500-6277-1
PB: 978-1-3502-3812-1
ePDF: 978-1-3500-6278-8
eBook: 978-1-3500-6279-5

Typeset by Deanta Global Publishing Services, Chennai, India

To find out more about our authors and books visit www.bloomsbury.com and
sign up for our newsletters.

Contents

Illustrations

Figures

Table

Acknowledgments

We would like to acknowledge the help of all the people involved in the production of *The Third Realm of Luxury: Connecting Real Places and Imaginary Spaces*, and, particularly our editor at Bloomsbury, Frances Arnold and her team. We also gratefully appreciate the support that we received to complete this book from Winchester School of Art's Research Fund at the University of Southampton. Lastly, we would like to thank all the contributors for sharing their expert knowledge and for their hard work, good humor, and patience, without which this project on the third realm of luxury would not have advanced from the imaginary to the real.

Joanne Roberts and John Armitage

1

The third realm of luxury: Conceptualizing the connections between real places and imaginary spaces

Joanne Roberts and John Armitage

Introduction

The growing importance of luxury in the everyday sociocultural and economic context is promoting the imaginaries of real and aspirant luxury consumers. This volume explores the connection between real and imaginary luxury consumed in what we refer to as "realms of luxury." We use the term realm for its capacity to denote a domain that may have a real or imagined quality, such that a realm may refer to a territory, as in a specific kingdom (e.g., United Kingdom), or an abstract imaginary sphere, such as paradise. Additionally, a realm may be used to indicate a domain that is not necessarily fixed in time and space. Indeed, realm evokes both real concrete places and imagined, even spiritual or transcendental, spaces. For our analysis we refer to the real places of luxury as the "first realm of luxury" and the imaginary spaces of luxury as the "second realm of luxury." To these we add a "third realm of luxury" where the first two realms exist and connect to generate a real–imaginary space of luxury. The fact that there are real places of luxury not only fuels the imagination but also creates countless unknown possibilities, some tangible others ephemeral, to be discovered and made "real" in the third realm by, and for, individuals, and, by association, extending to some degree into a collective social consciousness. Unlike luxury in the first realm, which is bound by resource limitations and the individual's capacity to consume, and luxury in the second realm, which (although limitless) remains in the minds of individuals, luxury in the third realm offers luxury businesses the opportunity to leverage consumers' imaginations to extend the demand for luxury goods and services that are invested with real–imaginary qualities to near limitless proportions. Consequently, through the exploitation of the third realm of luxury, the imaginaries of luxury consumers are increasingly being commodified according to the logic of advanced capitalism.

Indeed, we argue that we live increasingly *in* the third realm of luxury. The very idea of the real, how we make sense of place, and the means by which we imagine are all becoming invested in, and developed through, the third realm of luxury. The rapidly developing real–imaginary spaces of luxury are thus becoming a key area for studying the issues associated with luxury. Hence, adopting a critical luxury studies perspective (Armitage and Roberts 2016), *The Third Realm of Luxury: Connecting Real Places and Imaginary Spaces* provides an original and significant investigation of the most important developments in the theories and practices of luxurious real places and imaginary spaces over the last fifty years. In doing so, it draws on issues and concepts from philosophy, visual culture, design history, sociology, literary theory, architecture, cultural anthropology, cultural geography, and critical luxury studies.

Throughout the history of civilization, luxury has held cultural and political significance (Berry 1994; Adams 2012). However, promoted by advocates including Adam Smith (1981 [1776]) and David Hume (1987 [1742]), luxury's economic importance increased, such that it is thought to have significantly contributed to the industrial revolution in eighteenth-century Britain (Sombart 1967 [1913]; Berg 2005). Today, luxury is an important economic sector. Certainly, its growth, fueled by rising prosperity, especially among the emerging countries, is outpacing general economic growth. In 2017, the consultancy Bain & Company estimated that the luxury market grew by 5 percent on 2016 to reach an estimated value of €1.2 trillion globally (D'Arpizio, Levato, Kamel and de Montgolfier 2017). Hence, the production and consumption of luxury contributes to welfare through the employment of hundreds of thousands of individuals across the world. In the UK alone, the luxury sector contributes £32.2 billion to the economy, accounting for 2.2 percent of gross domestic product, directly employing 113,000 people, contributing £5.2 billion to the Exchequer through tax and National Insurance, and generating exports valued at £25 billion (Walpole 2017: 5). In addition to the direct positive economic impact of the production and consumption of luxury on, for instance, employment and taxes, the luxury sector has beneficial indirect influences, through spillover effects, on to other parts of the economy, including through the skills and innovation it promotes. Moreover, through the growing economic strength of the luxury sector and those consuming its products and services, including the growing ranks of the middle classes across the globe, and, importantly, the super-rich,[1] it has gained renewed cultural and political significance in contemporary society. The rapid rise of luxury business since the 1980s coincided with the economic restructuring, deregulation, and privatization following the widespread introduction of neoliberal economic policies. Such policies accelerated economic globalization and left individuals exposed to the vagaries of international markets. While some individuals prosper in this highly competitive neoliberal environment of reduced government intervention, others struggle without the support of the state. The consequence of growing inequality was further accentuated by the global financial crisis of 2008 (Piketty 2014). The fortunes of luxury brand companies and their consumers are intimately linked to the economic system with all its capacities to shape the sociocultural and political environment. It is for these reasons that a critical appreciation of luxury, including its spatial expressions, is required.

Furthermore, luxury has continued to shape places and spaces. Through its influence on cities, luxury contributes to the construction of what Paris (2017) calls "prestigious places," improving the built environment with potential benefits for all, directly through an improved quality of life and through attracting overseas tourists and the subsequent creation of jobs in the hospitality and tourism sectors. Accordingly, luxury impacts on real places, including, for instance, the design of retail outlets (Crewe 2016), shopping malls like Crystals at CityCenter, Las Vegas (Sharr 2016), homes (McNeil and Riello 2016), and tourist locations (Thurlow and Jaworski 2012; Calefato 2014). The effect of luxury on real places is of course not novel. For example, Annette Condello's (2014) *The Architecture of Luxury* elaborates on a range of tangible places of luxury from the Greek colonial city of Sybaris in Southern Italy founded in the eighth century BCE up to late nineteenth- and early twentieth-century locations in the US cities of New York and Chicago. But what is new in the contemporary era is the *scale* of the impact that luxury is having on the built environment. Hence, discussions of luxury and space tend to focus on real places, including how wealthy consumers of luxury, namely the super-rich, affect housing in capital cities (Atkinson, Burrows, and Rhodes 2016) and transform urban and rural landscapes in locations ranging from London and Kentucky to Ireland and St. Barts (Hay 2013). Moreover, while this volume adds to this body of work through consideration of real places of luxury, from the interior of automobiles and apartments to the homes of autocratic leaders, home and hotel interiors, museums and estates, free ports and California vineyards, it goes beyond the contemplation of the real places to consider the imaginary spaces that luxury evokes.

Similarly, luxury in the sphere of the online or virtual world is one form of imagined space of luxury that has received much attention in recent years, with the rise of social media and online fashion retailers like the Yoox Net-A-Porter Group and Farfetch that specialize in the sale of luxury online. Yet, studies focus on concerns such as the challenges of marketing luxury online (Okonkwo 2010) or how luxury is produced and consumed through luxury brand websites (Rocamora 2016). Digital luxury certainly involves an imaginary element of relevance to this volume, which examines how the interaction between real places of luxury such as retail stores can promote imaginary luxury and how imaginary luxury, including that stimulated by digital technologies, influences the real places of luxury. Clearly, real retail environments have evolved as a result of online luxury, by developing and focusing on experiential aspects of shopping, as the case of Burberry, which has been at the forefront of using technologies to enhance its stores and access to its merchandise, so clearly demonstrates (Roberts and Armitage 2017).

However, the aim of this book is to go beyond the interaction of the real and the somewhat limited—and limiting—imaginary stimulated by digital manifestations of luxury driven by marketing and advertising. For the contributors to this volume, the imaginary includes the very nature of being in and experiencing luxury in the concrete exterior and social world to the innermost personal imaginings of the individual. In this way, as editors, we offer an original contribution to appreciations of luxury and its impact on real places and the imaginary spaces of individuals and social groups. Moreover, we argue that the connections between real places and imaginary spaces produce a third realm of luxury, a realm of luxury that has yet to be explored in a systematic fashion and which the contributions to this volume investigate.

In this opening chapter, we examine the interaction between luxurious real places and imaginary spaces and we introduce and expand on our idea of the third realm of luxury. We begin by elaborating the nature of luxury before exploring the idea of connecting real places and imaginary spaces. We go on to argue that the interplay and interdependencies between these two spatial realms of luxury is today exposing a third realm of luxury arising from the nexus of real and imaginary luxury. Through our expansion of the idea of the third realm of luxury in this chapter, then, we offer an original conceptual approach to understanding and analyzing the spatial aspects of luxury. We provide the context for the contributions to this volume, all of which analyze luxury in a real place and its connection to imaginary spaces. We close this chapter by highlighting how each contribution offers evidence of the significance of the third realm of luxury.

Luxury: From an idea to a reality

In the present-day developed nations, luxury is ubiquitous in the sense that the term luxury is attached to an increasingly wide array of objects, services, and experiences. For instance, in London, as elsewhere, it seems that every new apartment or housing development is marketed as luxury real estate. Whether marketers' use of the label luxury is always valid is of course debatable (Roberts 2018). Luxury is usually associated with expensive, rare, and refined products and services of the highest quality consumed in the context of a rich and comfortable lifestyle lived in sumptuous surroundings, from the plush interiors of luxury homes to affluent urban districts and comfortable rural locations. Luxury as "luxus" in classical Latin implies effeminate sensuality, a passion for splendor and pomp, and "luxuria" indicated excess, extravagance, and moral weakness (Adams 2012: 7–8). Luxury is also viewed as unnecessary, superfluous, or an indulgence and, as such, its moral justification is open to question (Roberts 2019). Christopher J. Berry's (1994) seminal study, *The Idea of Luxury*, defines luxury as the antonym of necessity, in that luxury is distinct from basic needs, which are non-intentional and universal. For Berry (1994), luxury occupies the realm of wants and desires. Yet, he also argues that luxuries must be the object of socially recognized desire, and, as such, capable of giving pleasure rather than merely relieving pain. Luxury is relative and therefore cannot be objectively defined because it depends on cultural, social, and individual contexts and meanings. Hence, a luxury can range from a small box of Charbonnel et Walker Champagne truffles costing £14 to a £32 million Sunseeker 155 private yacht. For those with busy lives, quality time of one's own or shared with loved ones can be a luxury. Luxury is, then, more than a term to describe a group of objects or services; rather, it is an idea.

Furthermore, though a luxury is normally something that one desires for reasons other than necessity, some luxury is consumed *as* a necessity to demonstrate one's position of power in society. Such conspicuous consumption was first analyzed by Thorstein Veblen (1899) in his study of the leisured class in the United States during last decade of nineteenth century. Contemporary luxury consumption of this sort is evident in, for example, the lives of heads of state and those among the top echelons of major businesses. This instrumental consumption of luxury may have its origins in desire, but, as individuals reach positions of power, what was once desired becomes a necessary accessory and, in some cases, is transformed into the authoritarian luxury elaborated by Featherstone (Chapter 3) in his study of the homes of autocratic leaders such as

Adolf Hitler and Donald Trump. Moreover, some luxuries may be necessities because they are the object of intense desire or intense identification. Therefore, Berry (1994: 41) defines luxuries as *"those goods that admit of easy and painless substitution because the desire for them lacks fervency"* (original italics). Consequently, not all unnecessary goods or services are luxuries to everyone.

For most people, desire, rather than necessity, drives the consumption of luxury. But whether such desire originates with the individual is doubtful given the promotion by advertisers and the mass media of the false social needs identified by Herbert Marcuse (1991 [1964]). Distinguishing between "true" and "false" social needs, Marcuse (1991 [1964]: 5) describes true needs as "the vital ones—nourishment, clothing, lodging at the attainable level of culture." In contrast, false needs are

> superimposed upon the individual by particular social interests in his repression: the needs which perpetuate toil, aggressiveness, misery, and injustice. . . . Most of the prevailing needs to relax, to have fun, to behave and consume in accordance with the advertisements, to love and hate what others love and hate, belong to this category of false needs. (Marcuse 1991 [1964]: 5)

Discriminating between true and false needs is important because, in advanced capitalist societies, where most true social needs have been fulfilled, the satisfaction of false social needs drives major segments of the economy. This is clearly illustrated by our analysis of the role of new media in promoting false needs for luxury goods and services (Armitage and Roberts 2014). Of course, in the contemporary era, luxury brands are active in cultivating the desire for their goods and services by deploying the full range of stimuli available in contemporary visual culture including fashion, photography, works of art, television, cinema, and social media (Armitage 2019).

Luxury as a branded good or service has attracted much research attention from scholars in the fields of marketing and consumer behavior. A luxury brand refers to a commercially provided good or service rather than an idea of luxury. Hence, a leisurely bath might be someone's idea of a luxury, but it would only be the outcome of a luxury brand if it were taken in a luxury bathroom, hotel, or spa or if luxury bath products were part of the experience. There have been many attempts to define luxury brands (Ko, Costello, and Taylor 2017). For instance, in relation to luxury brands, Chevalier and Mazzalova (2012) argue that a luxury product must have a strong artistic content, be the result of craftsmanship, and be international, while Allérès (1990) identifies luxury in terms of three levels of accessibility: inaccessible—exclusive unique items; intermediate—expensive replicas of unique items; and, accessible—factory produced in large production runs. Drawing on a review of the luxury brand literature, Ko, Costello, and Taylor (2017: 2) define a luxury brand as a product or service that consumers perceive to:

1. be high quality;
2. offer authentic value via desired benefits, whether functional or emotional;
3. have a prestigious image within the market built on qualities such as artisanship, craftsmanship, or service quality;
4. be worthy of commanding a premium price; and
5. be capable of inspiring a deep connection, or resonance, with the consumer.

In the contemporary era, we are also witnessing a proliferation of terms, such as "new luxury" or "mass luxury" resulting from the efforts of traditional brands to trade up as well as the drive for profits among luxury businesses by offering products and services to a wider global market (Kapferer and Bastien 2012). Such changes also reflect the fragmentation of the production process, such that the design process may involve significant artistic inputs and craftsmanship, but the final luxury goods and services can be mass-produced in low-cost locations without any loss of quality (Thomas 2007). The democratization of luxury (Kapferer and Bastien 2012), characterized by the shift to mass luxury, has been accompanied by the emergence of the idea of "meta-luxury" (Ricca and Robins 2012) and "über luxury" (Quintavalle 2013) to make a distinction between mass-produced luxuries and those luxuries that remain exclusive, often because they are rare or the result of high levels of skill and craftsmanship, and their cost renders them accessible only to the super-rich. Examples of such luxuries include bespoke tailoring, haute couture, and individually designed items from jewelry to private jets and yachts. Despite the rhetoric of exclusivity, however, the major luxury brands identified in, for example, Deloitte's (2018) annual report on luxury goods operate in mass markets, albeit in international rather than national markets.

The academic literature concerning luxury is expanding rapidly, reflecting its growing importance in the economy and sociocultural contexts. Nevertheless, as Gurzki and Woisetschläger's (2017) analysis of this literature suggests, research continues to focus on luxury's history as a social phenomenon and as a means of signaling status, as a cultural product and carrier of cultural meaning, and marketing and consumer behavior issues, including luxury brands as a source of identity and brand equity, and how to create a luxury brand as well as issues concerned with authenticity including counterfeiting. Research that considers its real and imaginary spatial dimensions is underdeveloped. This is no doubt because, in today's economically developed nations, the idea of luxury is overwhelmingly associated with the very real luxury goods and services available in specific local and global markets. While this market manifestation of luxury dominates luxury discourse, there is also another dimension of luxury that is imagined by the consumer. This imaginary luxury, though having the appearance of independent creation by the individual, is no less commodified than the mass-produced luxury branded goods and services available in the marketplace. Indeed, the real luxury goods and services distributed by the luxury brand companies depend on the allure of luxury created in the imaginary. Hence, the imaginary fuels consumers' desires for luxury goods and services in specific places.

As noted, the neoliberal market system has supported the expanding demand for luxury and the growth of the luxury sector. This growth not only results from the increased prosperity and therefore the ability of individuals to afford luxuries but is also stimulated by the promotion and privileging of the individual's desires above the needs of the community and society. No longer viewed as excessive in the face of poverty and growing inequality, luxury becomes an expectation for the successful individual. Luxuries, like the Rolls-Royce Ghost Black Badge automobile described by Armitage (Chapter 2), become a reward for successfully competing in the neoliberal market system. Moreover, luxury brands, through the construction of "heritage stories" (Cox 2013) and present-day associations, support identity formation (Belk 1988; Brewer 1991) and appeal to the individual's simultaneous need for a sense of distinctiveness and belonging. Rather than engaging in real local communities, consumers seek, through the consumption of luxury brands, to identify with the set of values proclaimed by Chanel and Patek Philippe, among others, as well as with the virtual and often imagined luxury brand communities that are stimulated by the marketing departments of multinational corporate luxury groups like Moët Hennessy Louis Vuitton (LVMH), Richemont, and Kering. Hence, branding and marketing promote an imaginary sense of belonging and community, senses that have been lost in the atomized competition that drives the neoliberal market economy (Bauman 2001). This imagined sense of community is aptly demonstrated by Samuel Austin and Adam Sharr (Chapter 7) who focus on the production and marketing of luxury in imagined notions of home and community in the "The Collective"—student-style housing for professionals priced out of London's housing market.

As the chapters in this volume illustrate, advertising and marketing are important for the creation of certain imaginary spaces. The skillful construction of visual and textual representations of luxuries in real places disseminated through traditional and new media stimulate imaginary spaces of luxury in individuals, fueling the false needs upon which the luxury brand business is crucially dependent (Marcuse 1991 [1964]; Armitage and Roberts 2014). Through advertising and the promotion of luxury, the personal imaginings of individuals are commodified. By extending their markets from the real into the imaginary realm, luxury brand companies expand the finite real consumption capacities of the individual to near infinite imagined possibilities. Luxury as a commodity is, then, constructed and consumed in specific real places, and it is also an idea, an aspiration, an illusion, produced and consumed in abstract spaces. Increasingly, luxury brand companies are harnessing the commercial potential of these imaginary spaces of luxury to sustain above market rate returns for their shareholders.

Connecting real places and imaginary spaces: Toward the third realm of luxury

From real places and imaginary spaces to a Thirdspace

To expand further on the connections between real places and imaginary spaces, it is necessary to explore the distinction between place and space. The terms place and space are often used interchangeably and regarded as synonymous, yet they can also be used to conceptualize two very different spatial phenomena. The nature of place and space as well as the relationship between them has been much discussed in the field of human geography (Hubbard, Kitchin, and Valentine 2004), and it is from contributions to this field that we take inspiration for our conceptualization of the spatial realms of luxury that we elaborate here.

Place represents a distinctive type of space that is constructed and defined by the lived experiences of people. In a sense, a place is named space like a specific city, park, building, or room, that is associated with distinctive activities. Place involves embodiment, of being in a place (Thrift 2003), and places are fundamental to belonging and a sense of identity (Hubbard, Kitchin, and Valentine 2004). In contrast, space is a much broader term that can be conceived of as an abstraction, for instance, as in Euclidean geometry. Additionally, space may be a function of social relations, socially produced and consumed (Lefebvre 1991a).

Henri Lefebvre (1991a) argues that spatiality goes beyond the dialectic between place and space to a "trialectics" of spatiality, which captures the differential entwining of cultural practices, representations, and imaginations (Hubbard, Kitchin, and Valentine 2004). In so doing, Lefebvre offers a three-way dialectic between spatial practice (perceived space), representations of space (conceived space), and spaces of representation (lived space) (Soja 1996). Building on Lefebvre's idea of a trialectics of space, Edward W. Soja (1996) proposes the notion of Thirdspace. He notes that, until the late 1960s, mainstream spatial imaginations revolved principally around a dual mode of thinking about space. The first mode he described as a Firstspace perspective and epistemology, "fixed mainly on the concrete materiality of spatial forms, on things that can be empirically mapped"; the second mode he described as Secondspace, "conceived in the ideas about space, in thoughtful re-presentations of human spatiality in mental or cognitive forms" (Soja 1996: 11). Soja goes on to argue that "an-Other" form of spatial awareness began to emerge from the late 1960s, which he referred to as Thirdspace. For Soja, this Thirdspace is a product of a "thirding" of the spatial imagination:

> the creation of another mode of thinking about space that draws upon the material and mental spaces of thinking about spaces of the traditional dualism but extends well beyond them in scope, substance, and meaning. Simultaneously real and imagined and more (both and also . . .), the exploration of Thirdspace can be described and inscribed in journeys to "real-and-imagined" (or perhaps "realandimagined"?) places. (Soja, 1996: 11)

Furthermore, Soja includes among the defining qualities of Thirdspace:

> a knowable and unknowable, real and imagined lifeworld of experiences, emotions, events, and political choices that is existentially shaped by the generative and problematic interplay between centres and peripheries, the abstract and concrete, the impassioned spaces of the conceptual and the lived, marked out materially and metaphorically in *spatial praxis*, the transformation of (spatial) knowledge into (spatial) action in a field of unevenly developed (spatial) power. (Soja 1996: 31; original italics)

We take inspiration from the understanding of real and imagined space developed in the work of Lefebvre and Soja to develop our idea of the third realm of luxury. This is because, in their spatial analysis, they identify the illusory nature of space and the interplay between real, concrete, places, such as six-star hotels and luxurious country houses, with imaginary, abstract spaces, including fantasies stimulated by depictions of luxury in advertising and other media, to create an-Other, which is simultaneously both real and imaginary and more. Yet, our idea of the third realm of luxury differs from Lefebvre and Soja's ideas in that our spatial analysis not only foregrounds the concept of the realm but also concentrates exclusively on the realms of luxury, and it is to these that we now turn.

The realms of luxury

For our purposes, the first realm of luxury includes real concrete places of luxury, such as a spacious luxury penthouse apartment in a desirable location, while the second realm of luxury refers to the imagined space of luxury, like a small apartment marketed and imagined as luxurious despite its confined size and less desirable location. The real places and the imaginary spaces overlap, one influences the other and vice versa, but their existence also affords a third realm that is more than the two together. Thus, since it is more than the sum of the first two realms, the third realm of luxury is where the first two realms exist as illustrated in Figure 1.1. In the third realm, the real and the imaginary connect to realize the real–imagined space of luxury as a "real" place where, for instance, the lived experience of the luxury consumer is played out in the small apartment packaged as luxurious. The fact that there are real places and concrete forms of luxury not only fuels the imagination but also creates countless unknown possibilities, some tangible, others ephemeral, to be discovered and made real in the third realm by individuals. It is in this way that property developers are able to sell what would once have been regarded as serviceable social housing as a luxury abode. Indeed, the third realm offers a multitude of opportunities for individuals and luxury businesses alike to discover new luxury possibilities.

Gaston Bachelard's (2014) philosophy of imagination in *The Poetics of Space* also contributes to our understanding of a third realm of luxury. He argues that spaces, such as those of the house, with its cellar and attic, of drawers, chests, and wardrobes, of nests and corners, and of nooks and corners offer images that bring together memory, perception, and fantasy that intersect and reverberate in unpredictable and unrealized ways. Hence, for Bachelard "imagination augments the values of reality" (2014: 25) such that we remake and reinhabit imaginings in our own unique way. Moreover, through the creation of such personal interpretations of luxury goods and services, individuals find a foothold

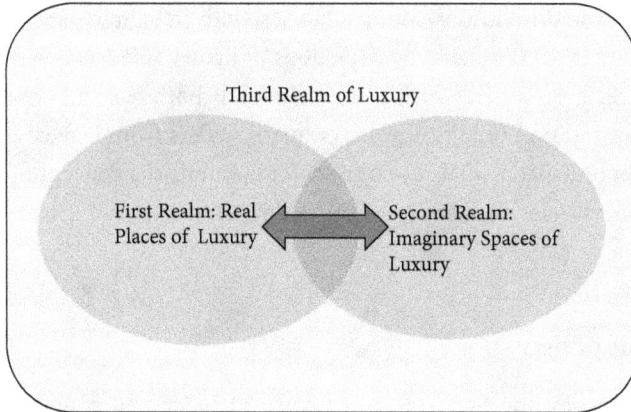

Figure 1.1 Connecting real places and imaginary spaces in the third realm of luxury.

in the advanced capitalist system, which, in this personal imagining, offers positive futures achieved through hard work and compliance with neoliberal market norms. In this way, resistance to the contemporary economic system is dissipated and gives way to imaginings of the possibilities of comfort and security available in the third realm.

Similarly, in the second edition of *Critique of Everyday Life* (1991b), originally published in 1958, Lefebvre points to what we refer to as the third realm in relation to the adoption of what would have been luxurious technologies at the time, such as washing machines, television sets, and electric cookers, in the sometimes dilapidated or squalid homes of French workers and peasants in the immediate post-1945 period:

> Far from suppressing criticism of everyday life, modern technical progress *realizes it*. This technicity replaces the criticism of life through dreams, or ideas, or poetry, or those activities which raise above the everyday, by the critique of everyday life from within: the critique which everyday life makes of itself, the critique of the real by the possible and of one aspect of life by another. Compared with lower or degraded standards of living, everyday life with all the superior mod cons takes on the distance and remoteness and familiar strangeness of a dream. (Lefebvre 1991b: 9–10; original italics)

Moreover, Lefebvre goes on to comment directly on luxury:

> The display of luxury to be seen in so many films, most of them mediocre, takes on an almost fascinating character, and the spectator is uprooted from his everyday world by an everyday *other* than his own. Escape into this illusory but present everyday world, the fascination of ordinary objects which scream

wealth, the seductive powers of the apparently profound lives led by men and women who move among these objects, all this explains the momentary success these films enjoy. (Lefebvre 1991b: 10; original italics)

Such insight remains relevant today; in a world characterized by depleted resources and pressures on real concrete places, the imaginary space and the allure of a life lived in luxury become ever more attractive. Hence, the spatially limited luxury real estate explored by Conley (Chapter 4) connects real places and imaginary spaces to produce a third realm of possibility and potential in the minds of consumers and the real places of the apartments presented as luxury despite their small size and less desirable location.

Of course, luxury has always coexisted in both the concrete places of, for instance, the opulent domestic interiors of stately homes, as well as in the illusory spaces of the dreams and desires of individuals and groups. But, we argue, it is in the past fifty years that imaginary spaces of luxury have escalated in significance. The end of the post-World War II period of growing prosperity in the advanced nations, following the oil crises and rising competition from the Far East in the 1970s, we suggest, provoked a retreat from the hard times of real lives and fueled the desire for better times played out in the imaginary. This last was an imaginary augmented by affordable goods advertised as luxuries through, for instance, the adoption of the language of Romanticism in the promotion of "cheaper" synthetic materials as luxurious in the context of 1970s' interior design (Turney, Chapter 5). Moreover, in the wake of the 2008 global financial crisis, many consumers have once again turned to the imaginary spaces of luxury as a retreat from the real and ongoing experience of austerity. This more recent mediated engagement with the imaginary has been assisted by the expansion of social media.

Imaginary spaces of luxury are facilitated not only in the individual's imaginary through the absorption of a host of visual media but also in the virtual environments and communities supported by globally connected digital technologies and social media platforms (e.g., Facebook, Twitter, Instagram, WeChat, Weibo, and YouTube). Such visual media provide stimuli for the dreams and fantasies of those who engage with them. For instance, social media users can play out their fantasies through the screen of a mobile telephone and share their dreams with an audience of followers. In so doing, they contribute to the promotion of luxury consumption and add to a social imaginary from which individuals draw their own personal imaginings. Undoubtedly, accessible real places of luxury, such as the department stores of Harrods and Bergdorf Goodman, or urban retail locations, like London's Mayfair or Los Angeles' Rodeo Drive, feed the dreams and aspirations that create imaginary spaces of luxury, and, in turn, these spaces fuel the desire for the consumption of luxury in real places. Additionally, through the possession of, or aspiration to own, a globally recognized Chanel handbag or Patek Philippe watch, or to drink a Château Mouton Rothschild 1945, people engage with an imaginary space, and, through engaging in social media, become members of an "imagined community" (Anderson 1991) indulging in the third realm of luxury. Through both the real and the imaginary, individuals attain moments of lavish indulgence such that we might refer to this state of being as luxuriating in the third realm of luxury: a space that is not actually real but is more than merely a figment of the individual's imagination.

Simultaneously, in search of ever-increasing profits, today's luxury brand companies are actively encouraging the desire for luxury at a real global and imaginary level. Although the global expansion, particularly into emerging countries, of the largely European luxury brand companies currently offers a means of maintaining their rate of growth, territorial expansion has its limits. In contrast, the spaces of the imaginary are infinite, and they hold the promise of ever-expanding demand for increasingly expensive luxury in a world of diminishing tangible resources. Through the intensification of desires nurtured in imaginary luxury space, consumers seem willing to pay ever higher prices for less and less. Consequently, securing a place in the imaginary spaces of luxury becomes a key objective for luxury brand companies. For, it is through the power of the imaginary that the reality of standardized and mass-produced "luxury" available in flagship stores is evaded in favor of an illusion of rarity and craft production. In such contexts, the often-conflicting realms of real and imaginary luxury coexist in a seemingly harmonious fashion. Indeed, it is here that we see the key developments occurring in the third realm of luxury.

Consequently, the sleek advertising and promotional activities of luxury brands, including product placement in films, stimulate memory, perception, and fantasy, encouraging false needs realized in the desire for luxuries goods and services. Accordingly, luxury businesses commodify not only real places but also the imaginations of consumers. Real places of luxury and imaginary spaces of luxury are combined and play on the individual's personal experiences of space as well as generic historical and futuristic representations of luxury. Thus, a third realm of luxury is generated, one which has collective and personal dimensions. By retaining the collective element, such as the luxury logo reproduced on multiple versions of the same "unique" handbag, business is able to gain economies of scale in production, while personal interpretation ensures that the individual receives an exclusive product; the mass-produced handbag takes on a unique personal meaning through a combination of the association with the luxury brand and the individual's own interpretations created through memories, fantasies, and imaginings. The individual's very own luxury handbag becomes a rare, exclusive, and unique purchase or what Lucien Karpik (2010) refers to as a singularity.

To clarify our notion of the third realm let us delineate the various realms of luxury in the example of the handbag outlined above:

1. The first realm of luxury is the luxury handbag that exists in real space and time. However, it is not the mass-produced one that the individual purchases; rather, it is the one-off version handmade by artisans.

2. The second realm of luxury refers to the type of unique handbag that exists in the first realm of luxury. Yet, for most individuals, this luxury exists in an imaginary space, which is promoted in luxury brand advertising and marketing campaigns to fuel the false needs but real desires of potential consumers.

3. The third realm of luxury is the real–imagined luxury handbag that the individual purchases, and which exists in a real–imaginary space within which the first two realms are actually located. Although the handbag may have been mass-produced, it is nevertheless imbued with imaginary qualities that are recognized as unique to its owner.

Therefore, the third realm is a knowable *and* unknowable, real *and* imagined lifeworld. Yet, through our analysis, the third realm is specifically related to luxury goods, services, and experiences. In the third realm, the connection between and blending of the real and the imaginary allow luxury brand companies to commodify the dreams, emotions, and the very being of a consumer. As Roberts (2018) has demonstrated, luxury brands leverage the unknown to promote their goods and services. Furthermore, because appreciating the nature of luxury often requires depth of knowledge only available to experts, consumers often rely on the marketing materials of luxury brand companies and are therefore vulnerable to exploitation (Roberts and Armitage 2016). Consequently, luxury provides one more field of activity through which advanced capitalism is able to colonize the inner most feelings, dispositions, imaginings, and uncertainties of individuals.

Exploring the third realm of luxury: The book

Having elaborated on the idea of the third realm of luxury and how it relates to the connections between real luxury places and imaginary luxury spaces, this chapter provides the context for the contributions that follow, all of which contribute in diverse ways to appreciate the spatiality of luxury through investigations of how the imaginary is shaped and reconstructed in relation to real places. The sequence of the chapters allows the reader to gain an understanding of the third realm of luxury through progression from the ontological spatial level to a variety of domestic interior and socially constructed spaces and on to how luxury facilitates the enclosure of exteriors and the creation of secret spaces, and, finally, how real places of luxury have given way to the imaginary space of the global market. In this final section, a brief overview of the contributions that follow is provided.

Hence, in the next chapter, "Being luxurious: On the Rolls-Royce Ghost Black Badge and beyond," John Armitage explores the nature of being luxurious through adopting a Heideggerian philosophical approach to enhance understanding of the being, time, and space of luxury. Providing an analysis of being, time, and space through engagement with a luxury automobile—the Rolls-Royce Ghost Black Badge—Armitage expands on what he refers to as the unique founding event of luxury, an event that draws on both the real luxurious place of the luxury automobile "with the horseshoe sweep design of the interior, cocooning you in a visceral experience of luxury"[2] and the imaginary spaces promoted by a combination of advertising and the consumer's desire to engage in a third realm of luxury.

The nature of being is also central to Mark Featherstone's contribution, "The architecture of authoritarian luxury," in which he considers the relation between luxury and political power through an exploration of the deployment of architecture by three autocratic leaders beginning with the Roman Emperor Nero, followed by Adolf Hitler, and, finally, Donald Trump. Drawing on Walter Benjamin's work on paranoid sovereignty, Featherstone develops a theory of authoritarian luxury. He employs Gaston Bachelard's phenomenology of homeliness to contrast a vision of paranoid place characterized as insulated from the outside with the idea of the home which is open to the spaces of imagination, to capture the meaning of two novel forms of luxury: the first, contained, objective, ontic luxury, and, the second, experiential, subjective, ontological luxury. Featherstone argues that the psycho-political struggle between these two dimensions of luxury can be observed in the cases of the three authoritarian leaders studied. Moreover, Featherstone argues that "Trump symbolizes the meaning of the third realm of luxury in contemporary America, where possessions of luxury things (ontic luxury) fuses with the promise of luxury experience (ontological luxury, or a universe without limitation) in the creation of a third space of luxury power."

By contrast, "Inhabiting luxury spaces," by Verena Andermatt Conley, is concerned with urban forms of dwelling and being luxurious. Increasingly, in the contemporary urban landscape, Conley suggests, long-standing communities are being uprooted to make way for redevelopment and gentrification. She focuses on this type of urban real estate development in New York and Boston, USA, to show how classical paradigms of luxury continue to be replaced by a proliferation of mass-marketed luxury products, just as Roland Barthes (1972 [1957]) and Baudrillard (2006 [1968]) noted over fifty years ago. Redeveloped and appropriately marketed with minimal furnishings and wide-angle photography, small apartments become luxurious homes. According to Conley, the illusion of space and luxury is created by architects and designers removing walls and using special lighting and cleverly placed mirrors. Hence, she argues, it is through an imaginary consumption of "luxury" that an ideology of identity and community is imposed. Here, again, we see the characteristics of the third realm of luxury where the real and the imaginary, together, generate an illusion of inhabiting luxury homes in the contemporary urban context.

The next chapter focuses on the domestic interior and the third realm of luxury in 1970s' Britain. In "A touch of the exotic: Sensuality as luxury in the 1970s' domestic interior," Jo Turney considers the appropriation of terms and images associated historically with luxury and their juxtaposition with 1970s' expressions of "luxury": specifically, sensory engagement and sensuality in advertisements for home furnishings. She argues that the fusion of traditional and modern furnishings reflected the zeitgeist and cultural values of the period. For Turney, debates surrounding the public in the private, the individual and the collective, the manufactured and bespoke, sex and sexuality, gender roles and sexual relationships, and the natural and synthetic are initiators of the consumption of, and discussions surrounding, new "luxury" home furnishings. The chapter reveals the role of advertising and marketing in generating imaginings of luxury and desire for household goods of real or imaginary luxury quality.

The interior is also the subject of Peter McNeil's contribution, "The emptying of the interior: Luxury, space, and the hotel effect in contemporary life." However, McNeil's focus is on the shifting concept of luxury in terms of its relationship between the space of the hotel room and the domestic interior, particularly in the period 1890–2018. McNeil traces the development of the luxury hotel from its origins in North America through to the contemporary era, along with the styles selected to convey luxury interiors from the eighteenth century to twentieth-century art deco, kitsch fantasies, "barefoot luxury" in

Southeast Asia, and present-day notions of generic "modern luxury." The "hotel effect," McNeil argues, has created a desire among the upper and middle classes to emulate the appearance of a contemporary hotel in their domestic lives. The real places of luxury hotels have fueled imaginary spaces of luxury such that they are being processed in the third realm of luxury to feed back into the real places of homes that increasingly emulate the sparsely furnished interiors of contemporary luxury hotels.

The role of luxury in imagining, producing, and advertising notions of home and community is considered in "'The Collective': Luxury in lounge space" by Samuel Austin and Adam Sharr. Exploring the marketing, architecture, interior design, and, particularly, what they refer to as the "lounge space" of the housing block called "The Collective," Austin and Sharr show how what is effectively minimal space student housing is presented as luxury to aspirational young professionals. "The Collective" is marketed as a community full of opportunity. Yet, as Austin and Sharr demonstrate, it is a community that, unlike the Narkomfin Communal House completed in Moscow in 1928 (a radical exercise in social engineering which sought to socialize previously private aspects of domestic life into the public sphere to consolidate a communist way of life), is a product of a neoliberal market system with its emphasis squarely on the individual. Again, we see the manipulation of the real and the imagined living and community space by marketing strategies and management policies that, through leveraging the real and imaginary, promote a third realm of luxury.

Yet, the third realm of luxury is not confined to the aspirations of those unable to acquire true luxury in the sense of the unique or rare objects or experiences. As George E. Marcus, in "'The third realm of luxury' as I experienced it in the legacies of Getty and the Rockefellers: Elite enclosure, 'as far as the eye can see...'" reveals, the third realm is as relevant to the elite as it is to the aspiring young professionals living in "The Collective." But, whereas most individuals do not have the luxury of being able to shape space into place in the most personally desired way, the rich and the aristocratic have always enjoyed the capacity to enclose themselves, to hide away from the wider world, guarding their own privacy and way of life. Exploring the spatial creations of such elites through the cases of the Getty Center in Los Angeles and the Rockefeller Pocantico estate near Sleepy Hollow, New York, Marcus reveals that the ability to enclose, or emplace, oneself, is never complete; rather, it is permeable at the edges of such enclosures and landscapes. Marcus shows how the elite are able to edit what they see, even if only in an incomplete way. The real world beyond their estate can remain largely hidden to them and vice versa.

The subject of the hidden, of the secret, of the unknown, or of the unknowable is a feature of the third realm of luxury. This theme is taken up in Joanne Roberts's "Secret spaces of luxury: Ignorance, free ports, and art," in which an ignorance perspective is deployed to consider the secrecy that is adopted in the lives of the super-rich and, particularly, in relation to their use of secure storage facilities located in free ports, where luxury goods, ranging from works of art to fine wines, are stored. Roberts reveals how the secrecy afforded by free ports gives rise to imaginary dimensions of luxury for the owners and for those who know little about such places. Fine art is taken as an exemplar to explore the changing nature of ownership brought about by the use of free ports as luxurious objects move from real places to imaginary spaces and beyond to the third realm of luxury.

In the final contribution to this volume, "Of space and time in California wine," Ian Malcolm Taplin discusses the transition of wine from a functional complement to food to a luxury product. He traces the history of wine and its rise to the status of a luxury good from medieval European production among Benedictine and Cistercian monks to the emergence of Bordeaux as a premier wine region and wine production in California, where Napa Valley has developed as a source of exclusive, high quality, wines that have acquired cult status in recent decades. Over centuries, wine has thus been transformed from a place-specific product consumed in local markets to a luxury desired and consumed in markets around the world. The real places of production enhanced through present-day viticulture knowledge and technologies are combined with the imaginary spaces of luxury wine promoted through the careful rationing of output to build cult status, branding and advertising, and the rating and awards systems, which make up what Karpik (2010) refers to as an "authenticity regime." As Taplin notes, "Fine wine has become the quintessential experience good, but its tangible properties derive not just from its future use value but in the aura that surrounds something that is impermanent." It is this aura that allows individual consumers to enhance the luxury and transform it into something that is of unique personal value. Removed from its original context, wine has therefore entered a new realm as a positional good whose value comes from the anticipated pleasure of drinking it, or merely possessing it; a pleasure that arises from the combination of the real and imaginary in the third realm of luxury.

Through the diverse contributions to this volume, the reader is offered an original introduction to the realms of luxury and, in particular, to the idea of the third realm of luxury as a distinctive understanding of how luxury pervades and connects the real and the imagined to produce myriad possibilities.

The interplay of the real and imaginary is evidenced in the vocabulary used to describe the very nature of being luxurious (Chapter 2), the architecture of authoritarian luxury (Chapter 3), and spatially compressed luxury real estate (Chapter 4) to the 1970s' trends in interior design (Chapter 5) and the contemporary influence of the minimalist hotel on domestic interiors (Chapter 6). Further contributions, through their consideration of the marketing of the communal housing of "The Collective" apartment block as luxury (Chapter 7), the privileged enclosures of the elite (Chapter 8), and the tangible global places of free port storage facilities and the transformation of the idea of luxury from a local place bound notion to a global imaginary conceptualization through the examples of art and wine (Chapters 9 and 10), reveal how the changing spatial reach of luxury generates real and imaginary luxury communities that connect in the third realm of luxury.

References

Adams, W. H. (2012), *On Luxury*, Dulles, VA: Potomac Books.

Allérès, D. (1990), *Luxe, Stratégies-marketing*, Paris: Economica.

Anderson, B. (1991), *Imagined Communities: Reflections on the Origin and Spread of Nationalism* (revised and extended edition), London: Verso.

Armitage, J. (2019), *Luxury and Visual Culture*, London: Bloomsbury Academic.

Armitage, J. and Roberts, J. (2014), "Luxury New Media: Euphoria in Unhappiness," *Luxury: History, Culture, Consumption*, 1 (1): 111–32.

Armitage, J. and Roberts, J. (2016), "Critical Luxury Studies: Defining a Field," in J. Armitage and J. Roberts (eds), *Critical Luxury Studies: Art, Design, Media*, 1–21, Edinburgh: Edinburgh University Press.

Atkinson, R., Burrows, R., and Rhodes, D. (2016), "Capital City? London's Housing Market and the 'Super Rich,'" in I. Hay and J. Beaverstock (eds), *International Handbook of Wealth and the Super Rich*, 225–43, London: Edward Elgar.

Bachelard, G. (2014 [1964]), *The Poetics of Space*, translated by M. Jolas, New York: Penguin.

Barthes, R. (1972 [1957]), *Mythologies*, translated by A. Lavers, New York: Noonday Press.

Baudrillard, J. (2006 [1968]), *The System of Objects*, translated by J. Benedict, London: Verso.

Bauman, Z. (2001), *Community: Seeking Safety in an Insecure World*, Cambridge: Polity Press.

Belk, R. (1988), "Possessions and the Extended Self," *Journal of Consumer Research*, 15 (2): 139–68.

Berg, M. (2005), *Luxury and Pleasure in Eighteenth-Century Britain*, Oxford: Oxford University Press.

Berry, C. J. (1994), *The Idea of Luxury: A Conceptual and Historical Investigation*, Cambridge: Cambridge University Press.

Brewer, M. B. (1991), "The Social Self: On Being the Same and Different at the Same Time," *Personality and Social Psychology Bulletin*, 17 (5): 475–82.

Calefato, P. (2014), *Luxury: Fashion, Lifestyle and Excess*, London: Bloomsbury Academic.

Capgemini (2017), *The Wealth Report 2017*, Capgemini. Available online at: http://www.worldwealthreport.com/

Chevalier, M. and Mazzalovo, G. (2012), *Luxury Brand Management: A World of Privilege*, 2nd edition, Singapore: Wiley and Sons.

Condello, A. (2014), *The Architecture of Luxury*, Farnham, UK: Ashgate.

Cox, C. (2013), *Luxury Fashion: A Global History of Heritage Brands*, London: Bloomsbury Academic.

Crewe, L. (2016), "Placing Fashion: Art, Space, Display and the Building of Luxury Fashion Markets through Retail Design," *Progress in Human Geography*, 40 (4): 511–29.

D'Arpizio, C., Levato, F., Kamel, M.-A., and de Montgolfier, J. (2017), *Luxury Goods Worldwide Market Study, Fall–Winter 2017*: *The New Luxury Consumer: Why Responding to the Millennial Mindset Will Be Key*, December 22. Available online at: http://www.bain.com/publications/articles/luxury-goods-worldwide-market-study-fall-winter-2017.aspx (accessed May 29, 2018).

Deloitte (2018), *Global Powers of Luxury Goods 2018: Shaping the Future of the Luxury Industry*, Deloitte Italy SpA. Available online at: https://www2.deloitte.com/global/en/pages/consumer-business/articles/gx-cb-global-powers-of-luxury-goods.html# (accessed June 1, 2018).

Gurzki, H. and Woisetschläger, D. M. (2017), "Mapping the Luxury Research Landscape: A Bibliometric Citation Analysis," *Journal of Business Research*, 77: 147–66.

Hay, I., ed. (2013), *Geographies of the Super-Rich*, Cheltenham: Edward Elgar.

Hubbard, P., Kitchin, R., and Valentine, G. (2004), *Key Thinkers on Space and Place*, London: Sage Publications.

Hume, D. (1987 [1742]), "Of Refinement of Arts," in *Essays: Moral, Political and Literary*, ed. E. Miller. Indianapolis: Liberty Press.

Kapferer, J.-N. and Bastien, V. (2012), *The Luxury Strategy: Break the Rules of Marketing to Build Luxury Brands*, London: Kogan Page.

Karpik, L. (2010), *Valuing the Unique: The Economics of Singularities*, Princeton, NJ: Princeton University Press.

Ko, E., Costello, J. P., and Taylor, C. R. (2017), "What Is a Luxury Brand? A New Definition and Review of the Literature," *Journal of Business Research*, Online First, August 31.

Lefebvre, H. (1991a), *The Production of Space*, Oxford: Blackwell Publishing.

Lefebvre, H. (1991b), *Critique of Everyday Life—Volume I*, 2nd edition, translated by J. Moore, preface by M. Trebitsch, London: Verso.

Marcuse, H. (1991 [1964]), *One Dimensional Man*, London: Routledge.

McNeil, P. and Riello, G. (2016), *Luxury: A Rich History*, Oxford: Oxford University Press.

Okonkwo, U. (2010), *Luxury Online: Styles, Systems, Strategies*, Basingstoke, UK: Palgrave Macmillan.

Paris, M., ed. (2017), *Making Prestigious Places: How Luxury Influences the Transformation of Cities*, London: Routledge.

Piketty, T. (2014), *Capital in the Twenty-First Century*, Cambridge, MA: Harvard University Press.

Quintavalle, A. (2013) "Über Luxury: For Billionaires Only," in J. Hoffmann and I. Coste-Manière (eds), *Global Luxury Trends: Innovative Strategies for Emerging Markets*, 51–76, Basingstoke: Palgrave Macmillan.

Ricca, M. and Robin, R. (2012), *Meta-luxury: Brand and the Culture of Excellence*, London: Palgrave Macmillan.

Roberts, J. (2019), "Is Contemporary Luxury Morally Acceptable? A Question for the Super-rich," *Cultural Politics*, 15 (1) 48–63.

Roberts, J. (2018), "Luxury and Ignorance: From 'Savoir Faire' to the Unknown," *Luxury: History, Culture, Consumption*, 5 (1): 21–41.

Roberts, J. and Armitage, J. (2016), "Knowing Luxury: From Socio-Cultural Value to Market Price?" in J. Armitage and J. Roberts (eds), *Critical Luxury Studies: Art, Design, Media*, 25–46, Edinburgh: Edinburgh University Press.

Roberts, J. and Armitage, J. (2017), "Luxury Fashion and Creativity: Change or Continuity?," in Tsan-Ming Choi and Bin Shen (eds), *Handbook of Luxury Fashion Retail Management*, 147–65, Singapore: Springer.

Rocamora, A. (2016), "Online Luxury: Geographies of Production and Consumption and the Louis Vuitton Website," in J. Armitage and J. Roberts (eds), *Critical Luxury Studies: Art, Design, Media*, 199–220, Edinburgh: Edinburgh University Press.

Sharr, A. (2016), "Libeskind in Las Vegas: Reflections on Architecture as a Luxury Commodity," in J. Armitage and J. Roberts (eds), *Critical Luxury Studies: Art, Design, Media*, 151–76, Edinburgh: Edinburgh University Press.

Smith, A. (1981 [1776]), *An Enquiry into the Nature and Causes of the Wealth of Nations*, Indianapolis: Liberty Classics.

Soja, E., W. (1996), *Thirdspace: Journeys to Los Angeles and Other Real-and-Imagined Places*, Oxford: Blackwell Publishing.

Sombart, W. (1967 [1913]), *Luxury and Capitalism*, translated by W. R. Dittmar, Ann Arbor: University of Michigan Press.

Thomas, D. (2007). *Deluxe: How Luxury Lost Its Lustre*, London: Penguin.

Thrift, N. (2003), "Space: The Fundamental Stuff of Geography," in S. L. Holloway, S. Rice, and G. Valentine (eds), *Key Concepts in Geography*, 95–108, London: Sage Publications.

Thurlow, C. and Jaworski, A. (2012), "Elite Mobilities: The Semiotic Landscapes of Luxury and Privilege," *Social Semiotics*, 22 (4): 487–516.

Veblen, T. (1899), *The Theory of the Leisure Class: An Economic Study in the Evolution of Institutions*, London: Macmillan.

Walpole (2017), *Thriving After Brexit: The Impact of Leaving the EU on the UK's Luxury Goods Sector and Policy Recommendations*, March, London: Walpole.

Being luxurious: On the Rolls-Royce Ghost Black Badge and beyond

John Armitage

Introduction

This chapter begins with a short conceptual account of being, time, and space in Martin Heidegger's (1962) *Being and Time* before progressing to a philosophical attempt to enrich our appreciation of them through analyzing being, time, and space together. Yet the aim of the chapter is to augment our understanding of the being, time, and space of luxury, four terms brought together to articulate the disposition or truth of "being luxurious" apprehended on the basis of the experience of a luxurious event, and which I call the unique, founding event of luxury, which is repeatedly happening as abundance, explicitly the event of the presence of sumptuous enjoyment itself. Consideration is therefore given to the key theme of being luxurious and to the significance of my argument concerning the presence of luxuriousness as a time and space. As the chapter's title implies, the idea of the being, time, and space of the Rolls-Royce Ghost Black Badge, an automobile that offers a new dimension of "pure luxury," with "added depth," is paramount in my theoretically specific contribution alongside concepts such as abundance and plentifulness. A conclusion is set aside for a critical appraisal of Heidegger's and my own philosophical work and my estimation of its probable impact. However, to appreciate my idea of being luxurious, we need to commence by examining Heidegger's major engagement with being, time, and space.

Being, time, and space

As Heidegger states in *Being and Time*, the idea of space had until the twentieth century occupied a humble position in philosophy where time and temporality had assumed a dominant position (1962: 418). The space of being received a significant injection of credibility and new thinking, I argue, through Heidegger's reconceptualization of space that avoids any attempt to effect a transcendental appropriation of space by time, to effect a dialectical identity between space and time, or any attempt to trace the spatiality of being as neither a space nor a being, or the tracing of the spatiality of being back to temporality, which cannot be sustained. Heidegger's underlying commitment, then, is to the finding of a satisfactory phenomenological analysis of the spatiality of being and of space. A whole history of Heidegger's withdrawal from "untenable" analyses of spatiality remains to be written, not merely of its temporalizing aspects and dimensions but also of the diverse modalities of the spatialization of being, I argue, which would at the same time be the history of his attempted elimination or exclusion of spatiality from the history of inner human time and temporality. We might comment that this history of inner human time and temporality substantially calls into question the whole project called *Being and Time*, given the implicit intervention spatiality must make for Heidegger to be able to describe the historical discourse and structures of inner human time and temporality in his own work on the problem presented by spatiality. It is on this basis that Heidegger sees his attempt to found being upon its ecstatic temporality. Yet it is also on this basis that he attempts to ward off the emerging "limit" or "menace" posed by spatiality concerning existential analyses of being and temporality. For it is precisely at this juncture where spatiality threatens Heidegger's privileging of the temporality of being, of temporality as the very *ground* (*Grund*) (an odd choice of terminology given that ground is associated with spatial concepts such as earth, soil, land, and field) of the ontological constitution of being, among which spatiality figures as temporal *distentia*, as temporal distension or enlargement, as spatializing *dispersion*, the spacing of the *dis-tancing*, and of the orientation characteristic of the spatiality of being.

A further contribution to this debate and to a temporal perspective on space is Heidegger's phenomenological comments on the foundational primacy of time for being in space, for a form of being that somehow excludes the human body or the spatialization of being in the world. For Heidegger seems to suggest that the passage from mind to body can be described as a subordination of the spatial themes of corporeality in favor of ecstatic temporality. Both his theoretical paradigms in *Being and Time* and the foundation of spatiality upon temporality, his securing of the independence of space with reference to time, his articulation of the dependence of being with regard to space, we might suggest, are today dominated by categories of temporality rather than by categories of space, as in the dominance of the *present* as the temporal dimension of concern, which is the mode of being of being delivered over to its concern-full everydayness, and by way of which, for Heidegger, its spatiality is also made manifest. As an example, we might cite Heidegger's designation of temporality as a foundation (*Grund*), as a primary dimension over space or the way in which for him time makes pure space manifest. Time's conditioning of the possibility of all representations and greater extension than space, its relationship to spatiality, its lack of obvious exteriority, and the privileging of interiority create a sense of space (which constitutes the world) in which the world, being, and their questioning are "turned" in another direction, toward hermeneutics, Greek philosophy, Plato, Aristotle, and the beginning of metaphysics. He argues that this attention to the question of the truth or meaning of being, to the questioning of thinking being, is a maneuver that allows him not only to deepen the question of being but also to reorient his attitude regarding the question of space, and to map his position in relation to "time-space" or *Zeit-Raum* (1989). Time and space stand, then, for Heidegger as the symbols of the wider contemporary question that is our decision about belonging to historical being or abandoning ourselves to what is not. But let us proceed with our interpretation of Heidegger's designation of temporality as a foundation by initially going back to the analytic of spatiality in *Being and Time* and its limits.

Of course, Heidegger's descriptions of space in the first section of *Being and Time* remain classics of the theme of the worldhood of the world and highlight some of the key aspects in his refusal to envisage the world as simply subsisting in space. Three leading issues are the following: first, making a break with the classical attitude for which the world did subsist, reduced to nothing but the totality of bodies in the objective space of Euclidian geometry, including the implications this has for a critique of the attitude of modern philosophy or its forgetting that geometrical space is itself constituted by an objectifying operation which can only be carried through on the basis of a world to which we are attached existentially and whose intrinsic spatiality we have to understand; second, the relation of the problem of space and of the spatiality of the surrounding world to being through calling into question ontological dualism or the rejection of the distinction between *res cogitans* (a thinking thing, as in the mind or soul) and *res corporea* (a bodily substance, as in its physical dimensions) to the extent that this distinction would, if operative, obscure the spatiality proper to human being while reducing the beingness of every natural being to *extensa* (to a substance or thing); and, third, the impact upon both being and human spatiality of the eclipse of any understanding of the effective modalities of our being in the vicinity of things with reference to the horizon and on the basis of the world. Being under conditions of modernity, therefore, entails living in an "a-cosmic" universe that is literally out of this world and thus capable of ignoring its human spatiality.

An influential account of those themes of attempting to rediscover the spatiality of being is offered by Heidegger when he sets out to describe the spatiality of the surrounding world. Heidegger sees those entities which present themselves with a primordiality that precludes their reduction to *res extensa* (to an extended thing) as distinguished by the use which beings make of them in their everyday lives. Where some might aim for an account of spatiality as *res extensa* or the in-itself of an objectivist ontology, Heidegger displays an awareness of presence and of modes of concernful involvement to produce a spatiality of those things which are close at hand, which are ontologically determined by their availability for utilization. Heidegger, then, remains committed to things presenting themselves as tools or instruments in their character of being-in-order-to: for instance, the hammer for the fabrication of the table or the construction of the house. Where others might miss this structure of being, which is determined by its reference to instruments revealing themselves as always already inserted into a whole, into an instrumental totality, Heidegger argues that the effect of paying attention to the totality of things, to their structures and use, can be illustrated by describing what happens in an office. The things found there are not disposed in such a way that each can be taken in isolation from the others. Together, and based on their relations with others, they determine the physiognomy of the room. What we encounter in the first place is the room in that susceptibility for signification which belongs to it: an office and not just a volume geometrically defined by the four walls which its simple things fill up. We discover the room, Heidegger also tells us, as a residential instrument—or, following Le Corbusier's functionalism—a "residential machine" (Frampton 2001). Thus, the uncovering of the environment in *Being and Time* is characterized throughout by a totalization of meanings and objectives, by our experience of connections, of linking instruments one with another, an analysis that never ceases to implicate both the spatiality proper to the being of an instrument and that is inherent in the whole into which it is inserted. Those entities which are available for utilization are entities whose "proximity" can only be determined regarding an oriented proximity which arises out of that concern which characterizes being in its everydayness. The being of the instrument only acquires its meaning regarding a practice, and its proximity is therefore that of its instrumental accessibility. This means that the being of the instrument does have its "place" where it can be found, but that place can only be found regarding other places with which it constitutes a network or a "totality" of places.

Heidegger, then, is a major theorist of place, arguing that, since it has itself to be situated, the condition of the possibility of a totality of places lies in a "wherein" (*Wohin*) in general, a wherein which has concernful involvement in mind from the first. The result is that everyplace must be referred to a "region," to a "side," all of which is already implied every time one specifies the place of a thing from "this side" rather than from "that side" as a function of the spatiality inherent in everydayness. However, in determining these regions in terms of a more general orientation upon the space of the surrounding world, one enormous being, the sun, plays a privileged role as both an ever-changing and yet constantly and regularly available "place" for the diverse and variable uses to which we put the light and the heat which these regions yield. Indeed, these regions serve to differentiate the celestial regions, which furnish pre-established points of reference for the terrestrial regions which these places occupy and articulate. Hence, the course of the sun and existential meaning are for us conjoined through notions of east and west, through the inalienable possibilities of being and as the uncovering of the spatiality of the surrounding world. Yet, while existentially relevant because it is founded on the spatiality of being, Heidegger's account of the spatiality of the surrounding world does presuppose the being of being, to whose spatiality it belongs essentially to adopt an orientation and to make distances disappear. Being's encounter with intra-mundane entities implies a "making space," an arrangement that makes possible a range of places upheld by gestures such as "displace" or "remove"—gestures which do not require the intervention of a theoretical attitude or the constitution of a geometrical space. Uncovering the spatiality of the world in the direction of its ontological presupposition, namely, the spatializing being of being, however, raises numerous questions concerning Heidegger's approach to spatiality in *Being and Time*.

For instance, as Günther Anders (van Dijk 2000: 101) has argued, Heidegger presents our encounter with the spatiality of the world and with its intra-mundane entities from the perspective of an already obsolete age—a restricted mode of involvement that is non-synchronous even with Heidegger's own era. Heidegger's paradigm, then, despite his talk of the modern office, is the lost world of the labor of the village artisan, of craftsmen and women toiling in their pre-capitalist workshop world oblivious to the world of capitalist factories, high-tech mechanisms, advanced forms of organization, and automation. Moreover, Heidegger's analysis of spatiality is not only "totalizing" in the sense that instruments and the places that belong to them are somehow "en-framed" in a system of reciprocal references, uncoverings, and uses but also surrounded by walls whose function is to close space down to allow being to orient itself in time, space, and everyday life. Preoccupied with revealing the spatiality of the world of everyday life, then, Heidegger reduces, neutralizes, or brackets the phenomenal appearance of open space, of nature (in fact, Heidegger excludes nature from his analytics of spatiality), of spectacle, of, in fact, the analytic of the sublime or questions of poetic vision. In other words, Heidegger's is a limited analytic, which only considers the spatiality of the world from the standpoint of its significance and of its practicality as a function of that specific existential which is involvement. Besides, what is one to say of those worlds in which instrumentality cannot be isolated inasmuch as the available entity/tool incorporates from the start other determinations and references than those of its utility alone? And how, based on its configurational aspects, can one fail to attribute to the spatiality of the world a metaphorical and symbolic tenor which, to some extent, already encompasses and surpasses the pragmatic significance that is uncovered across our everyday lives? Finally, the analytic of spatiality in *Being and Time* suffers from the absence of any investigation bearing on the constitutive spacing of *Mitsein*, of being with others, which impacts not only upon our understanding of the space of the world (spaces and distances of a cultural order) but also upon any consideration of the spatiality of being itself as well as upon the question of *Jemeinigkeit*, of mineness, that is to say, the question of selfhood or identity. How are we to understand being's character of being "mine" if we do not take into consideration the "here" and "there" constitutive of intersubjectivity which, from the start, manifests itself as an inter-corporeal phenomenon? Again, we rejoin the question of embodiment which the very project of *Being and Time* failed to articulate more exactly in its connection with the question of spatiality and of the question of mineness.

As Heidegger's statements suggest, his new awareness of space, which prompted the emergence of a new analysis of the spatiality of the world, has been accompanied by arguments on a transformed sense of nature, the spatiality of the world and of being. We might interpret this to mean that relations between the world and everydayness, entities, modes of being, temporality, history, and the question of the spatiality of the world, and the case for the disclosure of the latter derived from temporality alone remain not only contentious but also, perhaps inevitably, incomplete.[1]

Being luxurious

While Heidegger's *Being and Time* introduces his thoughts on space from the perspective of the twentieth-century human sciences, his interest is in being, time, and temporality rather than in being luxurious. Being luxurious, I argue, must be conceived of in such a way that it includes an attempt to achieve an impure or profane appropriation of space by the time of desire, to achieve a dialectical equivalence between space, time, and impurity (inclusive of impure looks, immoral countenances, and signs of nastiness and overindulgence). Here, I shall attempt to trace the spatiality of being luxurious as *another time and space of being*, of being outrageous. The tracing of the spatiality of being back to temporality thus becomes a project concerning the time-space of the luxurious, of the extravagant. The issue is whether such a project can be maintained, and, in addition, however attractive such a project might be, whether it is possible to discover an acceptable phenomenological examination of the time-space of being luxurious. I am not attempting to provide an entire history of the time and space of excess since that would be impossible within the context of a single chapter. Instead, I will document the temporal features of desire and its aspects of want as well as the varied modalities of desire's torments when temporalized and spatialized as being luxurious. I argue that the history of inner human time, temporality, and the spatiality of luxuriousness has not so much been removed or rejected from cultural history but has been neglected or marginalized, particularly concerning individual human beings and their luxurious habits. This history of the inner human time of luxuriousness and the temporality of self-indulgence does not significantly call into question the entire project of *Being and Time* (wherein the realm and concept of the luxurious is never mentioned). Rather, such a history raises the question of *another* whole project named "being luxurious," which is my explicit intervention into the time and space of the voluptuous, where our accounts of the luxurious, histories of idleness, discourses of bacchanalia, and the organizing of the inner human time and temporality of excess are works on the problems posed by the time and space of the luxurious. Hence, I see my contribution as a post-Heideggerian effort to *supplement* our understanding of the foundation of being, to augment our appreciation of being through an idea of luxuriousness as an ecstatic time-space wherein people are essentially joyful. Unlike Heidegger, I am not concerned with the boundaries or threat presented by spatiality but with existential studies of people leading "soft," luxurious lives, with being and time under conditions where people let their feelings run. Thus, the time-space of indulgent, luxurious flowing is not understood as a time-space of danger but, instead, as a privileged time-space where the time-space of being luxuriously wealthy, for instance, becomes, if not a ground, then an *event of presence itself, another time and space*, the temporal-spatialization, perhaps, of our conception of leisured individuals in a bygone luxurious age, individuals brimming with delightful things, and with the ontological constitution of being luxurious. Temporality and spatiality therefore begin to appear as temporal yet also spatial displays of luxury, as spatialized diffusion, dissolution, and *liquefaction*, as in the precious pearl which Cleopatra, the last active ruler of Ptolemaic Egypt, dissolved and drank as a luxurious expression of love to Mark Antony and portrayed in *The Banquet of Cleopatra* (Figure 2.1), a painting by Giovanni Battista Tiepolo completed in 1744 and now in the National Gallery of Victoria in Melbourne, Australia (Ullman 1957). The painting depicts the conclusion of a bet between Cleopatra and Mark Antony as to which one could provide the most expensive feast. As told in Pliny the Elder's (1991) first-century CE *Natural History*, Cleopatra wins the bet: after Mark Antony's feast, Cleopatra drops a rare and precious pearl from her earring into a cup of vinegar and drinks it once the pearl has dissolved. The third person depicted by Tiepolo at the banquet table is Lucius Munatius Plancus, at the time Antony's friend, who was to determine the winner of the bet. Such temporal-spatial distancing, dispersion, and dissolution through a precious pearl can only be described as the proclivity typical of the time and space of being luxurious.

My contribution to temporal-spatial understanding is different from Heidegger's, although I do retain a phenomenological conception of sumptuousness if not his argument for the foundational preeminence of time for being in space. This is because I am concerned with a form of being luxurious that *includes the human body* as an important site of the temporalization and spatialization of being luxurious in the world. Furthermore, Heidegger appears to overlook the fact that the journeying hither and thither between the luxuriant reality of the body and the luxurious imaginary of the psyche is a journeying not only from a *place* to a *space* but also to another, perhaps *third realm*, in our case, the third realm of being luxurious. Unconcerned with subordinating spatial corporeality to ecstatic temporality, I am, in its place, concerned with *elevating the event of the presence of spatial corporeality within luxurious temporality*, with luxuriousness given its proper "place" so that it can, finally, "appear." Divergent from Heidegger's conjectural exemplars in *Being and Time*, I do not seek to found but to *elevate* the temporality and spatiality of the subject of the luxurious to create a discourse that accepts the anxieties of the luxurious and that recognizes, for example, our corporeal *dependence* upon the times and

Figure 2.1 *The Banquet of Cleopatra* by Giovanni Battista Tiepolo (1743–44), oil on canvas (2,503 × 3,570 mm); National Gallery of Victoria, Melbourne, Australia. Wikimedia Commons (Public Domain).

spaces of luxurious grass spangled with wild flowers, upon the *sight* of villages situated amid the most luxurious groves. What I am trying to express is that sense of our dependence upon being luxurious with regard, for instance, to the "space" of a woman's luxurious hair. Certainly, the luxurious today is also increasingly governed by categories, times, and spaces of "unhealthy" flesh, by the temporal *presence* of an "unhealthy" abundance of flesh in the form of the so-called "obesity crisis" (Shugart 2016). The temporal-spatial element of the luxurious is of concern, therefore, because it is a style of being of being, of everyday sumptuous enjoyment, wherein indulgence is, somewhat removed from Heidegger's world, made obvious in all its temporality and spatiality. Consequently, we might sidestep Heidegger's description of temporality as a foundation or ground, and concentrate, instead, on my account of time-spaces as *elevated events*, as being luxurious, as principal facets of, among other things, the time and space of being impure, of how for me the subjective time-space of the consciousness of luxuriousness presences not so much "things" as the subjectification of desire, of luxuriousness apparent as pure intentionality. Time-space accordingly conditions an entire array of luxurious opportunities, from representations of sexuality to the touching and caressing of the time-space of the human body: "You came to me this morning and you handled me like meat," intones singer-songwriter Leonard Cohen (2009) in his "Recitation" featured on his *Live in London* album: "You'd have to be a man to know how good that feels, how sweet." These relations of temporality and spatiality take us into the "sin" of luxuriousness, into both its superabundant exteriority and its favoring of interiority as immoral luxuriousness. Our sense of this time and space, of the composition of the realm of the luxurious, is one wherein the realm of being luxurious starts to become a *quest*: a quest to turn Heidegger's thought in another direction, toward a hermeneutics of luxuriousness, a philosophy of adulterousness and debauchery, filth, brothels, and the metaphysics of shamelessness. I argue that we need to pay less attention to the quest for the truth or meaning of being and pay more attention to the quest for the truth or meaning of being luxurious: to the quest for thinking being luxurious as a productive form of "weakness" or "softness," "feebleness," "frailty," "flimsiness," and "fragility," as a move that permits us to widen or spatialize the quest for being luxurious and to reorient our approach concerning issues of time and space, and to chart our location with regard to the fertile time-space that is the *Zeit-Raum* of luxuriousness and superabundance. Thus, for me, the time-space of luxuriousness is a sign of the wider contemporary quest to *belong to historical being* sooner than a sign of the assumed contemporary quest to abandon ourselves to the routine use of, or pleasure in what is excellent or expensive, whether food, dress, furniture, or machines of any sort. In a word, the time-space of luxuriousness is representative of our contemporary quest, of our decision, to save ourselves. Thus, in continuing with my reinterpretation of Heidegger's designation of temporality and spatiality as a foundational event, we first need to advance through an analysis of temporality and spatiality beyond the confines of *Being and Time*.

Evidently, Heidegger's explanations of space in *Being and Time*, while models of the genre, remain problematic because the subject of the luxurious characteristics of the worldhood of the world is wholly absent: where, for example, is the desire to give and receive flattery? Leonard Cohen (2009) again: "I'm good at love, I'm good at hate, it's in between I freeze. Been working out, but it's too late, it's been too late for years. But you look good, you really do, they love you on the street. If you were here I'd kneel for you, a thousand kisses deep." Hence, and without wishing to disparage Heidegger's refusal to imagine the world as merely existing in space, I do want to draw attention to *another world*, a paradise lost to Heidegger, and that is the time and space of fun and games, of luxuriousness, feasting, and dancing.

Such problematic issues are, however, not simply confined within Heidegger's description of space. Nor are they limited to breaking free from traditional outlooks on the world and its maintenance, to being, to bodies, to the objective space of Euclidian geometry, and to the disregarding of geometrical space, or to the preparation of objectifying operations. What, for instance, are the philosophical implications of a world of luxuriousness? And how might we offer a critical understanding of luxurious time and space? The problem of the temporality and spatiality of the adjoining world to luxurious being is, for example, also connected to the problem of the temporalities and spatialities of today's adjoining world to luxurious being in terms of the great inequalities of fortune. These inequalities are, for instance, detailed in Thomas Piketty's (2014) *Capital in the Twenty-First Century*, which both uncovers the alarming facts about present-day inequality and makes the case that we are well on the road to re-establishing "patrimonial capitalism," a society and a culture controlled by oligarchs who inherit rather than earn their vast wealth. Being luxurious can, then, be questioned because it sets up and/or maintains ontological, moral, and sociocultural dualisms based on the acceptance of the division between the opulent temporalities and spatialities of the "super-rich" (Roberts 2019) and the impoverished temporalities and spatialities of what we might call the "super-poor." Such divisions, when and where operational, I suggest, *obscure* the temporalities and the spatialities of *both* human beings used to great luxury *and* those human beings used to great austerity. These divisions therefore shrink, contract, and shrivel the beingness of every human being. This divisive temporal and extensive feature of being, temporality, and human spatiality may, of course, appear outwardly as, say, the refined and intense enjoyment of the super-rich. But, in fact, often, the effect of inequality upon being, temporality, and human spatiality is such that the world of luxury, while convincing itself that it is "doing good" through acts of "haute philanthropy" (Nickel 2015), is indulging in an interpretation of the effective modalities of our being luxurious that is less to do with the creation of enjoyment and more to do with the continued creation of grief. Lost in a world of luxurious "things," the horizon of the new working super-rich—from Microsoft's Bill Gates and Amazon's Jeff Bezos to Facebook's Mark Zuckerberg—shifts to learning the luxury of "doing good" and on behalf of "the world" (Freeland 2013). Being luxurious, consequently, can result in living in a third realm, in a world brimming with dreams of perfection; a world that is a sort of garden of un-enlightenment wherein individualized worlds of luxury are increasingly equipped to discern only one's own human temporality and spatiality and to disregard that of others.

On the Rolls-Royce Ghost Black Badge and beyond

In endeavoring to explain the topic of uncovering the temporality and spatiality of being luxurious, my goal is to clarify the temporality and spatiality of the adjoining world in terms of luxurious enjoyment. I understand those sumptuous entities which show themselves with an exquisite primordiality as a temporal garden or elevated ground that precludes their reduction to spatiality. Yet, contrary to Heidegger, I am less concerned with distinguishing the instrumental use which beings make of entities in their everyday lives than I am with discerning the furnishing out or supply of different kinds of luxury, with being luxurious entailing entities that represent articles of luxury removed by their character and costliness out of the ordinary everyday category of human needs. My purpose in accounting for luxurious temporality and spatiality as a temporal-spatial extension, as the in-itself of an objectivist ontology, is to consider them as "things" that are conducive to enjoyment. In other words, I want to show an alertness to the presence of comfort and ease, to well-being, to security, to relaxation, to contentment, and to methods of concernful involvement with "things" *other than* those considered the necessities of life. For such a presence and these methods of concernful involvement create a temporality and a spatiality of "things" that are close at hand but, by way of their proximity to our human desire, are ontologically *undetermined* since their "handiness" is not for use but for the provision of diverse types of luxurious, often dispensable, "things." For me, therefore, much of this is not about necessary things presenting themselves as tools or instruments but about luxurious "things" presenting themselves as *self-seeking pleasures.* These "things," much like Heidegger's things, *may* have the quality of being-in-order-to: for example, the hammer for the manufacture of a luxury automobile or the building of further motorized merriments. Yet, I argue, the structure of being luxurious is governed not by its reference to instruments revealing themselves as always already incorporated into a whole but by its reference to self-seeking pleasures disclosing themselves as always already assimilated into a whole realm of expensive luxuriousness. Such self-seeking pleasures, when considered as a totality, I suggest, can only be revealed in their effects not by paying attention to the totality of Heidegger's things but to the totality of "things," by which I mean their structures and their supplying of varied sorts of luxury or abundance. I shall illustrate what I mean by describing and analyzing what I argue is taking place in the luxuriously abundant realm of the Rolls-Royce Ghost Black Badge, which is mainly purchased by the entrepreneurial crowd, those who establish businesses and employment on their

Figure 2.2 The Rolls-Royce Ghost Black Badge. Photograph reproduced by courtesy of Rolls-Royce Motor Cars.

way to generating wealth (Figure 2.2) and described by Rolls-Royce in the text that follows.[2]

Ghost Black Badge

For the Fearless

Ghost never compromises. And with Black Badge, that purpose is intensified to a whole new level. A darker aesthetic transforms Ghost Black Badge into the ultimate statement. Its striking stance exudes confidence, hinting at the refined power that lies waiting under the bonnet. It's time to discover your bolder side.

Sculpted by shadows

As a design statement, Ghost embodies simplicity. But Black Badge adds a potent edge to its presence. This is a more tenacious, more dynamic incarnation of luxury.

The Spirit of Ecstasy is now as dark as a shadow—her bold silhouette drawing you deeper into the night. Paint is deepened to a luxurious black, and high-gloss dark chrome elements transform the front grille to create a dramatic contrast to the LED headlights. Flashes of dark chrome along the bodywork accentuate Ghost Black Badge's subtle sculpting, carried through to the darkened boot lid and exhaust pipes. The Rolls-Royce badge also embraces a darker side, a mark of refined craftsmanship.

Ghost Black Badge's contemporary profile is elevated by the stunning 21″ carbon fiber composite wheels. Developed exclusively for Black Badge, the wheels' design is based on Italian supercars of the 1960s—strong, sculpted and geometric. The self-righting Rolls-Royce monogram remains upright even when the wheels are in motion.

Enter a new dimension

Discover pure luxury—with added depth. A mix of innovative, technically-crafted materials and bold upholstery transform the interior of Ghost Black Badge into a space designed to make you feel like anything is possible. Ghost's sculpted, luxury seats are a place of power from which you can take control of the road. Setting your braver side free.

Comfort is built into every inch of Ghost Black Badge. Its svelte lines envelop you in a deeper, darker luxury—creating an air of pure confidence. Bold two-tone leather upholstery, shown here in black and Tailored Purple, draws the eye, while the cabin is transformed by the stunning technical fiber fascia. Crafted from aerospace-grade aluminium and carbon fiber threads, the dashboard glimmers with possibility.

Deep chrome air vents darken the whole cabin to match the aura of the exterior. And other subtle touches—such as the exclusive Black Badge clock with orange-tipped hands—make the interior of Ghost Black Badge a thrill for the senses. Complete the ambience with an optional Bespoke Starlight Headliner, bringing the allure of the night sky inside.

Clearly, the "things" to be found in a Rolls-Royce Ghost Black Badge are not positioned in such a way that this appliance for comfort can be taken in isolation from other "things," such as the brilliancy of its "darker side" and the luxury of "the ultimate statement" that far surpass anything that other such motorized spaces can show. Collectively, and based on their relations with other such intensities and levels, as well as with a "stance" that "exudes confidence," these "things" determine the physiognomy of the abundant realm that is the Rolls-Royce Ghost Black Badge. What we encounter in the first place is the rich temporality, which Rolls-Royce christens our "bolder side" in that susceptibility for sculptural signification that belongs to shadows: a "design statement" and not just a voluminous luxury automobile geometrically circumscribed by the "simplicity" which its luxurious things "fill up." Being luxurious, then, is about much more than just filling up our lives with things; it is about filling up our lives with "things" such as the presence and dynamism of a Rolls-Royce Ghost Black Badge. We *discover* the Rolls-Royce Ghost Black Badge as "the incarnation of luxury," I argue, and not as a residential instrument or functional machine. Rather, we *uncover* the spiritual environment of being luxurious temporally and spatially through a totalizing yet varied number of sociocultural meanings and intentions, whether those of ecstasy or of a silhouette "drawing us deeper into the night." Our experience of seeing "luxurious black" is thus one of transformation, of connecting self-seeking people with dramatically contrasting yet pleasurable times and spaces, one with another. Any study of being luxurious must therefore implicate the spatiality proper to being but, distinct from Heidegger, I am less concerned with the being of instruments than I am with the temporal-spatial whole of self-seeking pleasures into which we insert ourselves, such as the "flash" of "dark chrome." For a good number of the entities associated with luxury are not merely obtainable for straightforward use: one thinks, for instance, of the "uselessness" of the Rolls-Royce Ghost Black Badge's "subtle sculpting" or "darkened boot lid and exhaust pipes." Yet, at the same time, such entities are in proximity to us, if not in the same way as the Rolls-Royce Ghost Black Badge's steering wheel or speedometer (Figure 2.3).

Figure 2.3 The Rolls-Royce Ghost Black Badge's Steering Wheel and Speedometer. Photograph reproduced by courtesy of Rolls-Royce Motor Cars.

Accordingly, while it is important to establish our oriented proximity to the Rolls-Royce Ghost Black Badge, which results from that concern which typifies being luxurious in its everydayness, it is also imperative to establish our oriented proximity to it concerning entities *beyond* the Rolls-Royce Ghost Black Badge's refined craftsmanship. Being luxurious thus results from a concern which should be described less in terms of the twenty-one-inch carbon fiber composite wheels of the Rolls-Royce Ghost Black Badge and more in terms of the "luxury-loving" Rolls-Royce Ghost Black Badge *owner* with a "bolder side," in terms of everyday human beings as luxury-loving animals who are always looking to enter that third realm. It is not, then, the being of the instrument, of "technically-crafted materials," and their meaning that concerns me but our self-seeking pleasures in terms of the possible discovery of "pure luxury," with "added depth," of our luxury-loving practices and their proximity to what can only be described as the transformative "soul" of luxury, that third realm of abundance whose luxurious accessibility is mediated by such entities as the interior of the Rolls-Royce Ghost Black Badge, by a space designed to make us feel that "anything is possible." This means that, instead of focusing on the being of the instrument, I argue for a focus on, for instance, human beings associated with the self-seeking pleasures of the Rolls-Royce Ghost Black Badge's sculpted, luxury seats, with human beings as a

Figure 2.4 The luxury-loving Rolls-Royce Ghost Black Badge owner taking control. Photograph reproduced by courtesy of Rolls-Royce Motor Cars.

luxury-loving species always on the lookout for a "place" of power from which they can take control (Figure 2.4).

How else can we explain our seemingly boundless desire not only for setting our "braver side free" but also for such "places" as the Rolls-Royce Ghost Black Badge's "svelte lines" where luxuriousness can be "found"? For such "places," whether in a deeper, darker, luxury or in the pure air of confidence, can only be "found" in relation to other luxurious "places" with which they establish a transformative global system or a totality of luxurious "places" associated with the glamor and aura of "confidence," the discovery of the "subtle touch," the "ambiance" of starlight, and the universal "allure" and totality of "the night sky."

Without denying Heidegger's standing as a foremost philosopher of place, I do, in contrast, as we saw above in the example of the Rolls-Royce Ghost Black Badge, argue that there are *other* times and "places" that must be "situated" "*elsewhere*," times and "places" that are conditioned by the possibility of "overflowing," by large quantities of "things." And, like Heidegger's totality of places, such a third realm of abundance also sits in a "wherein" but a wherein of *plenty*, a wherein in which concernful involvement is predicated on an imaginary time and "place" where we seek all that is good, from the abundance of fresh water to untold riches. The consequence is that this third realm of abundance can be signified as a region that is a "*wonder to behold*," as a side that may be "sinful" or "graceful." This third realm of abundance is suggested whenever we identify the time and "place" of an abundant "thing" from *this* "superfluous" side sooner than from *that* "superfluous" side as a function of the majestic temporality and spatiality characteristic in the gift, given voluntarily without payment in return, that is the plentiful third realm of everyday life. For this reason, in establishing these regions that are sensations to witness, that are an abundant third realm, positioning ourselves toward the copious times and spaces of the adjoining world is also a matter of privileging light and air. Indeed, it is a matter of the appreciation of beautiful views on a sunny day, of the variable and nevertheless continually and frequently accessible time and "place" for the miscellaneous and changeable supply of assorted varieties of luxury to which we put such light, air, and beautiful views: one thinks, for example, of the millions of people worldwide who regularly spend their time where sunbathing takes place, simply sitting or lying in the sun in order to make their skin darker. It is a matter of distinguishing the otherworldly regions that are a wonder to behold, which provide pre-established points of orientation for the earthly regions that are a marvel to observe, which these abundant times and "places" inhabit and express in terms of the riches that they offer. Furthermore, while the *course* of the sun and its existential meaning are for us adjoined through ideas of east and west, they are also connected through sublime concepts of *number* (e.g., the Sun's diameter is 109 times that of Earth) and *many* (e.g., the Sun formed approximately 4.6 billion years ago), through the incontrovertible possibilities of being luxurious and as the revealing of the temporality and spatiality of the adjoining world of large numbers of "things." Existentially pertinent since it is instituted on the profuse temporality and spatiality of being luxurious, my interpretation of the temporality and spatiality of the adjoining world, as distinct from Heidegger's, does not so much assume the being of being, with its temporality and spatiality belonging and oriented to making distances vanish but, more exactly, presupposes being's encounter with intra-abundant entities that indicate a making time and space for abundance. This last is thus an understanding which makes imaginable a variety of ample times and "places" supported by acts such as abundant movement and removal, acts which involve the intervention of a new and different speculative approach centered on the appreciation of, for instance, fabulous houses, good "things," and the composition of comfortable rather than geometrical space. Uncovering the lavish temporality and spatiality of the world in the direction of its ontological presupposition thus necessitates the temporalizing and spatializing of the being of being luxurious, of questions regarding a post-Heideggerian method of understanding luxurious spatiality, being, and time.

In contrast to Heidegger, I am not concerned with portraying our encounter with the spatiality of the world but with intra-abundant entities and unlimited kinds of participation that take as their example the recuperated world of the leisure of men and women and the plentiful world which corresponds to them, such as the abundance of butterflies and flowers that adorn the cliffs during spring and summer holidays. For my examination of abundant temporality and spatiality is not only "overflowing" in the sense that self-seeking states or pleasurable conditions and the superfluous times and "places" which belong to them are someway "liberated" but also because they offer a more than sufficient supply in terms of *plentifulness*, mutual generosity, exposed liberality, and abundance. Breaking down the walls of "necessity," the purpose of abundance is to *open up an ecstatic space* to let being luxurious position itself in times of plenty, in the "places" of the heart, and in everyday lives often driven insane by loving the Other just a little too much. Heidegger is therefore too engrossed with disclosing the spatiality of a world that is bereft of the tortured sensitivity of the artist, of a world that is deprived of the everyday abundance of life and love. We must not, then, downgrade, deactivate, or bracket the phenomenal appearance of the ecstatic spaces of abundance but, as in the untamed nature described in Jack London's novel about a sled dog called "Buck," (a St. Bernard and a Scotch collie cross) *The Call of the Wild*, (and wholly absent from Heidegger's world), recognize and investigate the temporality and spatiality of the plentiful supply of the good things of life:

> There is an ecstasy that marks the summit of life, and beyond which life cannot rise. And such is the paradox of living, this ecstasy comes when one is most alive, and it comes as a complete forgetfulness that one is alive. This ecstasy, this forgetfulness of living, comes to the artist, caught up and out of himself in a sheet of flame; it comes to the soldier, war-mad on a stricken field and refusing quarter; and it came to Buck, leading the pack, sounding the old wolf-cry, straining after the food that was alive and that fled swiftly before him through the moonlight. He was sounding the deeps of his nature, and of the parts of his nature that were deeper than he, going back into the womb of Time. He was mastered by the sheer surging of life, the tidal wave of being, the perfect joy of each separate muscle, joint, and sinew in that it was everything that was not death, that it was aglow and rampant, expressing itself in movement, flying exultantly under the stars and over the face of dead matter that did not move. (London 1993: 76–77)

Distinct from Heidegger, then, Jack London's entreaty is to engage *with*, if not *in*, the force of ecstasy, the world at the peak of life *and beyond*. Hence, London not only acknowledges the inconsistencies of living in ecstasy but is also willing to examine temporality as forgetfulness, spatiality as aesthetic ecstasy, plentifulness as a kind of insanity or refusal, and directing and announcing, exclaiming, struggling, escaping, rushing, and happiness as all part of the enjoyable "things" in life. With a view to opening up Heidegger's somewhat unsatisfactory analytic, therefore, I am trying to analyze the temporality and spatiality of the world from the perspective of its importance for supplying our wants and of its usefulness as a function of that existential which is immersion in delight, which is everything that is not death, which is uncontrolled liberality, pleasure in movement, and jubilant plenty. This is not a world of instrumentality, tools, and utility but a world of self-seeking splendor, satisfying riches, and of men and women, such as the Duke of Westminster and Coco Chanel, doing nothing but fishing if they so please until boredom, idleness, and lethargy drive them elsewhere (Morand 2008: 201). In taking this approach to the temporality and spatiality of the world, I am addressing abundance as a symbolic order of want and ruination that includes and often exceeds the practical importance of the feeling for luxury that is revealed through our everyday life of unlimited wealth. Any analytic of luxurious spatiality, being, and time should, therefore, include an examination bearing on the constitutive timing and spacing of being luxurious *with others* under conditions that are overflowing with abundance to the extent that one can no longer distinguish oneself from them in this shared world. This is because if we wish to comprehend the times and spaces of the world of abundance (the times, spaces, and distances of a cultural regime of self-indulgence), then we must also ponder the temporality and spatiality of being luxurious itself and the issue of luxuriousness as plentifulness, namely, the issue of luxurious selfhood or luxurious identity. Appreciating the nature of being luxurious, of plentifulness, should, then, allow for the "here" and "there" constitutive of luxurious intersubjectivity predicated on copious amounts and quantities. Revealing itself as an inter-corporeal occurrence of abundant copiousness and bountifulness, ampleness, lavishness, and profuseness, the issue of luxurious embodiment becomes an undertaking less to do with being and time and more to do with conveying their links with the issue of abundant temporality and spatiality and of the issue of one's own plentifulness.

Consequently, as my post-Heideggerian account proposes, I argue for a fresh responsiveness to time and space as plentifulness, as the relatively high quantity or number of "things" present in other "things" or a new analysis of the temporality and spatiality of the world *as* an abundant third realm. In a word, I argue for an altered perception of the character of abundance. For me, therefore, the temporality and spatiality of being in the world *is* luxurious.

Conclusion

I began this chapter with a conceptual explanation of being, time, and space in Heidegger's *Being and Time*. However, I would like to end it by making a plea for further philosophical efforts to supplement our understanding of being, time, and space as something luxurious, as something lavish. My initial goal in the previous pages was to expand our appreciation of the being, time, and space of luxury, of the nature or reality of being luxurious. As I have endeavored to demonstrate, being luxurious is not a thing but an abundant experience, a luxurious event of historical being that opens up an ecstatic space wherein we can be present to our authentic selves. Opening up that singular originating event of luxury corresponds simultaneously with bringing ourselves into our own selves, and with elevating ourselves on a recurrent basis. This is because the opening up of the ecstatic space of abundance is also an event of the presence of splendid enjoyment that retreats, and this retreat is a part of what is unique to, among other experiences, being luxurious. The importance of my case regarding the presence of luxuriousness as a time and space, then, is that, at certain times, and in certain ecstatic spaces, luxurious events determine what being, time, and space *are*, including the being, time, and space of the Rolls-Royce Ghost Black Badge. Yet, for all that the Rolls-Royce Ghost Black Badge or any other luxury automobile presents novel aspects of "pure luxury," with "added depth," what is vital to bear in mind from a philosophical viewpoint is that our ideas and experiences of luxury also retreat, to become a form of abundance that "has been" as well as a form of plentifulness that, in the instant of being in existence, also refuses the future.

In conclusion, we can appreciate that critically appropriating Heidegger's philosophical work is valuable insofar as he draws our attention not only to the event but also to significant issues relating to being, time, and space. What Heidegger does not do, however, is call attention to the important question concerning being luxurious wherein being is inclined to disappear within the event of luxuriousness. Consequently, rather than consider the event of luxury as being luxurious, the mission for further research is to try to consider being luxurious as an event that elevates us to an ecstatic space that expands. For the elevation of being is not separate from the event of luxury; rather, it is only within the event of luxury that there is an ecstatic space at all or any possibility of being luxurious.

References

Cohen, L. (2009), "Recitation," *Live in London*. New York: Columbia.

Dijk van, P. (2000), *Anthropology in the Age of Technology: The Philosophical Contribution of Günther Anders*. Amsterdam: Rodopi.

Frampton, K. (2001), *Le Corbusier: Architect and Visionary*. London: Thames and Hudson.

Freeland, C. (2013), *Plutocrats: The Rise of the New Global Super-Rich*. London: Penguin Books.

Heidegger, M. (1962), *Being and Time*. Oxford: Blackwell.

Heidegger, M. (1971), "Building, Dwelling, Thinking," in M. Heidegger, *Poetry, Language, Thought*, 145–61. New York: Harper and Row.

Heidegger, M. (1978), "The Origin of the Work of Art," in M. Heidegger, *Basic Writings*, 139–212. London: Routledge.

Heidegger, M. (1989), "Time-Space," in M. Heidegger, *Contributions to Philosophy (From Enowning)*, 263–71. Bloomington: Indiana University Press.

Heidegger, M. (2009), "Art and Space," in G. Figal (ed.), *The Heidegger Reader*, translated by J. Veith, 305–10. Bloomington: Indiana University Press.

London, J. (1993), *The Call of the Wild*. London: Penguin.

Morand, P. (2008), *The Allure of Chanel*. London: Pushkin Press.

Nickel, P. (2015), "Haute Philanthropy: Luxury, Benevolence, and Value," *Luxury: History, Culture, Consumption*, 2 (2): 11–31.

Piketty, T. (2014), *Capital in the Twenty-First Century*. Cambridge, MA: Harvard University Press.

Pliny the Elder (1991), *Natural History*. London: Penguin.

Roberts, J. (2019), "Is Contemporary Luxury Morally Acceptable? A Question for the Super-Rich," *Cultural Politics*, 15 (1): 48–63.

Shugart, H. A. (2016), *The Obesity Crisis in Cultural Context*. Oxford: Oxford University Press.

Ullman, B. L. (1957), "Cleopatra's Pearls," *The Classical Journal*, 52 (5): 193–201.

3

The architecture of authoritarian luxury

Mark Featherstone

Ontic luxury things and ontological luxury space

In his *Origin of German Tragic Drama* (2009), Walter Benjamin reflects upon the condition of tyranny in early modern German drama. The king sits uncomfortably upon his throne. The world is a maelstrom of events, and he is crippled by indecision. As his grip on power slips away, his sovereignty becomes an unbearable weight. Under these conditions, his palace, his luxurious seat of power, starts to feel like a prison. Paradoxically, he responds to incarceration by retreating further and further into his castle until there is nowhere else to hide, and he must confront the reality of his kingship. His palace, the architectural representation of his power, is a crumbling ruin, and he is a nobody. He is the same as everybody else. Now the splendor and grandeur of his office, which he once somehow believed came from within him and separated him from others, collapses onto *something else*. This *something else*, which is characterized by the end of vertical power and authority captured and symbolized in *luxurious things*, is a horizontal space that looks like death from the perspective of the king who has spent his life trying to escape the gravity of the natural world where everything is in everything else. But seen from the other side, this horizontal space beyond the outer limits of authoritarian power, beyond the edifice of the palace, the *luxury place* that marks the king out in his constructed difference, is *luxury space in itself* because it represents immersion in the universe that ruins grand architectural design and forms the ontological basis of radical political democracy. This is real luxury, *ontological luxury* beyond those fine things that desperately try to capture it and use it for the purposes of authoritarian power, and the philosophical basis of the idea of communism. Following Benjamin's (2009) vision of power consuming itself, my objective in this chapter is to explore the limits of luxury things and specifically luxury places. Centrally, I want to show how the grandeur, splendor, and finery of what I want to call *contained luxury* (or luxury things) is fated to crumble and open out onto something else, something more basic, namely the *experience* of *ontological luxury* where everything connects to everything else and *ontic separation* (the containment of the experience of luxury in the thing, the object) gives way to *ontological continuity*.

In order to explore this situation politically and show how luxury is an inherently spatial condition, I propose to read the difference between *the ontic representation or containment of luxury* and *the ontological reality of the experience of the luxurious in itself* through an analysis of authoritarian architecture, which I suggest can be seen to turn off notions of home and homelessness, security and insecurity, and vertical power and its collapse into horizontality. The key symbol here is the seat of authoritarian power, the palace, which I want to suggest captures the ontic or everyday meaning of luxury (the luxurious object, or first realm of luxury) and represents a strategy for the *solidification* or *concretization* of power (imaginary luxury, the second realm of luxury, where one no longer suffers under the humiliation of limitation), in the emergence of what we might call the luxury sign (which fuses object and idea in the third realm of luxury). However, even though the palace is perhaps the luxury sign par excellence, which fuses finery and power in the concept of authoritarian luxury, it also creates the possibility of the violent collapse of vertical sovereignty into real luxury (ontological luxury) characterized by horizontality and continuity. This is precisely how the French writer Georges Bataille understands the authoritarianism of the architectural (Hollier, 1992), which, in his view, symbolizes a Hegelian obsession with systemization and a Freudian drive to deny the reality of the ontological trauma that makes us human. In this vision, architecture is the concrete representation of Freudian bodybuilding that Deyan Sudjic (2005) writes about through the idea of the "edifice complex." In Sudjic's work, the notion of the edifice complex becomes a metaphor for the desire of tyrants to represent their political power architecturally, but a more sustained psychoanalysis of the term reveals that this idea could have much deeper roots in normal psychology. If the idea of the edifice complex emerges from the Freudian concept of the Oedipus complex *misheard*, Sudjic's play on faulty hearing potentially reveals a deeper connection. Where Freud's Oedipus marks the emergence of lack and desire in the experience of the individual, and more profoundly the origin of limitation in human life, Sudjic's edifice complex potentially names the process which sees the limited individual build a self and a world in order to overcome their inherent sense of their own inadequacy. In this respect, the discipline of architecture relates to self-making and bodybuilding, as well as to the construction of massive buildings that represent the power and authority of the individual in concrete form. The massive building is, therefore, not only symbolic of the hardness of the self impervious to attack but also paradoxically a representation of the inherent weakness of the Oedipalized individual who can never really overcome the traumatic experience of patriarchal prohibition. This is why desire never runs out, and the lust for grandeur and splendor that seizes hold of the tyrant who desperately needs to defend his destroyed self seems endless. Where the normal individual, who experiences Oedipal repression *within reason* and is able to find some free space to exert self-control, feels no need to dominate the entire world, it is likely that the psychological emergence of the tyrant or authoritarian ruler is characterized by absolute domination with the result that they develop a sadistic, controlling, personality set on the reconstruction of self, other, and the entire world. Of course, even the world is never enough, precisely because external grandeur and splendor can never take away the yawning abyss inside the self, which is why tyranny is a kind of madness that knows no limits.

This is "the housing problem" of the tyrant or the authoritarian leader that I propose to explore through reference to first-century Rome, the ur-place of tyrannical luxury, where Nero sought to concretize his rule through the creation of massive buildings, and centrally the Domus Aurea, that could represent his godlike status on earth. Nero's problem was, however, the same one that plagues every authoritarian in history, which is that the very attempt to concretize power through luxury places and luxury things eventually undermines the absolute security it was set up to produce and opens out onto the other mode of luxury, ontological luxury beyond the ontic sphere of the everydayness. In the Roman case, endless expansion, the civilization of the natural world, and the creation of the greatest empire ironically seemed to destabilize the emperor and throw him into a state of psychotic uncertainty. As Rome spread out and covered the world, luxury items flowed back to the city from Lydia (Roman Asia), to enable the super-rich to live lives of excess (Dalby 2002). Under these conditions, the great consumers of the ancient world sought to escape from the reality of natural limitation through fine things, but the result of this estrangement threw them into a state of existential instability, which Lewis Mumford (1968) writes about in terms of psychopathology. According to Mumford, the expansion of the city, and the elevation of the imperial elites through the consumption of luxury things, led to a state of purposeless materialism and a form of madness that would grip Nero and lead to his suicidal confrontation with his political opponents, who eventually included pretty much everybody in the entire city. The thanatological history of Nero's reign is well known and includes the apocalyptic fire that consumed the city in 64 CE, the emperor's construction of the Domus Aurea in the name of a vision of solar ideology based upon the truth of excess and consumption, and finally the transformation of suicide (the practice of "opening one's veins") into a form of political luxury that moved the suicide from the sphere of ontic splendor to the universe of ontological luxuriousness captured by Seneca (2014) in his *Natural Questions* where he writes of the upward abyss of outer space and the endless continuity of existence itself (Featherstone 2016).

Moving beyond Rome, I take up the modern example of Nazi Germany, and in particular Hitler's construction of luxurious domestic spaces, which were designed to convey an image of refinement, restraint, and cultural superiority. In contrast to the very visible excesses of Nero's Rome, Hitler's luxury, best captured in his Alpine Berghof, was set up to capture the significance of the *Volk* and root the Fuhrer in the land in the face of the chaos of Weimar and the modern condition more generally. We cannot see inside Nero's Domus Aurea for the sake of comparison, but images of Hitler's house show a staged space, rather than somewhere one might live. Although there is little doubt the house was carefully set up before photographs were taken, the restrained refinement of the Fuhrer's place screams anxiety and a desperate desire for cultural recognition. Everything is in its proper place, and Hitler's house speaks to a need for order, organization, and a paranoid refusal of the outside and its otherness. In this way, the high design luxury place is set up to oppose ontological luxuriousness in itself, even though Hitler's project followed a similar path to Nero's attempt to escape from reality. That is to say that Hitler's search for domestic control and cleanliness, which was repeated on the political stage in the form of the attempt to secure *Lebensraum* (living space) in Europe, ran into its limit in the murderous excesses of the Holocaust, which ultimately cost the Nazis military victory. Under the immense pressure of this obsessive compulsive desire for cleanliness and perfection, Hitler's own domestic luxury, which initially took in the panoramic mountain views of the Bavarian Alps, closed down until he found himself cornered in his Berlin bunker. As the Red Army advanced, he finally ran out of his own living space and shot himself in a suicidal refusal of the reality of luxuriousness in itself where everything is in everything else, and there is no prospect of paranoid escape from others.

Finally, in order to conclude my chapter, I move beyond the reactionary modern luxury of Hitler and Nazi Germany to consider the luxuriousness of postmodern America. Where the Nazis sought to use images of cultural refinement and natural homeliness in order to promote a vision of ethnic cleanliness and orderliness, the story of luxury in America recalls the Roman case where luxury was about class, rather than racial difference, though it would be possible to make the case that America remains a racialized state. In much the same way that luxury came to Rome through imperial conquest, post-World War II America became the world's consumer, taking on the role of stimulating productivity in the industrial and post-industrial powers that needed to rebuild in the wake of the war. As Yanis Varoufakis (2013) points out in *The Global Minotaur*, the post-1945 global system was founded upon the American consumer's desire for ever more luxury. While the American commitment to research and development drove technological innovation on the home front, the consumer's desire was the engine of growth in the rest of the world, including Germany and Japan, which is why neoliberal political and economic theory made the free market individual able to make rational choices about what and what not to buy sovereign. With the benefit of hindsight, it is now clear that this model, particularly from the 1980s onward, was founded upon easy credit and the creation of a mountain of debt that was entirely unsustainable, but this was less clear at the time because there was no sense that the party would ever end and debts would have to be repaid. Thus, easy credit and a lax attitude to financial regulation supported a boom in the American housing market with the result that everybody could buy their own place and escape the reality of limitation into the fantasy space of ontic luxury (luxury things). Everybody became a homeowner until the overheated market collapsed under the weight of massive numbers of defaults on high risk loans and the fantasy of escape into the luxury house collapsed into the reality of luxuriousness in itself defined by limitation or, in this case it might be better to say, universal indebtedness. In this context, universal indebtedness means the social interdependence of everybody upon everybody else, which is, of course, one way of writing about the luxurious immersion of the self in a communistic social whole. But while this condition is real, the kind of sociological and political correlate of the philosophical, ecological condition of luxurious intimacy and continuity, it is intolerable from the point of view of neoliberal, and in fact liberal, ideology because these theories make the individual sovereign and try to deny its dependence on others and the world. From this perspective, indebtedness is always a temporary state. Although we may spend most of our lives in the red, from the point of view of liberal and neoliberal thought, the ideal situation is living in the black because this represents the truth of individualism where the self is independent of others and out on its own.

Being independent, being out on one's own—this is the American dream, the fantasy of ontic luxury, where the individual is truly sovereign and no longer needs to rely on others. This is precisely the American fantasy, the fantasy bound up with owning one's own home, which has been punctured by the financial crash and resulted in the election of Donald Trump whose appeal rests on his promise to save normal Americans from their collapsing individualism, their collapsing independence, and sense of sovereign selfhood. Although he had no experience of political office, "the desperate" could vote for Trump because he appears to embody what it means to be a rugged individual, a strong man out on his own, who lives a life of ontic luxury and says he knows what it takes to save the empire (Kellner 2016). On the basis of his life lived out on screen, it is clear that Trump himself is a bundle of anxieties, has a highly vulnerable sense of self, and constantly feels under siege (Kellner 2016, 2017). But he clearly meets these problems relating to egoistic insecurity head on through building strategies concerned with shoring up his sense of self. He throws up buildings, most famously the phallic Trump Tower in Manhattan, writes his global brand name everywhere he finds open space and over everything he can transform into a luxury object, and seeks to destroy anybody who threatens his fragile self-identity. In this way, Trump builds himself in concrete, words, images, and luxury objects in the name of sealing himself off from the reality of the world. It is thus no surprise that the insecure chose to vote for Trump. He models inadequacy and wrote the book on how to respond to this situation by building himself a world of ontic luxury sealed off from the ontological reality of luxuriousness in itself. But this is, I would argue, the real tragedy of Trump's American brand of authoritarian luxury. While Nero was a real tyrant and Hitler soon seized absolute power, Trump emerged in perhaps the home of modern democracy! There is no doubt that Joe Six-pack cast his vote for Trump on the basis that he thought he could fight his corner in the way he fights his own, but the truth of Trump is that his defensive narcissism, and his anxious obsession with cleanliness and the purity of ontic luxury, means that he is "locked in" and lacks empathy for other people simply because understanding and recognition are feelings founded in the humility of interrelatedness, communication, continuity, and the open spaces of ontological luxury in itself. Against this state of immersion, Trump is a paranoid leader who occupies sealed spaces characterized by exorbitant displays of wealth and wants to hide in ontic luxury in order to escape from the horror of openness. However, before I reach Trump, and an exploration of the authoritarian luxury of contemporary America, in the next section of my chapter I propose to explore the phenomenological meaning of the house and the home in order to situate my analysis of *ontic luxury places* and *ontological luxury space*. On the basis of this work, which relies upon a reading of Gaston Bachelard's (1994) *Poetics of Space*,

I propose to take up and analyze Nero's luxury places and final suicidal collapse into luxury space, before moving forward into a consideration of Hitler's Nazi construction of luxury domesticity in the Bavarian Alps. Following this work, which will close through reference to the transformation of Hitler's Volkisch Berghof into the only five-star hotel in the Berchtesgaden region, I move on to explore the role of luxury in postmodern capitalism before concluding in an exploration of the politics of luxurious in the case of Trump.

Home, unhome, and the housing problems of the rich and famous

In his *The Poetics of Space* (1994) Bachelard quotes Baudelaire's *Paris Spleen* (2009), noting that there is no place for intimacy in the palace. This is because the very grandeur of the place—"those golden ridden walls . . . the solemn galleries" (Baudelaire 2009: 47)—leaves no room for openness, vulnerability, or real interaction. The very concept of the palace suggests uprightness, verticality, remoteness, and the inhumanity of the sovereign. This is a place of ontic luxury that represents and captures the symbolic, posthuman, function of kingship. It is not meant to be homely. For Bachelard, the house is by contrast a metaphor for humanity. He explains that the house is our first cosmos, where we are simultaneously open, vulnerable, and humble, as well as feel safe and secure enough to think big thoughts and imagine the abyssal depths of reality. The real house, the house that becomes a home, is thus small enough to capture our imperfections, and also comfortable in ways that reflect the ontological luxury we find in the house of being where we relate to everything and lose ourselves in the world. On this basis, Bachelard explains that the basic form of the house shelters, provides comfort, and opens out on to the experience of immersion in the universe. In this way, he explains that the house is the non-I that grounds and enables the development of the I. Although Bachelard never mentions individual psychoanalysts and could not have known of the object relations theorists who wrote after him, his vision of the house and the home which enables us to grow is comparable to D. W. Winnicott's (2005) idea of the secure space that emerges from our first relationships with our parents and enables our later psychological development. Bachelard is clear that the home cannot be a hostile place, because by definition a house would not be a home if it was colored by hostility, but there is a sense in which he overlooks the fate of those who reside in violent and abusive houses which similarly produce psychological types who later seek to build fortresses in order to bolster their ruined selves. However, Bachelard is less interested in violent places, which might produce tyrants and authoritarian leaders, and more concerned with the way the enclosed being of the home opens up onto the great outdoors.

The home is, in Bachelard's view, a place that brings the outside in and welcomes relationality. In order to capture this idea, he refers to Baudelaire's use of the terms "vast" and "vastness" and explains that these words are less about megalomaniacal constructs built by the obsessive possessed by the edifice complex and more references to the openness to the infinite spaces of luxury in itself. Although the tyrant's palace may be a huge place and represents the very height of ontic luxury, it will never measure up to luxuriousness of "the house of being," simply because its function is to wall people in and keep others out. Its very hardness means that it is opposed to relationality. It is like Bachelard's "defensive shell," unrelated, and similar to Heidegger's (2001b) rock, *worldless*. But in much the same way that the palace pulls back from space in order to evade relatedness, it also seeks to blast off into the atmosphere in the name of escaping the earth. This is why sovereign places so often comprise towers because verticality screams superiority and being above others who remain stuck on the ground. Inside the palace itself, rooms seem to spread out and there appears to be oceans of space, but this is illusory and designed to draw the visitor's eye away from the fundamental paranoid enclosure of the place. The palace is, therefore allergic to those small spaces and corners that Bachelard treasures because the sovereign understands them from the point of view of the paranoiac. They reduce his sense of self, limit his vision of ontic luxury, and represent what he cannot stand to confront—his own smallness, his own vulnerability, his own closure upon himself. By contrast, Bachelard reads small spaces in a completely different way. In thinking about nooks, crannies, corners, and other dark places where creepy-crawlies live, Bachelard finds the possibility of the entire universe. In his view, these shadowy places "deny the palace" because their smallness, their intimacy, their homeliness, opens out onto horizontal vastness, universality, and the continuity of everything with everything else.

However, consideration of Nero's first-century imperial excesses shows that the ontic luxury of the palace is actually continuous with the emergence of luxury in itself because it is impossible to ever escape corners. Although the tyrant's strategy appears to be concerned with bodybuilding, locking himself in, and shutting out the great outdoors, the reality of the situation is that extreme, ontic luxury ends up opening out onto the ontological space of interconnection and immersion because the fine things set up to contain the idea of luxury are in the end unable to effectively hold the sense of difference and separation they are meant to convey. At this point, ontic luxury, the luxury of perfect things, becomes an absurdity that reveals the true objective of the tyrant's paranoid strategy, which is concerned with bodybuilding through objects. What is the objective of this strategy? It is an escape from the horror of the vulnerable self that is compelled to resist continuity with the world because it cannot accept its own fragility. Once this happens though and the base objectivity of the tyrant's world becomes clear, his strategy of sealing himself off in a universe of transcendental finery (the palace and his wider world of luxury objects) collapses and his self crumbles toward the ontological truth of life where there is no independent organism or thing that is somehow out on its own. In spatial terms, we can understand this process through the tyrant's attempt to escape the dark corners that *must* form the boundary of his palace through techniques meant to draw the eye to the massiveness of his place and, by extension, his powerful and endless self. The problem of the corner resides in its simultaneous representation of closure, intimacy, and immensity, which the tyrant must seek to evade in the name of the paranoid integrity of his self. He cannot tolerate the small, because his identity is premised on his refusal of vulnerability; the intimate, because he cannot stand closeness to others on the basis that this might involve recognition of his ontological dependence on them; or ironically the immense, because vastness threatens to empty his self in the truth of the continuous being of existence itself. This theory of the politics of place and space essentially provides a model for understanding the function of luxury and the luxurious in Nero's Rome.

Reading Andrew Dalby's (2002) exhaustive survey of imperial luxury, we learn that it was the military expansion of the city that enabled the import of luxurious goods, but what he never really explains is how we should understand the *indulgence* of the Roman elites. Although Dalby explains the extent of the luxury goods entering Rome from Lydia, he never really touches upon the second concept in the subtitle of his book, which is indulgence. It is this blind spot in Dalby's work that I think it is possible to explain through the idea of bodybuilding and centrally the notion of escape from the privation of the limited self. In this respect, bodybuilding refers to both the visual impact of the display of the luxurious, which raises the self above others in a representation of power and authority, and the consumption of and indulgence in the luxury that can be seen to efface the boundaries of the self by taking away its sense of lack. For Peter York (2005) who wrote the book on tyrants' homes, the authoritarian leader is a kind of eternal teenager caught up in the endless identity crisis that Erik

Erikson (1995) writes about in his work on adolescence, who uses luxury to try to bolster his weak sense of self. Since this symbolic strategy never really works, the desire for luxury is endless, and the leader eventually descends into madness concerned with the desperate defense of his broken self. Where Nero's Rome is concerned, I think this is precisely the process Victoria Rimell (2015) explains when she opposes the apparently contradictory spatial trajectories of the city toward, on the one hand, absolute expansion and globalization and, on the other hand, paranoid contraction and closure toward bunkers and corners. In the first instance, imperial expansion and military conquest enabled the luxurious erasure of limits and the forgetting of the boundaries of the self. The luxury goods coming back from Asia enabled this process on the level of individual psychology. However, the problem with this approach is that the self was then subject to the possibility of psychotic collapse and fragmentation with the result that defensive formations came back on to the scene in order to attempt to shore up the identity of the self. Of course, the problem with this move is that it then led to the subsequent, paranoid fear of smallness and corners that led to expansion outward in the first place. In Nero's case, this confusion of grandiose expansion and paranoid contraction can be understood through his cult of solar kingship, where the emperor sought to identify with the sovereignty of the sun in order to elevate his own position (Champlin 2005).

As Bataille explains in various works, but most clearly in *The Accursed Share* (1991), the sun confirms the priority of the concept of luxury for understanding life because its heat and light enable existence itself. Since there is no economic return in the case of the solar economy, and the sun simply burns and will continue to burn until there is nothing left to consume, Bataille writes of its energy in terms of cosmological luxury and suggests that this is the model for how we should understand every other form of earthly luxury. Although life persists on the basis of metabolic cycles, its overall persistence is beyond exchange and is, therefore, a kind of gift or luxurious supplement to the nothingness that would otherwise (cease to) exist. The irony of Nero's adoption of solar ideology in order to support his kingship is, therefore, that the sun's sovereignty is entirely premised on consumption and in the end its own destruction. The power of the sun is founded in radiation and the extension of heat and light through space, and the only way in which it represents containment and contraction is in its long road toward burn out and extinction. There is probably little doubt that Nero's solar ideology was partially concerned with realpolitik, and an attempt to communicate to the people that he was their provider of heat and light, but on a deeper level I think we can also think about the way that the emperor's identification with the sun was symbolic of the trajectory of his reign, which was characterized by, on the one hand, the consumption of ontic luxury things and the dissolution of boundaries that might indicate the limitation of the massive self and, on the other hand, by the desperate, paranoid attempt to retain some sense of identity and preserve his own position within an empire that seemed permanently on the verge of collapse, precisely because of the confusion between the drive to expand and the need to contract and protect its insides.

The turn through these two alternatives, comprising the attempt to globalize the self beyond all boundaries through the consumption of ontic luxury and conversely situate identity within the high walls of the palace that omits no strangeness, may be seen to represent the death drive of Nero's Rome, which found expression in three key events. In 64 CE, Rome burned to the ground in an apocalyptic conflagration that could be understood in terms of the consumption of the ontic luxury of the city by the natural forces of luxury in itself. Although there is little evidence to support the claim that Nero himself started the fire, or fiddled while the place went up in smoke, it is possible to make the case that the destruction of the city reflected his thanatological desire to escape from the containment of everydayness into the wide open spaces of ontological luxury where there are no boundaries, but only vastness and continuity. Following the destruction of the city, however, Nero famously constructed his Domus Aurea or Golden House in order to seek to contain his kingship in a building representative of his supreme power. But even here ontic luxury pointed toward the endlessness of ontological luxury. The gold of the house was symbolic of Nero's infinite reach, and the building itself was constructed to catch the sun and reflect the emperor's universal sovereignty (Champlin 2005). Ancient sources explain that a massive statue of Nero stood by the entrance to the complex and a huge banner carrying his image hung in the grounds. Responding to this desperate bodybuilding exercise, Pliny the Elder (1991) explained that the Domus Aurea was representative of the insanity of the age. He continued that the problem with Nero's edifice was that it had come to occupy the entire city. Driven upward and outward by his paranoia, Nero sought to escape his vulnerability through the endless expansion of his self in expressions of ontic luxury, but the problem with this strategy is that in the end his megalomania expanded beyond all possible containers and led to a psychotic situation on the borderline between absolute smallness and infinite reach. Nero was cornered by his political opponents and whichever way he turned there was no way forward, but into the wide open spaces of death (Featherstone 2016).

Although there was a long tradition of suicide as a means of escape from the profanity of the body and everyday reality for the immersive space of what Freud (2010) calls the oceanic in Greek and Roman thought, Chris Berry (1994) points out that the Ancients were for the most part down on ontic luxury because they thought it led to softness of character. By contrast, Berry points out that luxury became a key organizing principle in modern thought because of its transgressive dimension. In economic terms, the desire for luxury things leads to expansion, because it feeds innovation, creativity, and development, but more generally the idea of luxury represents the overcoming of limits that captures what it means to be modern. Where the traditional premodern economy tended to be founded upon need, the modern economy drew on the luxury complex of imperial Rome and made desire its key idea. However, the problem with this situation is that it brought about a general crisis of containment, authority, and sovereignty, that Susan Bernstein (2008) writes about in terms of space, place, and building. Following my reference in the opening passage of this chapter to Benjamin's (2009) tyrant who has no idea which way to turn, Bernstein's focus is on how building and architecture could make sense of the wide open spaces of modernity and how place could structure experience in order to oppose the schizophrenic state of the world. She starts her fine work *Housing Problems* (2008) by explaining how modern architecture represents what she calls the *architectonic* or art of system-building. Connecting this idea to the Hegelian tradition, she turns to Heidegger's theory of building, which she explains avoids the functionalism of this idea of architecture through a notion of gathering and bridge-building.

In "Building Dwelling Thinking," Heidegger (2001a) explains that bridge-building links separate places and has the potential to gather together what he calls the fourfold of earth, sky, mortals, and divinities in a form of relatedness that undoes binary structures characterized by means, ends, here, there, and inside, outside. For Bernstein, this vision of continuity represents the unconscious supplement to Hegelian architecture that tends to break up space and construct discreet places. In her reading of Heidegger, she notes that building offers shelter and contains, but equally remains open to the outside. In this respect, building should never construct paranoid places that are somehow cut off, but rather create a situation where *Dasein* (being there) becomes *Insein* (being in), through the exposure of the finitude of the self in its relationship with everything in its surroundings. Against this vision, which effectively comprises a philosophy of ontological luxury through the immersion of the self (*Dasein*) in space (*Insein*), Bernstein sets out a history of German construction through reference to Goethe's (2016) essay "On German Architecture" where *building* becomes synonymous with *bildung* (self-formation, bodybuilding) and homemaking turns out to be about throwing up sealed, secure places for the defense of the self. In this passage, Bernstein reads the idea of cultural *edification*, where the word edification comes from the Latin *aedes* meaning *temple* or *house* and *ficare* which translates as *making*, in terms of a kind of homebuilding project concerned with the discipline of the sensuous and the mastery of life (*the architecture of the edifice*). Although Bernstein only mentions Hitler in passing, it is clear that Goethe's theory of edification became part of the Nazi strategy for the creation of culturally superior men and massive buildings (edifices) reflective of their ethnic superiority. According to this approach the openness of ontological luxury in itself, which is precisely what Heidegger means when he talks about the house of being, is contained, disciplined, and sublimated within ontic luxury and a strategy of cultural refinement set up to tame the wildness of life.

On the basis of the history of work on the psychoanalysis of Nazism, including Klaus Theweleit's (1987, 1989) massive study of the proto-Nazi Freikorps, we know that the Nazi problem with the wildness of life is that they were terrified of the possibility of the disintegration of their poorly formed selves and sought to oppose this through brutal violence toward anybody who seemed to represent openness to the world and the creation of a myth of cultural superiority that was similarly concerned to insulate them from the ontological continuity of being. In terms of building, this fearful psycho-politics was represented by Albert Speer's efforts to model the architecture of the Third Reich on Rome and even think about strategies for making sure Hitler's empire could survive its own collapse in the form of beautiful ruins. Where the Germans were critical of Rome was in their view that the empire's edifice complex forgot about and lost connection with the dynamism of life, but in the Nazi case even their myth of Germanic nature, the mountains, and the forest was framed and contained by a cultural ideology fixated upon the refusal of luxury in itself. Where Heidegger (2001a) wrote of the authentic house of being, Nazi building was always technical, inauthentic, and defined by the attempt to escape continuity through monumentality and a level of refinement and ontic luxury opposed to the openness of sensuous existence. In much the same way that the Romans sought to drive out ontological luxury through imperial expansion and the creation of a kind of world house without corners, the Nazis sought *Lebensraum* in Europe on condition that this space or place would be absolutely self-identical and homogenous. It would, in other words, be absolutely controlled and free of others (the *Untermenschen*, etc.).

In her study of Hitler's home, Despina Stratigakos (2015) explains how this obsession with ontic luxury, containment, and the control of space and place was represented in the Fuhrer's own domesticity. She shows how Hitler's house was a kind of dead place, defined by a desperate need to present the image of a normal, stable, heterosexual man. Against the cultural chaos of Weimar, Stratigakos refers to Heinrich Hoffman's popular work *The Hitler Nobody Knows* in order show how Hitler became identified with Germanic myth, the Alps, and the forest, and a sense of stability and natural order in the face of the turbulence of modernity. This mythology was reinforced by the Fuhrer's own home, Berghof, on the edge of Berchtesgaden, which looked out onto the mountains and identified Hitler with the land, the people, and living space. But this view of the Alps, what Stratigakos (2015) calls Hitler's "Alpine seduction," and the appearance of the embrace of the ontological luxury of the natural world was always framed and staged, and the interior of Berghof was a picture of sky-high anxiety and a desperate attempt to control everything through refinement and ontic luxury completely unrelated to the sensuousness of the world. Although this character study of Hitler's domesticity may seem peripheral to the real problem of Nazi totalitarianism, reading Zygmunt Bauman's (1991) work on the Nazi obsession with order and cleanliness shows how the leader's paranoid attempt to exert control upon everything eventually found its culmination in the Holocaust and the attempt to construct a living space, or world house, free from verminous others who lurk in dark corners and corrupt the refinement, purity, and ontic luxury of this utopian building project with decadence and the monstrous ontological continuity of luxury in itself. It is, of course, this obsessive compulsive megalomaniacal drive toward cleanliness that eventually led to the military defeat of Nazis.

From Nazi to American luxury

Hitler's Alpine house, Berghof, was bombed by the British in early 1945, even though the Fuhrer had already retreated to his Eagle's Nest and, following this, the Berlin bunker where he would eventually end it all. As a result, the Nazi attempt to discipline and order ontological luxury was consumed in the fires of the collapse of their dark utopian project doomed by the hubris of imperial overreach. Although Hitler's attempt to capture the world in a place of absolute cleanliness and ontic luxury ended in suicidal self-destruction, which from the point of view of Bataille (1991) would symbolize the emergence of the truth of ontological continuity beyond containment, the savage irony of the destruction of Berghof in 1945 is that Intercontinental opened a luxury hotel on the site in 2005. This hotel, or house which is never really a home, became the Kempinski in 2015. The Kempinski promises guests executive mountain views and a *luxperience* of the Berchtesgaden area, but nowhere mentions its former resident even though its own presentation of ontic luxury and high cultural refinement is chillingly reminiscent of the approach to housebuilding and homemaking of its former owner. In much the same way that Hitler's home was empty of life, a kind of tomb that represented the Fuhrer's necrophilic suspicion of the expansive nature of existence that spreads out into space, the Kempinski Hotel is an idealized house, but never a home, a place that one passes through, rather than lives in. Images of the place suggest a building constructed in the name of luxury objectivity and a kind of corporate sense of identity which is never really alive, but instead captured in a kind of mortified, commodified vision of what it means to be at peace because one is no longer really in the world.

In this respect, the Kempinski's approach to ontic luxury is strangely continuous with the Nazis' thanatological strategy for the escape from the openness of life into the closure of refinement and monumentality, even though its own very managed late capitalist vision of the luxurious represents the American victory over the Nazi Reich and the emergence of the global, neoliberal empire in the late twentieth century. Although the American defeat of totalitarianism in 1945 was thought to be a turn away from the utopian dreams of European modernity that became the nightmarish dystopias in the form of Nazism and Stalinism, perhaps what the continuity of Hitler's Berghof and the Kempinski, Berchtesgaden really represents is what Laurence Rickels (1991) calls the *Germanicity* of post-World War II Americanism and the capitalist dreamworld. In the wake of the destruction of 1945 luxury, the pursuit of luxury and the consumer society more generally became the motors of capitalist growth and the democratization of the good life in America, as well as later in the rest of the world, including, by the 1990s, China, India, and other parts of the global South. In the American context, where the individual was always king, this pursuit of the capitalist dream took the form of housebuilding and homeownership, which would allow the individual to make their own way in the world. However, the problem with selling the idea of the dream home to everybody in the name of the escape into a place of ontic luxury is that it soon became unsustainable. By the 1980s, when everybody wanted to be a king and everybody wanted to own a palace, the American economy continued to expand on the basis of the creation of huge mortgage debts that eventually became unsustainable because they were more or less completely disconnected from real economic value. In the wake of the global economic crash of 2008 and the subsequent recession that threatened to destroy the luxury economy, which promised people escape from the natural limitations of the self in others and a world that is absolutely intolerable in capitalist ideology, it is no surprise that Americans voted for their own luxury leader, Donald Trump, who ironically promised to save the people by restarting the American economy and bringing luxury back home. In this respect, Trump symbolizes the meaning of the third realm of luxury in contemporary America, where possession of luxury things (ontic luxury) fuses with the promise of luxury experience (ontological luxury, or a universe without limitation) in the creation of a Thirdspace of luxury power or, what I am calling in this chapter, authoritarian luxury.

It is easy to read Trump in terms of a symbolic representation of capitalist inequality and react with incredulity to his election to high office, but it is also possible to understand his very appeal through his vulgar displays of ontic luxury and his sky-high anxiety and violent reactions to others, because what these behaviors capture is a desperate need to escape from vulnerability, need, and openness to the world that plagues the majority living under conditions of neoliberal capitalism in a state of low economic growth. Caught in this situation, who would not want to escape into ontic luxury, who would not want to take off and hide deep inside the verticality of Trump's Tower? Reading Michael D'Antonio's (2015) excellent biography of Trump, it is clear that his own family story is one of escape from vulnerability and openness through making money, buying, selling, and building property and taking flight into ontic luxury. Long before the Kempinski took over Hitler's home in Berchtesgaden setting up the idea of the Germanicity of American power, Friedrich Drumpf left Germany for the land of the free. Looking to make his fortune in America, Friedrich headed out to the Yukon in order to make money off the back of the ultimate luxury mining operation, the Klondike Gold Rush. But Friedrich was no miner himself and instead made money by setting up a hotel for weary prospectors. Following in his father's footsteps, Donald's own father Fred also made money from property in New York City and socialized his son into a militarized way of life where existence itself is characterized by Darwinian struggle and a universe where there is nothing between security and insecurity, winning and losing, and life and death. Under these conditions, I think the young Donald came to unconsciously understand the link between money, success, and the trappings of ontic luxury and the possibility of escape from the horror of vulnerability that is necessarily represented by the ontological truth of reality where everything is open to everything else.

Taking flight from the humble reality of luxury in itself, Donald moved up in the world of his father who made money from the Brooklyn property market by buying up buildings in upscale Manhattan. Under the influence of a narcissistic complex comprising feelings of threat, persecution, and grandiosity, Trump set to work on his iconic tower, finishing in 1983. According to D'Antonio (2015), Trump made it clear that the objective of his tower was to gather up "the best people" and refuse the rest in a kind of capitalist rerun of the Nazi obsession with cleanliness and order. Beyond his family connection to Germany, it is this sadistic tendency involving the defense of his own ego through the attack on others that Doug Kellner (2016, 2017) and Henry Giroux (2016) point to that most clearly links Trump to Nazi bodybuilding. Akin to Theweleit's proto-Nazi Freikorps, who made themselves feel strong by attacking and destroying others, Trump's vision of America is one where power comes from struggle, conflict, and warfare. As Michael Kranish and Marc Fisher (2016) point out in their biography of The Donald, Trump is driven by a weak sense of self, a fear of failure, a terror of becoming nothing, and he responds to this through monumental bodybuilding projects, branding the entire world with his name and attempting to seal himself off into a world of luxury. What is the objective of all of this, but to insist upon his identity, to assert his control over the world, to make himself somebody, and to make himself exist? Yet the tragedy of this approach, which seeks to make use of luxury objects and luxury things, what I have been calling here ontic luxury, in order to seal the self off from the world and defend an authoritarian personality horrified by the possibility of ontological luxury in itself, is that it is entirely unsustainable and cannot lead anywhere but collapse back into the reality of what Bataille (1991) called continuous being where vulnerability and openness are normal. Although Americans voted for Trump to "Make America Great Again" and to give them back some sense of identity, my conclusion is that the future probably resides less in the kind of ontic luxury The Donald wants to push and more in understanding the ways in which smallness, humility, and the intimate open out onto the massive, the vast, and the immense. This is where I think we find the meaning of ontological luxury in itself and the possibility of a sustainable world founded upon the idea of ecological balance beyond the paranoia of ontic luxury.

References

Bachelard, G. (1994), *The Poetics of Space*, Boston, MA: Beacon Press.

Bataille, G. (1991), *The Accursed Share: An Essay on General Economy, Volume I: Consumption*, New York: Zone Books.

Baudelaire, C. (2009), *Paris Spleen*, Middletown, CT: Wesleyan University Press.

Bauman, Z. (1991), *Modernity and the Holocaust*, Cambridge: Polity Press.

Benjamin, W. (2009), *The Origin of German Tragic Drama*, London: Verso.

Bernstein, S. (2008), *Housing Problems: Writing and Architecture in Goethe, Walpole, Freud, and Heidegger*, Redwood City, CA: Stanford University Press.

Berry, C. (1994), *The Idea of Luxury: A Conceptual and Historical Investigation*, Cambridge: Cambridge University Press.

Champlin, E. (2005), *Nero*, Cambridge, MA: Harvard University Press.

D'Antonio, M. (2015), *Never Enough: Donald Trump and the Pursuit of Success*, New York: St. Martin's Press.

Dalby, A. (2002), *Empire of Pleasures: Luxury and Indulgence in the Roman World*, London: Routledge.

Erikson, E. (1995), *Identity and the Life Cycle*, New York: W. W. Norton and Co.

Featherstone, M. (2016), "Luxus: A Thanatology of Luxury from Nero to Bataille," *Cultural Politics*, 12 (1): 66–82.

Freud, S. (2010), *Civilization and Its Discontents*, New York: W. W. Norton and Co.

Giroux, H. (2016), *America at War with Itself*, San Francisco, CA: City Lights Books.

Goethe, J.-W. (2016), *The Essential Goethe*, edited by Matthew Bell, Princeton, NJ: Princeton University Press.

Heidegger, M. (2001a), *Poetry, Language, Thought*, New York: HarperCollins.

Heidegger, M. (2001b), *The Fundamental Concepts of Metaphysics: World, Finitude, Solitude*, Bloomington, IN: Indiana University Press.

Hollier, D. (1992), *Against Architecture: The Writings of Georges Bataille*, Cambridge, MA: MIT Press.

Kellner, D. (2016), *American Nightmare: Donald Trump, Media Spectacle, and Authoritarian Populism*, Rotterdam: Sense.

Kellner, D. (2017), *American Horror Show: Election 2016 and the Ascent of Donald J. Trump*, Rotterdam: Sense.

Kranish, M. and Fisher, M. (2016), *Trump Revealed: An American Journey of Ambition, Ego, Money, and Power*, New York: Scribner.

Mumford, L. (1968), *The City in History: Its Origins, Its Transformations, and Its Prospects*, San Diego, CA: Harcourt.

Pliny the Elder (1991), *Natural History: A Selection*, London: Penguin.

Rickels, L. (1991), *The Case of California*, Baltimore, MD: Johns Hopkins University Press.

Rimell, V. (2015), *The Closure of Space in Roman Poetics: Empire's Inward Turn*, Cambridge: Cambridge University Press.

Seneca (2014), *Natural Questions*, Chicago: University of Chicago Press.

Stratigakos, D. (2015), *Hitler at Home*, New Haven, CT: Yale University Press.

Sudjic, D. (2005), *The Edifice Complex*, London: Penguin.

Theweleit, K. (1987), *Male Fantasies, Volume I: Women, Floods, Bodies, History*, Minneapolis: University of Minnesota Press.

Theweleit, K. (1989), *Male Fantasies, Volume II: Male Bodies: Psychoanalyzing the White Terror*, Minneapolis: University of Minnesota Press.

Varoufakis, Y. (2013), *The Global Minotaur: America, Europe, and the Future of the Global Economy*, London: Zed Books.

Winnicott, D. W. (2005), *Playing and Reality*, London: Routledge.

York, P. (2005), *Dictators' Homes*, London: Atlantic Books.

4

Inhabiting luxury spaces

Verena Andermatt Conley

There all is order, and beauty,
Luxury, peace and pleasure

Charles Baudelaire, "Invitation to the Voyage"

Over half a century ago, in *Mythologies* (1957), Roland Barthes defined luxury as
"le mousseux": in other words, whatever is foamy, frothy, light, airy, and useless.
Looking at how laundry soaps and detergents were advertised in print media,
he noted that pure luxury was susceptible to the encroachment of marketing
in an increasingly aggressive consumer culture. A decade later, in *Le système
des objets* (1968), Jean Baudrillard pointed out that with the rise of seriality
and mass-marketing, luxury referred to a model form, that is, to whatever is
unique. Next to the model, marketers used gimmickry to disguise the serial
status of commodities they purveyed and put on public sale. Strategists sought
to give average consumers the illusion of buying a "unique," high-end, or luxury
product. At the same time, in the realm of the foyer and home, this shift in
economy gave consumers a semblance of agency and freedom of choice when
they set about arranging and furnishing their own spaces. Since they suddenly
no longer had to conform to an inherited symbolic and generally patrilineal
hierarchy, budding families were—in theory at least—free to create their interior
space. Baudrillard argued that this new freedom was mainly a marketing ploy
that smoothed over increasing spatial compressions and paucity of habitable
space. The stratagem also furthered consumerism that placed emphasis on
things new and in fashion. As if by miracle it tendered to a massive public an
illusion of freedom and agency.

Luxury and habitable spaces

Today, the findings of Barthes and Baudrillard are still partially valid. However, the term "luxury" itself continues to evolve under the dictates of marketing and publicity. Assisted by the engineering of new technologies, global consumerism has witnessed a sizable increase in demographic numbers and greater spatial compression. In practically every urban environment, luxury has become part of what might be called a mainstream imaginary through which we create our daily reality. By way of captivating images and text, the *idea* of luxury strives toward what is increasingly an illusion of the unique and the model form of a serial commodity. Vital for the global economy and subtending a new social hierarchy based on unprecedented riches (and correlative misery), it can be asked if "luxury" can still refer to the excess, the useless, or the unique. As a term of marketing, luxury drives the world, be it from the advertisement of consumer goods to fashion and the food industry, from travel and leisure to the real estate market and interior design, to mention only a few. For the purpose of our topic, in the paragraphs that follow, I will focus on the relation between luxury and urban real estate. I will ask how the question of "luxury" is mobilized to market urban dwellings and furnishings in order to produce habitable spaces. What does the term "luxury" promote? What does it gloss over?

In *Spatial Ecologies* (2012), I asked how it is possible to invent habitable spaces. I examined the relation of space to inhabiting and *habitus* in the sense of opening areas of possibility in otherwise unyielding or even repressive political orders. Here, I focus less on the transformation of oppressive places into more existentially defined spaces (Certeau 1984; Baudrillard 2006) than on the ways in which global consumerism primes and tracks subjects so that, as a result, they no longer think outside of norms that are imposed on them and that completely reify them (Crandall 2011; Hansen 2015; Massumi 2015). Earlier, I examined the possibility of inhabiting mental and physical spaces through movement. I explored how everyday practices and minor deviations lend a certain consistency, a thickness or *épaisseur*, to one's existence. Here I will take the inverse tack. I will argue that by way of simulation contemporary marketing of "luxury" prescribes, defines, and imposes fixed ideas of space and habitation. Put otherwise, the coupling of *space*—that had been understood in terms of an existential relation—with *place*, no longer holds because the modeling of habitus predetermines creation and invention.

A brief history of a term

In an era that thrives on the celebration of wealth and the making of money for money's sake, consumer goods tend to be advertised in terms of luxury for sale purposes though oddly, according to any online dictionary, the use of the term is less frequent today than it was in the nineteenth century. We are told that, derived from Latin, meaning splendor, excess, "luxury" dates from the seventeenth century. In France, under the absolute monarchy, luxury was the prerogative of the king. Luxury helped make the monarch the object of adoration of his subjects who could never dream of occupying his place. Attributes of luxury included shine, glitter, and even bedazzlement (Marin 1988). It so completely separated the king from his subjects that when Nicolas Fouquet, the superintendent of finances, hired Charles Le Brun to build the château of Vaux-le-Vicomte to rival the luxury of Louis XIV, the latter had him imprisoned before appointing the same architect to design Versailles. No one could exceed the luxurious appearance of the king.

In the nineteenth century, with the advent of the bourgeoisie and a rise in commodity fetishism, usage of the term increased in popularity at the same time that its meaning was being reassessed. Industrialization and rapid urbanization in France were well documented in the novels of Honoré de Balzac who in many of the ninety plus volumes of *La comédie humaine* (1999) described the new intensity of city life. He relishes in the description of new luxuries as well as miseries of this kind of life in the city that, to the contrary, poets like Charles Baudelaire will want to escape. In "Invitation to the Voyage," first published in *Les fleurs du mal* (1998), Baudelaire writes of an elsewhere where everything is "ordre et beauté, luxe, calme et volupté" (order and beauty, luxury, peace and pleasure). Emphasis is placed on the calm atmosphere and the pleasure and luxury the setting can afford. In a different vein, the growing importance of luxury is also the focus of Emile Zola's novel, *Au bonheur des dames*, serialized in the review, *Gil Blas*, before being published in its entirety in 1883. The novel traces the transformation of an economy that promotes the broad reach of luxury goods, seen in concert with their democratization when available in department stores or through mass-marketing. Zola's novel emphasizes the very availability of "luxury" products now within the reach of an eagerly consuming public. Similarly today, luxury is less the excessive, the unique or the scarce than, increasingly, the accessible, the reproducible—that which, advertisers tell us, must be possessed and owned, but has uncommon exchange value and may be advertised as unique. If with Louis XIV luxury had subtended an absolute hierarchy and a world order, it is now becoming a lure. Luxury itself has grown out of a term that is used as an incentive to consume and as part of a marketing strategy aiming to confer upon the buyer an elegant identity and stature. "Luxury" products constitute an entire spectrum from low to high end. With the proliferation of these goods, "luxury" itself has, in a sense, been cheapened.

In the real estate market, it becomes a series of check-offs on a prospective buyer's or even renter's list: marble countertops, ceramic baths, top-of-the-line appliances, and so on. Only the brand name changes according to an individual's buying power. Luxury exists at different levels and no longer only in the absolute. In believing themselves belonging to a mobile society, people will try to increase their earning power to accede to so-called "luxury" goods associated with more prestige that invasive advertising strategies mirror in front of every consumer's eyes. Advertisement creates an aura of immanence of sorts that reifies and commodifies. While luxury may once have referred to the intangible, it now appeals increasingly to standardized products that come in different price ranges. Consumers are even looking for a certain standardization that will legitimize their identity.

Waning existential territories

Since World War II, as already documented by Barthes and Baudrillard, "luxury" has definitely lost its blinding luster and shine. Having been democratized, it has become the new normal, that is, without which products cannot be sold and without which people are given to believe they can no longer exist. Echoing Merleau-Ponty, Michel de Certeau, seeking to transform a static place into a more mobile space, had written in *The Practice of Everyday Life* in a chiastic turn of phrase that *space is existence and existence is spatial* (Certeau 1984: 117). While place was often defined by a repressively symbolic order, space, made possible through physical or psychic mobility, was said to provide an additional existential dimension. With the emphasis on luxury in the realm of consumerism, what Certeau had invoked has become, as it were, an object of history. The spatial dimension, it was felt, enabled people to think, to invent new relations, to create territories other than those charted and imposed by technologies of the state. In the words of Gilles Deleuze and Félix Guattari, an existential dimension was made possible with the smoothing of striated environments, that is, with the creation of openings in a rigidly sedimented order that enabled subjects to think otherwise (Deleuze and Guattari 1987: 474–500). Today, this previously hieratic state of things has been replaced by the persuasive powers and even the dictate of marketing strategies already analyzed by Barthes and Baudrillard and exquisitely parodied by Georges Perec in *Things* (1965). Marketing immerses the consuming subject into the commerce of things. It causes people to adhere to a spatial order rather than create their own. A plethora of mainly digital marketing firms with trendy names (Expandtheroom, Lounge Lizard, Ruckus Marketing), global consulting firms (Boston Consulting Group, Bain, McKinsey), helped by celebrity bloggers who launch advertisement friendly websites or, even more effectively, non-celebrity bloggers on social media now assist in continually tracking and priming subjects. They mirror imaginary spaces such as immaculate condos with ultramodern furniture in which computer-generated people, smiling, sit or stand around so as to instill a desire or, better, a craving for a space and objects marked as "luxury." The image of a space and objects among which prospective buyers can see and feel themselves move about gives them a sense of belonging and inclusion.

Existence itself is based on the possession of goods defined as "luxury," from the condo itself to its contents. Baudelaire's *volupté* and pleasure and Barthes's sublimely "priceless" uselessness give way to the useful and above all to exchange value. Marketing websites advertise themselves as "purpose-driven." Space is no longer affiliated with concepts or tactics that theorists had cultivated between the late 1960s and 1980s to loosen or fracture the perceived repressiveness of symbolic places, state technologies, and even nascent consumerism. In today's luxury market, spatial thinking of this sort is all but forgotten. Today, forms of spatial thinking and of "creativity" belong to strategies of marketing. Always under the sign of luxury, conceived and realized by "starchitects" and award-winning celebrity teams of designers, a prearranged living space is now linked in the buyer's—or renter's—imagination as a fact of basic existence. An overabundance of marketing services tells or shows prospective clients how to furnish and move through a space. When put up for sale, condos are carefully "staged" by an expert team with the latest stylish furniture, the likes of which the interested party is invited to buy in order to be. Merleau-Ponty's dictum (2012) that Certeau mobilized has clearly lost its spiritual dimension. It functions in an entirely material and static way. Space is not defined through the relation between things or people (Latour and Hermant 1999), but is assumed to be preexisting, a container to be filled with a series of mandatory "luxury" objects destined to be replaced when they are no longer in fashion.

Third realm of luxury

Must-have items branded as "luxury" come in different price ranges. They all bear a similar appearance because of the constraints of fashion. As Baudrillard had noted, the shift from an interior space dictated by a symbolic order to another, an order aiming at putting people in control of their own arrangements, was often a simple ploy to mask the loss of space. With compression on the increase in cities and their surroundings, "make belief" inheres in objects. Carefully chosen, branded goods can seemingly transform even the smallest spaces into luxury habitations. Refurbished workers' cottages in Cambridge, Massachusetts, that date to the nineteenth century are advertised, equipped with Bosch appliances, ambient LED lighting, kitchen islands with USB docks, dramatic twenty-eight-foot open-plan living, dining rooms and kitchens. In New York City, the now historic McDougal-Sullivan Gardens, a former low- to middle-income housing project, was revamped by means of similar strategies— though not without protest—to appeal to (and perhaps become a defining trait of) the upscale, hipper, more artistic citizen. To qualify as "luxury," dwelling spaces are now required to include a minimum of prerequisite items. Helped by clever wide-angle photography, the image imprinted on the brains of the prospective buyers, no matter if before or after their visit, occludes cognition of real space. To create the illusion of luxury in urban spaces that are, paradoxically, often quite common, small, and dark, developers recruit "teams" of architects and designers. They ingeniously produce "make-believe" spaces by removing walls, a strategy that in the text accompanying the images employs a vocabulary that underscores the stylishness of "openness and flow" simulating larger rooms. Emphasis is put on illumination. *Lux!* Small quarters and low ceilings are offset by special lighting as well as the addition of skylights to produce a mirage of more extensive space. Through clever positioning of mirrors, far from those the psychoanalyst Jacques Lacan (1966) had theorized in his work on the mirror stage in the halcyon days of existentialism, they become substitute windows that simulate additional depth.

Next to these revamped older places, new upscale condos such as those being built in the towers rising on top of the former railroad yards of the Metropolitan Transit Authority in New York City, the so-called Hudson Yards between 30th and 34th Street West are also marketed with emphasis on luxury. The condominiums look sizable mainly because of the floor-to-ceiling glass windows and the open floor plans that are *de rigueur* (Figure 4.1). At Fifteen Hudson Yards, above floors reserved for businesses, living quarters are advertised in

Figure 4.1 Luxury condos at Fifteen Hudson Yards. The image shows the standardization of the condos. Fifteen Hudson Yards rendering, courtesy Related-Oxford.

terms similar to those describing the older dwellings, although they are slightly higher pitched. Next to the usual "luxury" items (stainless steel appliances, spot lighting, etc.), the advertisements offer prospective buyers the possibility of a "custom made" bathroom or kitchen. The choice consists mainly of two shades of gray for cabinetry and tiles that can be viewed and visited on the web. Now, no longer sublime (or "priceless"), luxury mainly refers to standardized products and spaces that marketers call "custom made." Despite the fact that the choice of colors and materials is limited, consumers who can afford to decide what they want will gain the illusion of entitlement, satisfaction, and an augmented sense of being.

In Certeau or Deleuze and Guattari, the concept of space had been linked to movement, invention, becoming, and the consistency of an existential territory. Contemporary space is designed for a prefabricated world of being, for (re)producing what Deleuze would call the "*calque*," the copy and not the tracing of a "map" (Deleuze and Guattari 1987). *Calquer* means to imitate, to copy, not to make a map or draw new connections in the world. Today, even the marketer's "model" is already a copy. Paradoxically, with all the emphasis on mobility, the contemporary world turns out to be quite static. To live in a space reshaped through positioning of purely material goods evacuates it of an existential dimension: it affords buyers and dwellers a place from where they can imagine themselves in a new social ladder whose echelons are defined by the possession of certain kitchen appliances or bathroom cabinetry. In a world where older forms of identity no longer have currency, luxury goods bestow a fleeting sense of belonging upon those with the means to buy into a given market.

The experience of luxury

As part of an exchange, luxury is experienced and consumed. In places like Fifteen Hudson Yards, the private dwelling spaces are complemented by public counterparts. (In other places, such as Boston, the ultra high-end luxury apartments tend to be built on the tops of hotels, among others, the Ritz-Carlton and the Four Seasons [Figure 4.2].) A phalanx of professionals manages the sites that occupy the lower floors of the glass tower, restaurants together with high-end fashion stores, art galleries, gyms, and green spaces. Their mission is to turn the dwelling "place" into a "complete and even holistic experience." Money buys "experience," and experience is the sensation of luxury.

The development of Fifteen Hudson Yards, the beacon of the entire project, began with the vanguard designers, Diller Scofidio and Renfro, founders of the interdisciplinary design studio DS+R, who won a prestigious MacArthur award. Aiming to integrate architecture, the visual arts, and the performance arts, they assisted in the design of a platform for what was to be an "immersive experience." And no holistic luxury experience would be complete without a team of landscape architects, preferably those baptized as "eco-landscape architects." Established firms such as NWB (Nelson Byrd Woltz) were instrumental in building a public green space connecting the area to the north end of the High Line, a 1.5-mile elevated greenway, built in 2014, that reconfigured a former New York Central railroad spur. NWB was asked to complement Hudson Yards' "uncommon living spaces" with a "common public space and walkways" that rejoin and extend the famous High Line in order to produce a democratic and open space where the inhabitants of the luxury condos can in principle—if not in reality—mingle with other citizens. In the description of the project, one architect, enamored with (and taking lessons from) theater, dance, and performance, calls the experience thus produced to be one of "immersion." A new and seemingly aqueous

Figure 4.2 Ultra high-end condos at One Dalton, Boston. The picture shows well the similarity between the condos and also between them and others such as those of Hudson Yards in New York. Courtesy of Pei Cobb Freed & Partners/Cambridge Seven Associates.

environment would abolish differences, to begin with, of class and social rank in order to make ambient luxury available to everyone.

A similar process is set in motion to transform not just a railroad yard but a former shipping canal, which happens to be one of the most polluted environments in North America, into the setting for luxury condominiums. In Brooklyn, the Gowanus Canal had been targeted for assistance from a Superfund in order to defray the costs of a governmentally sponsored clean up. The eponymous neighborhood is now marketed with images of people kayaking on the canal in front of "luxury" apartment buildings (Figure 4.3). A recent article in *The New York Times* (Newman 2017) documented how German students who visited the site had read about the sunsets on the canal in a tourist brochure. A team of publicists accompanying them thought they could use the idea of a glowing sunset to market the nearby condominiums. The imaginary appeal to luxury items bathed in an aura of dusk was aimed to completely gloss over the irreparable ecological devastation.

When developers began turning to Brooklyn, after Park Slope and Carroll Gardens, the Gowanus was next in line. In 2015, Juan-Andres Leon wrote

Figure 4.3 365 Bond Street, Gowanus, Brooklyn with the hues of sunset in the original color image and kayaks in the foreground to make the buyer, renters forget about pollution. Courtesy of The Lightstone Group.

about Gowanus and the attempt to overcome its toxicity through development. Emphasizing the health risks people are willing to take in order to live in a conveniently located neighborhood near Manhattan, Leon noted how, with the arrival alongside the canal of Whole Foods, one of the first upscale grocery stores, the developers of Gowanus attempted to change its image. In 2015, the neighborhood was still stigmatized by the known presence of chemical toxins. Two or three years later, clever advertisement of the neighborhood has all but eradicated the memory of the extensive mercury poisoning in the sludge that Consolidated Edison had left as its lasting legacy. Meanwhile, real estate prices and rents have skyrocketed. One of the online advertisements for the condominiums for the neighborhood reads:

> Gowanus cuts its own distinctive path, much like the mile-plus-long canal of the same name that helps define the neighborhood. Industrial in look, it manages to feel small scale: filled with intimate rock clubs, upstart breweries, hip restaurants and, of course, a shuffleboard hangout. Art studios, galleries and green businesses dot the streets, while a walk near the banks of the Gowanus itself has an undeniable rough-hewn charm.[1]

Luxury condos such as those at 363 Bond and 365 Bond alongside the canal are for sale or even more often for rent. Carefully staged images help construct the place and transform it into a third realm of luxury. Aggressive marketing obliterates any lingering doubts about the site itself. As elsewhere, communities and buildings are advertised as being "for tomorrow." Under the guise of being cutting-edge and ultramodern, the apartments and condos are described as follows:

> Designed for avant-garde living, 363 Bond Street brings everything you've come to expect in luxury Gowanus apartments for rent to a neighborhood that's refreshingly unexpected. Situated in Brooklyn's hottest new community, our apartment homes offer the most desirable location to work, live, and play. Landmarked by the Gowanus Canal, the neighborhood was formerly an industrial shipping center and is home to the Carroll Street Bridge, the oldest of the four retractable bridges in the country. Recently, Gowanus has become an urban utopia where art, industrial architecture and innovation meet, creating the ideal modern urban setting. 363 Bond Street creates an authentic living space mixing curated art collections from local artists with the luxury amenities you desire in your next home.[2]

Luxury is to be expected when moving to Gowanus. It belongs to the rhetoric of the "urban experience" alongside "culture," while completely obliterating the real and menacing dangers posed by toxic build-up, especially in the increasing likelihood of storm surges caused by rising oceans and the effects of global warming on climate and weather. At Gowanus, like elsewhere, the expectation of luxury comes with a mixture of products and with atmosphere created, we are made to believe, by carefully chosen—or, as the buzzword would have it, "curated"—artworks that provide the total immersive experience.

Under condo availability we read:

> Arrive home to True Inspiration in Your Gowanus Apartment. . . . Whether you choose one of our studio, 1-bedroom or 2-bedroom Gowanus apartments, you're destined to be impressed at 363 Bond Street. Our apartment homes are designed with comfort and luxury in mind. We offer spacious, distinctive floor plans with high-end, luxurious amenities like custom Italian cabinetry, stainless steel appliances by Bosch, hardwood flooring, and washer and dryers in your home. A select number of our apartments also feature a private terrace for you to enjoy. Click below to learn more about each available floor plan that 363 Bond Street offers and to see what homes are available now.[3]

The appeal to luxury via products and the illusion of a personalized "home" masks the serial construction in a thoroughly polluted environment. A pseudo-existential dimension is reintroduced through the use of "home." More upscale condominiums also become "residences" or "estates." The marketing strategies emphasize life in luxury and enjoyment that are both "but a click away." Though the apartments at Gowanus are cheaper than those at Hudson Yards, they are advertised in a very similar manner: luxury comes in different price ranges.

The advertisement adds: "Your life is a Work of Art . . . and here it reflects on every surface. From Tristan Eaton's colossal poolside mural to the gallery vibe that welcomes you inside, a curated collection from local artists gives our luxury Brooklyn apartments an authentic style."[4] The appeal of luxury brings together with top-of-the-line appliances, flooring, teams of so-called high-end designers, the integration of art into the daily life to provide an avant-garde, yet also holistic and enriching experience that can be bought with any sizable amount of money you are willing to put up for rent. "Curate the Luxury at Gowanus," read an online publicity that recently popped up on my computer screen while I was reading an article about politics in *The New York Times* (May 11, 2018). To curate luxury can be seen as an invitation to organize and update what is "happening and cool" (Rosenbaum 2012), in other ways, to manage what is already pregiven.

Marketing luxury

True luxury—what would be unique, ineffable, unnecessary, without purpose—if it still exists, has withdrawn from view. Most "luxury" has been standardized and (at the risk of falling into the Marxian idiom) its exchange value carefully calibrated. The ongoing shift in what, thanks to ubiquitous marketing, passes for luxury can best be discerned in the entangled words and images of advertisement. The element of freedom that Baudrillard noted in 1968 has morphed into an obsession and a compulsion of simple cravings and "must haves" researched by teams of publicists and consulting firms that push people to fill a shrinking space. Under the impact of the strategic appeal to the imaginary condition of a space of luxury, stress is placed on how to inhabit a place according to what advertisement dictates. Baudrillard, Barthes, Perec, as well as Jean-Luc Godard in *Two or Three Things I know about her* (1966) had raised similar concerns. With tongue in cheek and deceptive irony, they had decried the influence of Madame Elle in the newly minted *Elle* magazine. Quoting from the magazine, Juliette Jeanson in Godard's film decries her husband's lack of "culture" when he professes ignorance of Madame Express's existence. Over fifty years later, the marketing strategy has shifted toward the quasi-mandatory addition of luxury to every item that will afford an illusion of self-worth and increase sales. At the same time as the model has gone global, luxury itself has become quite serial.

To stimulate sales of new spaces, marketers deploy strategies from fashion branding. While branding bestows exchange value on the object, fashion gives people the incentive to buy as Barthes, and Walter Benjamin before him (1999), had remarked. Branding will bestow the stamp of luxury and aura on a product. Fashion will create desire; it will make it indispensable while already spelling its ultimate demise. Fashion changes with the whims of architects and designers who must continually reinvent what will pass for the next luxury space. These days, if floor-to-ceiling windows and "flowing" open spaces suggest a world of circulation without borders and obstacles, luxury furnishings in today's chaotic world come in the shape of ultramodern, sleek—preferably Italian—designs that confer upon the space and appearance of utmost simplicity and order. If in the seventeenth century luxury was defined as baroque (a model, as Maureen Dowd [2016] remarked, that is kept by Donald Trump whose interior in the Trump Tower was referred to by his biographer, Timothy O'Brien, as being like "Versailles and Louis XIV on acid," that is, in "bad taste") and kept as an ideal into the nineteenth century, today, the emphasis tends to be on simple lines. Color palettes are mostly discreet, emphasizing white, beige, brown, black, and dark blue tones punctuated by a few color splotches. Straight lines of tables, sofas, and chairs adjacent to pendant lighting are *de rigueur* where luxury condominiums are advertised. Furnishings in publicity pictures or open models rarely seem to deviate from this style, though newer, softer, more rounded forms are beginning to appear, requiring changes and, as a result, become a market for new purchases. Dictionaries list austerity as one of the antonyms of luxury. However, contemporary spatial furnishings are quite austere and their colors discreet. And it is precisely this austere look, a giveaway for luxury that carries a high-end price tag. It echoes, in a sense, Baudelaire's narcotic utopia where everything would be "order, beauty and luxury." But while Baudelaire's luxury was that of a dark, paneled drawing room in amber light, its contemporary avatar is said to be light, fresh, and airy. It entirely disregards the messiness of today's world. Interior design companies, like the Italian firm Flexform, which calls itself a family enterprise but is nonetheless of a global reach, advertises one of its collections, MOOD, in an online catalog under the heading, "An Intimate Look" that speaks for itself:

> Intimate and elegant. That is the atmosphere that can be breathed through the Flexform MOOD collection. Warm and sophisticated ambiences, shimmering

fabrics and soft shapes suggest to our senses An Intimate LOOK, a statement that describes the entire Mood world. The collection travels in an ambience where the taste extends between retro and deco. It takes inspiration from the models of the past by reinventing and by making them leaner and lighter. The allure and the taste of the memory pieces are enhanced, by contrast, by contemporary architectural contexts that surround them with the images. The light and original chromatic research of the materials flows among the photographic narration telling about places and comforting atmospheres, where the spectator perceives an enveloping and pleasant cocooning effect. Sofas, armchairs, tables, chairs, beds generate a sort of soothing island and try to create a welcoming nesting-refuge, protecting ourselves from the outside chaos. Silence as trend. The soothing silence of objects, feeble tones and rounded curvilinear aesthetic, never intimidating, never sharp-cornered. Mood offers an ecosystem of objects supported by harmony. Once seen, Never forgotten. (Flexform, Mood collection catalog. Online)[5]

The repression or forced oblivion of a world of social contradiction, political chaos, and environmental degradation is *de rigueur*. The collection is said to "travel" in an ambience between past and future, while through their photographic "narration" the images tell the consumer about comforting atmospheres and cocooning effects. The trend toward silence is generated through the new curvilinear aesthetic of the objects. With this collection said to offer an ecosystem of things in concert and harmony, we are far from Baudrillard's perception in 1968 of a certain freedom for people to reinvent their own space; from Certeau's invention of the quotidian through verbal or physical movements in the apartment or the street; from the making of maps and connections for which Deleuze and Guattari had been advocates.

An ecosystem as the one glossed above tries to convey a mood through objects that fill a static space. The interior space becomes an imaginary refuge. Luxury condos are advertised as a retreat from the world. If immersion there is, it is turned inward where, as the Italian firm declares, angles are no longer sharp but rounded. The mood is tempered. It is a cocoon, a nest, a niche. Silence becomes a shelter from outer chaos. Rather than embracing life, inhabitants put themselves in a bubble of imaginary self-sufficiency. Luxury buyers segregate themselves, while they also congregate among their happy brethren (to be with "good people," as the advertisement for Hudson Yards reads). From their chrysalis, they can look down on public spaces where immersion is left to those who harbor the illusion that when walking on the High Line they count among Certeau's wanderer-*flâneurs*.

Is there true luxury?

With ubiquitous marketing, where then are the real spaces of luxury? Where are the uselessness and excess? If excess comes with a price tag, the froth comes, perhaps, with the myriad services advertised for the owners of some of the more upscale spaces such as in those at Fifteen Hudson Yards in New York City, One Dalton, or PIER 4, Boston. These range from grocery shopping to pet services, childcare, assistance by sommeliers for a wine cellar, event planners, runners, and the like. True luxury, more than the object itself, resides in the more intangible extras, in the services that enhance "the experience" of these "lifestyles." Belonging to what long ago Jean-Paul Sartre called the "pratico-inert," these extras are, however, far from useless. They truly help the inhabitants to become more productive, to make more money to consume more luxury products, and in the process further refine and redefine the term.

We could, of course, also add that these high-end luxury places where a temporary model reportedly costs as much as twenty single-family houses in a nearby neighborhood (Teitell 2018) replace a more rigid social hierarchy of times past with a more fluid counterpart, based on money, which in accord with the myth of America is still believed to be within everyone's reach. We could also add that consumption of all these luxury items is based on the extraction and destruction of the earth's materials (Parikka 2015) never mentioned in the official advertisements that abundantly tout farm-to-table restaurants with sustainable sourcing. Eco-conscious living too has become a marketing gimmick, from the freshness of organic produce to the soothing quality of products. Extraction of precious metals from the earth, the waste of material, and the fact that luxury contributes happily to the destruction of resources and biodiversity go unstated.

The promotion of luxury condominiums is a worldwide phenomenon. We focused on a few places in New York and Boston. Similar sites can be found in Shanghai, Hong Kong, Lagos, Mumbai, Abu Dhabi, Milan, Paris, or London. Yet there are still many inhabitants for whom luxury might be, for example, running water or a toilet. The emphasis on luxury, even as a devalued concept, celebrates the social contradiction and underscores the gap between the haves and the have-nots. It also shows the values of a world where existential space and "existential territories" are rare and where, as Félix Guattari (2000) put it, an equivalence between material, natural, and intangible goods reigns supreme.

Perhaps, we can claim, true luxury will always have something to do with inhabiting in an existential sense. If existence is spatial, it can only be so in areas outside of the invasive space of advertisement. Recently, there has been much talk to the effect that the ultimate luxury in today's world is silence. Silence would quiet the inner and outer cacophony using vacuous terms like "luxury." Yet again, silence too has already been coopted by businesses selling not only furniture but also EEG (electroencephalogram) headbands to quiet the inner chatter of our brains in order to make us more focused and productive. Real silence would have to open onto the world rather than simply promote a retreat into a "cocoon" of the kind described in advertising brochures for luxury condos. The luxury of a silent space would be, in the words of Gilles Deleuze and Félix Guattari, the possibility to do away with today's deadening and deafening insistence on the *décalque*, the mindless copying of things. The silence would allow one once again to open to the tracing of maps and the creation of time-spaces that are part of a care of the possible so necessary for the composition of today's world.

References

Balzac, H. de (1999), *La Comédie humaine*, ed. Pierre Dufief and Anne-Simone Dufief, 4 vols, Paris: Omnibus.

Barthes, R. (1957), *Mythologies*, Paris: Éditions du Seuil.

Baudelaire, C. (1998), *The Flowers of Evil*, translated by J. McGowan, Oxford: Oxford University Press.

Baudrillard, J. (1968), *Le Système des objets*, Paris: Éditions Gallimard.

Baudrillard, J. (2006), *The System of Objects*, translated by J. Benedict, London: Verso.

Benjamin, W. (1999), "Paris, Capital of the Nineteenth Century," in *The Arcades Project*, translated by Howard Eiland and Kevin McLaughlin, 14–26, Cambridge, MA: Belknap Press of Harvard University Press.

Certeau, M. de (1984), *The Practice of Everyday Life*, translated by Steven Rendall, Berkeley: University of California Press.

Conley, V. A. (2012), *Spatial Ecologies*, Liverpool: Liverpool University Press.

Crandall, M. (2011), *Gatherings*. Available online at: https://vimeo.com/21346731.

Deleuze, G. and Guattari, F. (1987), *A Thousand Plateaus*, translated by Brian Massumi, Minneapolis: University of Minnesota Press.

Dowd, M. (2016), "Monsieur Vogue," *New York Times*, December 21. Available online at: https://www.nytimes.com/2016/12/21/fashion/andre-leon-talley-melania-trump-donald-trump-anna-wintour.html (accessed March 20, 2018).

Godard, J.-L. (1966), *Two or Three Things I Know About Her*. The Criterion Collection, 2009.

Guattari, F. (2000), *The Three Ecologies*, translated by Ian Pindar and Paul Sutton, London: Athlone Press.

Hansen, M. B. N. (2015), *Feed-Forward*, Chicago: University of Chicago Press.

Lacan, J. (1966), *Les écrits*, Paris: Seuil.

Latour, B. and Hermant, E. (1999), *Paris, Ville Invisible*. Available online at: http://www.bruno-latour.fr/virtual/index.html (accessed February 20, 2018).

Leon, J.-A. (2015), "The Gowanus Canal: The Fight for Brooklyn's Coolest Superfund Site." Available online at: https://www.sciencehistory.org/distillations/magazine/the-gowanus-canal (accessed March 20, 2018).

Marin, L. (1988), *Portrait of the King*, translated by Martha Houle, Minneapolis: University of Minnesota Press.

Massumi, B. (2015), *The Power at the End of the Economy*, Durham, NC: Duke University Press.

Merleau-Ponty, M. (2012), *Phenomenology of Perception*, translated by Donald Landes, New York: Routledge.

Newman, A. (2017), "Can Gowanus Survive Its Renaissance?," *New York Times*, November 13, 2017.

Parikka, J. (2015), *The Anthrobscene*, Forerunners Series, Minneapolis: University of Minnesota Press.

Perec, G. (1965), *Les Choses: Une histoire des années soixante*, Paris: Julliard.

Rosenbaum, S. (2012), "Content Curators Are the New Superheros of the Web," April 16. Available online at: https://www.fastcompany.com/1834177/content-curators-are-new-superheros-web (accessed May 12, 2018).

Teitell, B. (2018), "At home, in Boston's Stratosphere," *The Boston Globe*, May 4, 2018.

Zola, E. (1883), *Au bonheur des dames*, Paris: G. Charpentier.

A touch of the exotic: Sensuality as luxury in the 1970s' domestic interior

Jo Turney

Introduction

The home is not the one tame place in a world of adventure;
It is the one wild place in a world of rules and set tasks

G. K. Chesterton, quoted in Garvey (2001: 47)

This chapter seeks to uncover the development of luxury as experiential; specifically, as a desirable experience or sets of experiences that can be articulated and obtained through ordinary consumer goods that hitherto would not have been considered "luxurious." With reference to the presentation of home furnishings in advertising in the UK in the 1970s, this chapter presents a discourse that considers new ways of "being" and/or experiencing the traditionally private domestic environment through the increasingly public display of home decor choices as demonstrating personal or bespoke taste (as furnishings always had done) but with the added dimension of sensual desirability, of a new language of pleasure (luxury) elevating the mundane and practical to near-orgasmic levels.

By discussing and analyzing popular culture sources alongside contemporary cultural and design discourse, the chapter draws parallels between a social trend toward ideals/ideas of permissiveness, as well as acknowledging transitions and the acceptance of equality legislation, and more general expressions of the zeitgeist surrounding new ways of "being." Such an emphasis is twofold; it acknowledges the conversational cultural backdrop of new ideas (popular culture) and expresses projections of ideal scenarios, which in turn reflect a sense of the "mood of the times." It is, of course, impossible to correlate this with any particular accuracy, particularly over such a wide temporal, social, economic, and geographical arena, so the chapter privileges the period 1970–74 and draws from diverse primary sources such as popular TV shows, magazine articles, and readily available bestselling popular novels and lifestyle books (e.g., Greer 1971; J 1971; Woodiwiss 1972; Morgan 1973; Adams and Laurikietis 1976). The advertisements selected for comment, and indeed for the research undertaken, all feature in nationally available "homes" magazines throughout the period specified and therefore to a certain extent can be seen as part of a general dialog surrounding the promotion of an "ideal home." This means that the research juxtaposes that which is part of a popular consciousness surrounding what it was to be modern with ideal visualizations of what this might look like and how it might be experienced.

Although we might recognize the well-known advertising epithet "sex sells," by discussing examples of advertising in this context, specifically identifying the language of luxury in conjunction with contemporary discourses surrounding sex and sensuality, as well as the private made public, the aim is to consider the home as an extension of the sexual, natural, or women's body; a space for sensorial exploration and heightened pleasure through touch. This sensory pleasure is, via the language and iconography of advertising during the 1970s, further defined and understood as an aspect of a "new" or different form of luxury. We might see this as "luxuriating," of indulging in unnecessary or excessive pleasures, and, because the emphasis was so overtly bodily and thus sexual, luxury or the practice of indulging in it became imbued with wantonness and the illicit, that which is private, desired, and inhabits the realm of fantasy or the imagination.

Such a claim might seem somewhat at odds with what was being sold: ordinary, household objects and surfaces. Yet, throughout the decade, advertisements for seemingly mundane products such as floor coverings, furniture, crockery, and wallpaper, all exploited the concept of tactility; the feel of the product on the skin inviting one's toes, fingers, and bodies to luxuriate in the warmth, depth, and quality of new surfaces. Such pleasures of the flesh were especially modern, offering the possibility to engage with objects in a pleasurable even desirable rather than practical way, and by association, elevate consumer goods and the home environment to new dimensions of experience, what also might be described as the third realm of luxury.

The modern home: The private becomes public

During the 1970s, the home and its design began a process of transformation in which the privacy of the domestic sphere, historically associated with women's work and stereotypes of femininity devised in response to nineteenth-century morality and biological determinism, became further feminized by the expression of space as corporeal. Domestic space was becoming indistinguishable from the domestic body. Such a statement might seem somewhat farfetched, but the home was undergoing a transformation in response to feminist discourse surrounding texts such as *The Captive Wife* (Gavron, 1966; Oakley, 1976), which drew attention to women's isolation in the home, juxtaposing the experience of being "at" home as a housewife with the experience of being a housewife; the woman becomes the environment and vice versa.

Concurrently, the home and its allusion to femininity or as a feminine environment was also being explored in relation to issues central to discourses in women's magazines: ideas of permissiveness and what it was to be "modern." For example, the May 1973 issue of *19* magazine, included articles discussing trends toward promiscuity (p. 177), abortion (p. 4), anti-establishmentism and "dropping out" (pp. 74–75), obscenity laws and pornography (pp. 86–89), knowing one's rights (p. 121), the Common Market (pp. 147–52), alongside the expected fashion, music, entertainment spreads, short romantic fictions, and horoscopes. It is clear that from just one magazine issue the traditional interests of women were merging with those that focused on overthrowing them; there was a new emphasis on personal freedom and empowerment. So, in Agony Aunt Virginia Ironside's discussion of promiscuity, she likens casual sex with acquiring life and entertaining skills (akin to "learning to play the piano") much like an addition to more commonplace accomplishments offered by a finishing school. She continues to use traditionally feminine genres to unpick a still, however popular it was claimed, taboo subject, by describing promiscuity metaphorically as an uncooked cake mix "too much makes you feel sick, but a lick or two is yummy" (p. 177). The language and topic are of the time, easily recognizable to the young women who made up the target readership, but the framing is echoing the familiarity of women's magazines of the past. The advice and discussion appeared as less directed; readers were encouraged to make up their own minds, rather than bowing to social convention or the views of a magazine editor. We might argue therefore that modernity was expressed through freedom (Lehman 2011), particularly freedom of choice and freedom to choose (Scanlon 2009), a semantic discourse that linked ideology and a state of being, with being oneself and making consumer choices accordingly.

As outlined, this was not an easy transition; the modern can only be defined as such when compared to its predecessor, so the old worked to underpin new ideas, to act as a support while also emphasizing the radical and exciting potential of those being proposed. Indeed, design throughout the decade was characterized by the juxtaposition of the old with the new, or a reworking of it, and frequently opposing value systems, which demonstrated a historical or traditional bias, were overtly positioned to accommodate the new. The period is characterized by a style chaos, punctuated by retro-gazing that saw the whole past century revisited and "reinvented" in some form. Likewise, "craftsmanship" and "artworks" were used to promote cheap laminates, wipe-clean wallpapers, and polyurethane faux leather armchairs. This lack of authenticity is central to the stigmatizing of the decade as one of tastelessness, as the reinvention and repetition (Binkley 2000) of past styles exemplify the formal and sentimental characteristics akin to Greenberg's definition of kitsch (Greenberg 1961). Nonetheless, the ideas being promoted were radical and also taboo, and the home was a site for reinvention, and reference to the past, authenticity and that which was "known," eased their passage into the language and practice of design as well as the British domestic interior.

Essentially, the making of the private public, what we might consider as looking behind and beyond the net curtains, was more than a home makeover; it was a revolution that revealed what was hidden and thus what was possible. So much like a striptease, the domestic interior was being uncovered, critiqued, and laid bare, while the social constructs that supported it and the relationships between the people that inhabited it started to literally get in touch with the environment, and also its ideology and the experience of "being at home." The emphasis on experience was important, not because people didn't know what home was like, but because being at or going home were ingrained with notions of tradition that did not sit comfortably with concepts of modernity. Indeed, notions of home, for both men and women were so much part of a popular psyche that was constructed around gender relations and stereotypes, the division of labor, and outdated concepts of marriage that it formed the basis of almost all British comedy from the postwar period to the mid-1970s. Primarily, marriage in this context was seen as emasculating, with the domestic interior dominated by a castrating wife, for example, *George and Mildred, Fawlty Towers, Carry On* films, where the comic praxis rested on latent misogyny and the male protagonist's attempts to regain a sense of potency through pomposity, stubbornness, and (generally failed) attempts to seduce younger and less masculine, single women (Hunt 1998: Heath 2014: 657). Such was the depth of this understanding, Slumberdown's 1974 advertising campaign for bed linen headed with the tagline: "From the day you buy a Slumberdown, your husband will be sleeping with another woman." The interplay between *double entendre* and marital expectation here toyed also with notions of the woman as consumer and dominant wife, and with notions of the husband as seducer as well as consumer of the product.

If popular concepts of home had been constructed around a model in which sexual relations were stagnant if not non-existent and potentially terrifying, the representation of the 1970s' incarnation was the opposite. The home was presented as a realm of fantasy in which both men and women could experience sensory, and specifically tactile, pleasure, a site of exploration and potential discovery, an awakening that was suitable for this new period of enlightenment. The repetition of phrases and words that demonstrated the sensory (e.g., touch, soft, moist, feel/ing) alongside those that alluded to hedonistic pleasure (e.g., luxuriate, reveal, recline) and those that specified body parts (e.g., a sofa that has "arms to hold you," chairs that have "attractive legs," or products that have "as many colours as you do") establish a language and narrative pertaining to the feminine and the tactile female body. This is not a "practical" female body, but a desirable one, and therefore the products described speak indirectly of sex, but not sex with your wife; this is a fantasy form of sex, and one in which that fantasy can be realized through the consumption of luxurious, but not necessarily expensive, furnishings.

The social anthropologist, Alison J. Clarke describes "'home' as a process, as opposed to an act of individual expressivity, in which past and future trajectories (inseparable from external abstractions such as 'class') are negotiated through fantasy and action, projection and interiorization" (2001: 25). And here, during the early 1970s, home became the site of this form of "fantasy in action"; the experience of home and the possibility of leading or experiencing the life one dreamed of was available in a multicolored, mass-market of goods, offering fulfillment based on individuals' lifestyle choices.

The development of the mass-market from the mid nineteenth century developed a cult and mythology of goods, which is underpinned by cultural fetishism. This means that consumerism, emerging at a time when spectacle was a fundamental component of what it was to be and experience the modern, is driven by a desire to consume, assimilate, and display goods (Stratton 2001: 26). This was made possible not merely by a desire for goods themselves, but via a system of techniques that established a narrative of desire, such as modern advertising, sales, and marketing techniques (Richards 1991: 49). It was the creation of this mythology of objects that Bowlby considers central to notions of shopping and pleasure; the "dream" of consumption, of time not working, in places and spaces of fantasy (Bowlby 1993) and what Thomas Richards describes as "the familiar imperatives of modern commodity culture, with its emphasis on status, eroticism, health and female sexuality" (1991: 71). So we see that consumerism is built on concepts and experiences of the spectacle, and this spectacle is articulated through the female body. This concept is developed by Guy Debord, who reconsiders commodity fetishism as "domination of society by tangible and intangible things" (2012: 36), which reaches its climax during spectacle in which the tangible is partially replaced with that which might be considered beyond or excessively tangible.

This moved consumerism beyond the engagement of the primary sense, sight, to include other forms of sensory engagement including sound (new developments in hi-fi equipment), smell, and taste (the reinvention of the gourmand). Consumers became witnesses to and participants in what Merleau-Ponty (1962) calls the "synaesthetic"—the fusion of all our senses in an overall bodily experience (Hecht 2001: 129).

Touch, as the only reciprocal sense, has been considered, certainly from the mid nineteenth century onward, taboo. Touch establishes an intimacy that disrupts the private and public self, challenging sociocultural hierarchies and norms. In the advertisements for home furnishings in the 1970s, the subtext of image and strapline are undoubtedly sexual, encouraging sensual and sensuous engagement with products, as well as with the home, offering the potential for a higher level of experiential interaction with one's surroundings through touch, and, by association, a clearer and fulfilling relationship with the private and sensuous self. But if this is taboo and takes place in the privacy of the home, how can new modes of thinking and being infiltrate the home?

It's only natural

The most obvious way in which new designs become part of everyday life is through stealth and assimilation, or pretending that they had always been *in situ*. As previously indicated, in terms of aesthetic, the decade borrowed ruthlessly from past styles, appropriating and reappropriating what was considered to have been "good taste." This can be attributed to several interrelated and well-worn sociocultural factors: (a) recognizable styles offered a sense of stability that counteracted the ephemerality that marked 1960s' design; (b) social mobility and access to credit, alongside the development of a neoliberal "Me" culture, allowed consumers to position and mark themselves through the style they exhibited in their home; and (c) design innovation in the period was not in terms of appearance, but in relation to science and experience, for example, ergonomics, user-centered interplay, psychology, development of chemical synthetics, and new manmade materials, so the emphasis on a "new" aesthetic was not a priority. This is a common practice, especially with new home technologies; a radio in the 1930s and a TV in the 1950s did not need to have a wood surround but did so to give the appearance of being "part of the furniture."

Popular interior design elements often repeated a fusion of high cultural form with affordability, as a means of addressing a wider spread of consumers, by reproducing aspects of historic, aristocratic, and luxurious taste and fusing it with modern technology, such as manmade fibers, plastics, wipe-clean surfaces, and so on, which emulated wealth and status. So, synthetic floor tiling was produced to emulate grand mosaics or lavish marbles, while wallpapers became textured, heavily decorated, and colored, referencing the decor of stately homes. Style and design, it appeared, became an exercise in imitation, and this imitation of accepted "good" or high-class taste became a vehicle for the expression of contemporary furnishing technology. The combined emphasis on nostalgia and an idealized home as a means of establishing security in an unstable climate can be also addressed as a need to create some sense of authenticity in an increasingly inauthentic world.

Another way in which authenticity could be expressed and experienced without critique was through nakedness. Not only did the unclothed body demonstrate a truthfulness, it was also considered the ultimate natural form— the perfect foil to the dearth of new synthetic fibers. For example, Arlington fabrics, new PU leather upholstery "Arlan" was marketed as having "even more colours and textures than you do," set against an "arty" series of photographs all of which detail segments of a woman's body. Each image is sexualized to the point of fetish, exemplifying Lacan's concept of lack and the rim (Cavallaro and Warwick 1998). In the composition, the woman's body is fragmented and brutalized, reduced to a series of parts that cannot be reconfigured into a whole. She has been cropped into a series of erogenous zones, akin to those that characterize pornography, with her "lack" or potential sites for penetration open and overt, for example, painted mouth, weeping eye, peach-like bottom, ear, pert bosom with erect nipple. Even when this "woman" (and it is likely many have been photographed to make this image) is visible, she is in a half-light, obscured by the media that intends to celebrate her. Here, PU leather is likened to skin, to the tactile surface of a woman's body; the consumer is invited to touch, to feel, how "natural" both are, implying that if one were to luxuriate on Arlan, the experience would evoke the naked flesh of a woman.

Likewise, adverts for laminates were presented as silhouettes of naked women, flesh merging with and substituted for a space-age synthetic surface in which the animate becomes laminate/inanimate, alive or dead, natural or artificial. The authentic woman is presented as a two-dimensional, less complex facsimile, easier to keep and control. There is no doubt of emasculation or castration here.

The bare breast is a particularly compelling motif in interior design during the period. The breast also featured as a surface design, appearing on mirrors, footstools, on fabrics, and as a dishwasher fascia made by Kitchen Aid. Along with more "traditional" or "appropriate" patterned surfaces, such as country gingham check, natural florals, tiles, even the Mona Lisa, the bare breast dishwasher cover sticks out like a, well, bare breast.

The single, bare breast has a long history as an allegorical emblem. From religious iconography and the Virgin suckling the Infant Christ, to the bounty of "Mother Nature," the breast represents abundance, plenty, and the primary role of women in building and nurturing nations. In this respect, we might consider the single breast in Freudian terms, as a parallel (if not equal) to the single penis or in relation to the slang "tit," which simultaneously embraces men and women, subject and object, the woman's breast, or an ineffectual male (Kaite 1995: 38). The breast is also (and it is always one part of the pair) a real, fleshy, and wobbly appendage that needs the constraint and restraint of a bra, and thus indicates the pleasure and wantonness of the female body (Gamman 2000). Indeed, the single breast is the most favored icon in pornography (Kaite 1995: 37). In these images, we are confronting the maternal and the sexual woman.

Although there are undoubtedly symbolic elements at play in advertising campaigns, the construct woman as a mélange of Eve, the Virgin Mary, and "Mother Earth," more practical and contextual issues develop a more pressing subtext; the naked body, in a contemporary domestic setting equates with a "healthy" sex life, albeit one in which women are presented and cast in traditionally iconic and idealistic, rather than edgy or contemporary roles.

The creation of a tactile and sensory/sexual home was not an overnight transformation and, even so, it is unlikely that many people decorated their homes with bare breasts. But, the domestic interior had been changing slowly since the postwar period, and by the 1970s its transformation was near complete. Less controversially, there was an emphasis on the senses as hardwood floors were replaced with soft, fitted carpets or warm to the foot lino; open fires were replaced with central heating; air fresheners and more perfumed cleaning products created a pleasant olfactory sensation. Better electrical circuitry facilitated the use of multiple lights in each room, thus offering a brighter and/or mood-enhancing visual ambience. This is what James Obelkevich describes as a "new sensory regime" (1994: 147) and later, "the tactile home." This can be seen as an extension of wider sociocultural shifts in attitudes and lifestyle, a letting go or of letting one's hair down as a sign of the zeitgeist (Binkley 2007: 10), and also as an expression of a "Me" culture, which privileged the personal over the collective. The home, once a space associated with communal living, had become a site of personal experimentation and pleasure. This is seen in the advertisement for Mazda lighting, which sees consumer goods transform the domestic space into a stage for a variety of leisure activities. Here, we see the mundane home transform into a site of pleasure, one not of chores or drudgery, but of "date nights" filled with sexy dances and delicious food. The desires of the inhabitants take center stage, literally beneath their "spotlight."

Research in social anthropology demonstrates that objects are major players in establishing and maintaining a sense of "home" (being at home) through familiarity, connectivity, and in forging narratives, whether conscious or not (Miller 1987). Anat Hecht (2001: 141) argues that these understandings are developed through the complementary evocation of memories of sensory engagement with spaces, people, and things. By evoking past pleasures, such as premarital dating in the Mazda advert, the home and its passions are remembered and reignited.[1] Mazda "turns you [and it] on."

The "other" woman and the experience of home

In relation to design, and much like the revival of styles as a means of promoting authenticity, one way in which touch, sex, decadence, and other sociocultural taboos had been incorporated historically into the sanctity of the home had been through concepts and representations of "Otherness." Such a position not only enabled the trade in luxurious and sumptuous goods but also created a mythology of peoples and places that at best considered "others" as childlike and at worst, deviant. In either case, goods from the non-Western world became synonymous with the exotic, which in turn became a byword for the erotic, and, by the nineteenth century, wallpapers, silks, drapes, sumptuous fabrics, ethnic patterns and motifs, and tactile goods became metaphors for the sexual female body. In the 1970s, this leitmotif was revived, with adverts for floor coverings and carpets featuring reclining, non-Western women in traditional dress, under straplines such as "Exotic and Readily Available."

We might consider this form of representation of both objects and space as a form of pornification; both illicitly sexual in relation to imagery and idea and commodity. As Berkeley Kaite suggests, "they enunciate phantasies which in some way elaborate a logic of seduction and desire" in which a "quintessentially private and intimate act is rendered public in its consumption" (1995: 1).

We may consider the discord between the public and the private as confirmation of either a loosening of morals or an "opening up" or acceptance of sexual acts, by way of the ubiquity of pornographic imagery and language in relation to domestic consumer goods. Indeed, the seeming and changing focus of Good Housekeeping magazine from homemaking to love-making was not lost on at least one reader. In a letter to the editor of Good Housekeeping, Mrs. Berman wrote:

> GH (Good Housekeeping) certainly has its surprise elements. Nowadays I am not sure whether to expect a sex manual or a housekeeping magazine. . . . It has become so sex oriented that soon you may have to deliver it in a plain wrapper! (Mrs. A. Berman, Pinner, Middlesex, Letter to the Editor, *Good Housekeeping*, June 1973)

One might also consider this emphasis on sexual pleasure, particularly at home, as a nod to women's sexual desires and experiences, acknowledging popular discussions about the female orgasm, premarital sex, and body politics. However, the centralization of both the space of the home and the goods within it is as an extension of or substitute for the woman's body establishes additional opportunities for and sites of penetration, thus challenging the home as a woman's "sphere" in which she has any sense of agency. This is Foucault's textural body, a place where biology disappears and pleasure comes from the text and its reading; in this case, the consumption of goods and space (Foucault 1980: 26). The woman becomes "part of the furniture." This, combined with the semiology of pornography, which relies on sexual difference (Kaite 1995: 2), creates an uncomfortable space, which emphasizes the instability of or challenge to patriarchy resulting from the move of feminism to the mainstream.

> The pornographic body, however, is constructed through its discursive arrangement: the body is not naked but adorned and dressed up, it is not disciplined in terms of sexual pathology but speaks to sexualities. Pornography as a discourse on sexuality constitutes the body, not vice versa. (Kaite 1995: 37)

The replacement of women by furniture (the animate with the inanimate) can be understood as an example of fetishism. In Freudian psychoanalysis, specific fabrics that are used in furnishings, such as velvet and fur (which in the 1970s we might equate or substitute with flock wallpaper and shag-pile carpets), are symbolic and fetishized as signs of female castration—the shock/anxiety of seeing or encountering the penis-less woman. The fetish object is considered necessary in halting repression or denial while facilitating full orgasm. Gamman and Makinen (1994: 42–43) consider the fetish object as representative of "the doing and undoing" of this knowledge, acknowledging and saving the subject from castration.

Sex at home: Consuming men consuming women

A focus on the woman as consumer had been well articulated through the early sections of the twentieth century, with the consumption of goods offering not only a means of articulating "feminine taste" (Sparke 1995: 74) but also a means of limited agency (Benson 1994: 187). It might be assumed that as equal opportunities became *du jour* during the period of study and that feminism started to move away from the margins (Black 2004: 116), that women's emancipation would be solidified by and articulated through their consumer power. Not so much; by the early 1970s, particularly in relation to home decor and furnishings, men started to be targeted hard by advertisers.

By targeting men as consumers, advertisers not only were able to speak in a new, direct language that acknowledged a more permissive society, but also drew on specifically British cultural forms and ideals. In many examples, sex sold, but not as an established ideal of a "happy ever after"; here, sex was raw, tactile, exploratory, and, ultimately, temporary. This is particularly evident in adverts for the Bremworth Ram, a wool carpet, that drew from the language of pornography and combined this with the iconography of "the bachelor," the fashionable, single man. The strapline in Bremworth's 1974 advertising campaign read: "The Bremworth Ram creates excitement in any room," which alludes to pleasure, the non-domestic, the tactile, and the sexual. When placed in combination with the accompanying image—a red, shag-pile carpet (a close-up of which begs the reader to run his fingers through it, to feel its depth) under the smooth green baize of a pool table and a chair, which is draped with a fur stole that simulates feminine legs positioned akimbo—the message is one of pure phallic pleasure. For example, the use of fur, a traditionally luxurious fabric, is emblematic of

Freudian fetish and the castrated female, while playing pool is reminiscent of the sex act, which involves potting balls into pockets with a phallic cue. Each element, from the use of words, the phrasing, to the visual coding, situates the Bremworth Ram (a name that suggests some form of animalistic "rutting") and directs the reader to male sexual pleasure, and here that sexual pleasure is fun, a "no strings attached"[2] game or sport, in which the consumer should compete and be in complete control over. This sentiment is expressed in a similar manner in an advertisement for double glazing in which it appears that the new windows are so effective at excluding drafts that women just want to discard their clothing. Although this advert plays to the ways in which the consumption of goods had the potential to improve one's sex life, it also expresses a British middle-class anxiety surrounding the unnecessary luxury of interior heating, which was considered "indecent" and a means to "soften" or "spoil" inhabitants.[3]

In another Bremworth advert (also 1974), the carpet becomes host and witness to seduction. Readers are confronted with what one assumes is a post-coital tableau: the part-visible "bachelor" with shiny shoes and crumpled clothing leans against the wall, slumped and lighting a cigarette. To his right is a trendy, masculine living space (open cocktail cabinet, whiskey in a glass, sleek, modernist furniture); to his left an ajar door. The carpet follows onward, leading the eye beyond the image, luring the reader to the role of voyeur, offering a peek at an abandoned woman's silver shoe and a segment of a pink, ostrich feather trimmed negligee. The explicit narrative is formed through the visual clues of seduction. The man is the central character; we assume that this is his place, and therefore we assume that he is a cultured and wealthy man, based on his choice of clothing, alcohol, and furniture (and obviously carpet). We also assume that he is sexually attractive, as the hastily cast-off women's clothes in the next room, along with his own crumpled garb and exhausted cigarette smoking, imply a frantic and passionate heterosexual encounter. Women's clothes are not only indicative of unnecessary luxury but also speak of a soft-porn aesthetic seen in British suburban sex comedies and much of the widely available European porn which adopted a domestic *mise en scène*. The discarded shoe, as if to tone down the explicitness of the narrative, echoes the Cinderella fairytale, substituting romance for raw or exploitative, casual sex.

There should be no real surprises here. The relationship to male desire and its relationship to both home and consumer goods is evidenced in Freud's concept of Family Romances.

> If we understand Freud's theorisation of desire as describing a culturally specific phenomenon, then it becomes a description of how, within the bourgeois-

originated nuclear family, the sexual aspect of desire is privileged and enhanced. Further, this form of desire operates in the space between what one has and what one wants, the person who is socially constructed to have an active desire, the male, will seek to reduce his anxiety by producing/acquiring what he wants. (Stratton 2001: 6)

The promise of permissiveness, and the loosening of morals, articulated in adverts such as these and in the mass media, women's magazines, and expressed in interior design, was certainly a popular theme, but one which remained predominantly an exception and ideal rather than a norm.[4] Nonetheless, the potential for sex without consequences, with, we assume, many unseen/ unknown partners, articulates and normalizes non-procreative acts within the domestic environment, and thus negates any form of women's ownership of that space. It also presents casual sex as hedonistic—underwritten by the use of phallic symbolism—as an unnecessary, but highly desirable luxury for the single man, obtainable for the price of a carpet. The seducer/consumer is seduced/ consumed and vice versa.

Summary

New materials democratized design but were also seen as "inauthentic" and consequently were promoted as "authentic" by associations with the natural and concepts of individual experience. Luxury was central to these concepts as it was the key to personal sensory, pleasurable (even unnecessary) experience negotiated through the domestic environment and consumer goods. The pleasure inherent in a tactile home, of surfaces that stimulated the mind, body, and eye, while recreating experiences reminiscent of the exotic and erotic, equally paid testament for a post-permissive generation's quest for a sense of the "real" in an increasingly inauthentic world, and of a desire for a place and state of mind which transcended the mundane.

Advertisements for seemingly mundane products such as floor coverings, furniture, crockery, and wallpaper, all exploited the concept of sensory, and by association, sexual experience; the feel of the product on the skin inviting one's toes, fingers, and bodies to luxuriate in the warmth, depth, quality of new surfaces. This was the third realm of luxury—experience beyond, but stimulated by, products that hitherto had not been considered luxurious.

However, this new luxury was built on an established language of sex and sensuality that was quintessentially British; arising from colonial concepts of the Orient and Otherness, the erotic was constructed as exotic (and luxurious). This essentially nineteenth-century concept was modernized through its juxtaposition with innuendo, pornographic imagery, and iconology, all of which was underpinned with a trajectory toward the self: personal acquisition, exploration, and pleasurable experience. The luxury and hedonism of the aristocracy of the past came home.

Likewise, objectification, most frequently understood as the animate made inanimate and applied to representations of women, was now, undergoing some kind of reworking of meaning, applied to consumer goods that were "enhanced" by the addition of allusions to women's bodies and/or attributes. This change of focus coincided with, or was a direct response to, varied approaches to lifestyle as an experience-based concept that presented consumerism as a means by which freedom of being or the expression of being modern was aligned with the praxis at which choice that was perceived to be one of individual free will met mass choice of goods within the mass-market. In other goods sectors, such as clothing or foodstuffs, the target consumer was a woman; in furnishings, it was a man. This was important because it demonstrated wider sociocultural concerns relating to gender stereotypes and new approaches to the home, which highlighted the sexual and revelatory potential of furnishings and consumer choice. One was not merely buying a sofa, for example, one was buying Parker Knoll's "Melissa," which would offer actual sensory delight through its surface and comfort, but equally embody the ideal woman and ideal sexual experience. "Sex in the sitting room" became less about sexual intercourse and more about sensory intimacy with one's possessions.

Products, therefore, became an extension of the body, the woman's body, and consequently the domestic took on almost fetishistic qualities. Ultimately, such advertising stimulated desire in a new way; this was less about "keeping up with the Joneses" and more about lust induced longing. Consumer goods became associated firmly with desire, and their promotion as "lifestyle" objects fueled a desire which gave the consumer access to a world of fantasy, a means of escaping the harsh realities of daily life. Luxury was feminized as the home, traditionally a sexualized, private space, became one of intimacy and sexual fantasy for the male consumer.

References

Adams, V. and Laurikietis, R. (1976), *The Gender Trap*, London: Virago.

Benson, J. (1994), *The Rise of Consumer Society in Britain 1880–1980*, London: Longman.

Binkley, S. (2000), "Kitsch as a Repetitive System: A Problem for the Theory of Taste Hierarchy," *Journal of Material Culture* 5 (2): 131–52.

Binkley, S. (2007), *Getting Loose: Lifestyle Consumption in the 1970s*, Durham, NC: Duke University Press.

Black, J. (2004), *Britain Since the Seventies*, London: Reaktion Books

Bowlby, R. (1993), *Shopping with Freud*, London: Routledge.

Cavallaro, D. and Warwick, A. (1998), *Fashioning the Frame: Boundaries, Dress and the Body*, Oxford: Berg.

Clarke, A. (2001), "The Aesthetics of Social Aspirations," in D. Miller (ed.), *Home Possessions: Material Culture Behind Closed Doors*, 23–45, Oxford: Berg.

Debord, G. (2012), *Society of the Spectacle*, Bread and Circuses Publishing. http://www.breadandcircusespublishing.com/

Foucault, M. (1980), *The History of Sexuality, Vol. 1*, New York: Vintage.

Frum, D. (2000), *How We Got Here: The 1970s*, New York: Basic Books.

Gamman, L. (2000), "Visual Seduction and Perverse Compliance: Reviewing Food Fantasies, Large Appetites and Grotesque Bodies," in S. Bruzzi and P. Church Gibson (eds), *Fashion Cultures*, 61–78, London: Routledge.

Gamman, L. and Makinen, M. (1994), *Female Fetishism: A New Look*, London: Lawrence & Wishart.

Garvey, P. (2001), "Organized Disorder: Moving Furniture in Norwegian Homes," in D. Miller (ed.), *Home Possessions: Material Culture Behind Closed Doors*, 47–68, Oxford: Berg.

Gavron, H. (1966), *The Captive Wife*, London: Penguin.

Greenberg, C. (1961), "Avant Garde and Kitsch," in *Art and Culture: Critical Essays*, 3–21, Boston, MA: Beacon Press.

Greer, G. (1971), *The Female Eunuch*, New York: McGraw Hill.

Heath, J. (2014), "'My Missus . . .': An Essay on British Comedy and Gender Discourses," *Journal of Research in Gender Studies*, 4 (1): 650–57.

Hecht, A. (2001), "Home Sweet Home," in D. Miller (ed.), *Home Possessions*, 123–48, Oxford: Berg.

Howes, D. (2005), "Hyperesthesia, or the Sensual Logic of Late Capitalism," in D. Howes (ed.), *Empire of the Senses*, 281–303, Oxford: Berg.

Hunt, L. (1998) *British Low Culture: From Safari Suits to Sexploitation*, London: Routledge.

Hunt, M. (1974), *Sexual Behavior in the 1970s*, Chicago: The Playboy Press.

J (1971), *The Sensuous Woman*, New York: Random House Publishing. https://www.amazon.co.uk/Sensuous-Woman-J/dp/0440178592

Kaite, B. (1995), *Pornography and Difference*, Bloomington, IN: Indiana University Press.

Kinsey, A., Pomeroy, W., and Martin, C. (1948), *Sexual Behavior in the Human Male*, Philadelphia: W.B. Saunders Company.

Kinsey, A., Pomeroy, W., Martin, C., and Gebhard, P. (1953), *Sexual Behavior in the Human Female*, Philadelphia: W.B. Saunders Company.

Lehman, K. J. (2011), *Those Girls: Single Women in Sixties and Seventies Popular Culture*, Lawrence, KS: University Press, Kansas

Merleau-Ponty, M. (1962), *Phenomenology of Perception*, London: Routledge.

Miller, D. (1987), *Material Culture and Mass Consumption*, Oxford: Basil Blackwell.

Morgan, M. (1973), *The Total Woman*, Old Tappan, NJ: F. H. Revell.

Oakley, A. (1976), *Housewife*, Harmondsworth: Penguin.

Obelkevich, J. (1994), "Consumption," in J. Obelkevich and P. Catterall (eds.), *Understanding Post-War British Society*, 141–54, London: Routledge.

Richards, T. (1991), *The Commodity Culture of Victorian England: Advertising and Spectacle, 1851–1914*, Stanford, CA: Stanford University Press.

Scanlon, J. (2009), *Bad Girls Go Everywhere*, Oxford: Oxford University Press.

Sparke, P. (1995), *As Long as It's Pink: The Sexual Politics of Taste*, London: Pandora Press.

Stratton, J. (2001), *The Desirable Body: Cultural Fetishism and the Erotics of Consumption*, Urbana, IL: University of Illinois Press.

Woodiwiss, K. E. (1972), *The Flame and the Flower*, New York: Avon.

The emptying of the interior: Luxury, space, and the hotel effect in contemporary life

Peter McNeil

The environment in which Lily found herself was as strange to her as its inhabitants. She was unacquainted with the world of the fashionable New York hotel—a world over-heated, over-upholstered, and over-fitted with mechanical appliances for the gratification of fantastic requirements . . .

Edith Wharton, *The House of Mirth* (2002: 222)

Life's not easy. You need to write your thank you notes. Silver needs to be polished. You need to join the adult human race and not just lounge around in front of the TV and have your bedroom look like a hotel room.

Frank de Biasi, interior decorator, "Interview," *New York Social Diary*, 2016

The emptying of the interior and its connection to generational change is much remarked upon today, from the pages of international financial supplements to the musings of New York taste-makers past. Whereas once the newly arrived rich, as well as the older monied elites, enjoyed living among antique furnishings, dense collections, and *ancien-régime* wood paneling, the dominant aesthetic in real estate advertising for high net-worth individuals and their "best-in-class" assets is for an "empty" look not seen since the modernism of the 1930s or the minimalism of the 1970s. Such a look is often compared to that of the luxury "hotel." The "grand hotel" when it developed 150 years ago on the North American eastern seaboard was far from "empty," but it did embrace some of the contemporary taste for depersonalization and modularity, as well as being a technological marvel. In this chapter, I consider the shifting concept of contemporary luxury as played out in the relationship between the hotel room and the domestic interior. In the late nineteenth century, the hotel represented the luxurious embodiment of a quasi-princely existence. Yet the hotel was always recognized as a strange space, slightly askew, not completely domestic, and effortlessly maintained. Its state of seeming perfection was made possible both by technology and new approaches to the organization of time and labor.

The "hotel effect" has created a desire among rich and middle class alike to emulate in their everyday and domestic lives something of the appearance of a contemporary hotel. The Airbnb or "disruptive sharing" effect has led to contemporary domestic spaces and hotel rooms appearing perhaps their closest at any time in history—hosts are unlikely to house very valuable items in "private" rooms that are let by the day. These are spaces in which collections of objects, books, and artworks are largely absent (being both too personal and valuable), where comfort and luxury are provided instead via textile, lighting, and technological and spatial play (large spaces in dense urban cities being the great luxury of our time), and in which the type of atomized existence that perturbs cultural commentators such as Sarah Schulman is played out. Real estate "stylists" deliberately under-furnish rooms in order to make them look larger in photography. Airbnb cultivates a "hipster" aesthetic in which a few artfully chosen industrial products—old typewriters, ladders, or macramé plant hangers—punctuate the room, and this look has in turn fed back into the so-called art hotels, a type of boutique hotel (many of the "retro" industrial products are in fact new reproductions of older mass-produced items). Newly built loft dwellings in Manhattan are designed to evoke the past but resemble newly built hotels and vice versa. Property development around the world and its widespread advertising has spawned a non-threatening approach to photography in which any consumers can supposedly imagine themselves—anything too personal or extreme is discouraged. On one level, this is a modernist nirvana—no need for extraneous decoration—but on the other hand, most modernists liked their collections arranged to their own tastes. Contemporary London property speculation in eighteenth-century Georgian spaces has used the idea that the Georgian was "minimal" (simple perhaps, but not minimal) to justify the destruction of much of the built environment. Such negation comes about in part because the popular view of Georgian environments, formed during the Arts and Crafts period (1890s) focused on plans and photographs of fragments and a type of "negative space" in which the textiles and furnishings of the period were lacking (McKellar 2007: 331). In areas such as Spitalfields, eighteenth-century windows are routinely smashed, interiors stripped out, and only the protected brick facades remain. Heritage is replaced with the "mass-produced" aesthetics and modern systems mentioned above.

Today, foods, entertainments, and experiences tend to be brought in from the outside; they are enclosed, private, "personal," and "bespoke" (when in fact most are highly scripted and marketed). It is less about community and more about privacy and perhaps even narcissism of the first truly globally connected peoples. This marks an ironic return to the inward-looking interior of the bourgeois nineteenth century that emphasized the separate spheres of public and private life, as well as a flight within luxury imaginings from an object-based to more experience-based luxury culture encompassing travel, food, and care of the self (fashion, beauty, fitness). Concepts of contemporary luxury promulgate this new desire, which inflects everything from the art market to interior design and the social and economic impacts of tourism. It relates to Richard Sennett's notion of the "corrosion of character" (Sennett 1998) that accompanies stratification of rich and poor around the world, gentrification of working-class neighborhoods and a new middle-ground aesthetic designed to neither provoke, stimulate, nor offend. As "luxury on tap" is now relative emptiness at home in terms of objects (whereby space, expensive material surfaces, and experience are the new luxuries), home and hotel appear more and more similar.

Grand hotel

"Grand hotels," replacing commercial traveler inns, were in large part a North American invention. They were public spaces with private bedrooms and shared, later, private, bathrooms, required for business travel and transactions. They were always held up to aesthetic scrutiny, being new, but often made to look old. Edgar Allan Poe, in his essay "The Philosophy of Furniture" (originally 1840), criticized the "display of wealth" in the New World "well-furnished apartment" which took the place of "heraldic display" and confused "magnificence and beauty." He criticized the "glare," "glitter," and "analogous errors" of the US interior (Poe 1967). The poet and aesthete Oscar Wilde continued the famous "put down" for New World architecture on his landmark speaking tour in the United States and Canada in 1882: "Luxury gives us the gaudy, the vulgar, the transient. It may help but it never creates art."[1] Wilde always stayed in the most luxurious hotel in any city, but he found the built environment lacked aesthetic coherence and authenticity; when he was asked "What do you think of our architecture?" he replied: "You have none."[2] Wilde commented at length on his dislike of the thick, white industrial porcelain that is still called "hotel china" (it resembles what is still used for catering and in American diners today): "All over the country, in all the hotels I stop at, they give me cups like this to drink my coffee or chocolate from. See how thick and clumsy it is. It is at least half an inch thick and so barbaric in form that one would think it was made in a barbarous, savage age.... It disgusts me to drink from it."[3] Wilde repeated the tale in different versions at least three times on his tour, contrasting hotel china with the simple porcelain wares used by Chinese laborers in San Francisco. A part of his irony was that contemporary, industrial aesthetics had debased contemporary taste and that so-called "primitive" peoples—in this case, poor and migrant workers—had better taste than the wealthy North Americans. Despite what the aesthetes felt, consumers persisted with such lavish and convenient hotels.

By 1900, the luxury hotel eagerly adopted modern and utopic ideas of time, motion, and modularity with the implementation of new technologies such as electricity, radio, and air-conditioning. The effect and possibly also the desire of such integrated technology was to efface all signs of labor. As well as new models of management, services, and catering, hotel entrepreneurs needed to decide on the look of their hotels. Developing at the time of Victorian taste, in which a densely cluttered domestic environment was considered tasteful and desirable, the grandest made use of "le goût Ritz" (Ritz Hotel taste), a transformed eighteenth-century French style (Figure 6.1). This style was also used in many of the first residential New York apartments (which merged hotel and residence) as well as the smartest British mansions. Hotels can be like a residence and vice versa—craftsmen from many countries were hired to build and furnish great houses in Britain, which, along with France, was a center of finance, learning, and art and considered a most desirable destination from which to conduct business in the nineteenth century. Men who relocated from other countries to live in Britain included German-born Sir Julius Wernher (1850–1912), one of the so-called Randlords, those from South Africa who had made a fortune in diamond and other mineral exploration; in the 1890s he refurnished his London residence, Bath House in Piccadilly (previously owned by Mr. Baring of the homonymous bank), and in 1903 bought and furnished the eighteenth-century Robert Adam designed Luton Hoo in Bedfordshire (today a luxury hotel and spa). The taste was "le goût Ritz," and Wernher was a part of the syndicate that had backed the Swiss hotelier César Ritz in creating the London landmark of luxury, in which every room had a private bath (McNeil and Riello 2016: 141). The interior of Luton Hoo was redesigned by Mewès, the very architect of the London Ritz, and it was later described by the architectural expert Ernst Pevsner as "Beaux Arts at its most convincing and indeed most splendid" (Christies 2000: 42).

Figure 6.1 Marie-Antoinette Room, Waldorf-Astoria Hotel, New York, *c.*1902. George C. Boldt, photographer. Courtesy Library of Congress Prints and Photographs Division Washington, DC 20540 USA.

The domestic interior "densified" in the nineteenth century. More and more objects, coverings, and also specialized spaces appeared. Manuel Charpy has emphasized that nineteenth-century taste was not a copy or amalgam of the century that preceded it but a unique bourgeois creation in which new modes of collecting, dealing, retailing, and image-making (both painting and photography) contributed to a distinctive consumption model of the nineteenth-century bourgeoisie. This new class of people engaged in an imaginative transaction with memory and the past, hence the taste for historicizing furniture and collections. Yet, at the same time, Charpy argues, they adopted an identity also built around mass production and fixed-price uniformity, which can be seen in everything from reproduction antiques to bathroom and kitchen fittings (Charpy 2007). Experts, artists, antique dealers, and architects were there to ensure the bourgeoisie did not make mistakes, and the "amateur" (meaning expert but not professional) vision was highly valued. New public spaces that sprang up in Paris following the French Revolution included museums, luxury hotels, and grand restaurants for the bourgeoisie (the aristocracy did not embrace restaurant going until the 1930s). In a similar vein, Simon Goldhill observes that the profusion of objects inhabiting a Victorian drawing room "speaks insistently not simply of a history of taste, but also of the interconnected forces of the industrial revolution, which changes the modes of the production of things, and the imperial project, which changes the modes of circulation of material objects and their owners" (2015: 1). Things do not have fixed value or determination but are always historically contingent. The desire for "things French" did not begin with the nineteenth century but was borne from the French Revolution itself: the Revolution "unleashed an earthquake not just in the world of governance and ideas but also in the world of things" (Stammers 2008: 295). Material culture itself—prints, porcelain, fans, and furniture—shaped views of European history before the professionalization of history in the 1870s via texts and documents (Stammers 2008: 313). We will return to the matter of "things" and objects consumed within luxury tourism and hotel experiences later, in a discussion of "barefoot luxury" in Southeast Asia.

The hotel room as luxury model/module

Molly Berger points out that the luxury hotel is an American eastern seaboard idea, not European, as many people might think. Her book *Hotel Dreams: Luxury, Technology, and Urban Ambition in America 1829–1929* outlines a century of a type of new management system, hierarchies and training, new technological systems, including lighting, plumbing, patented locks, steam heat, and enormous onsite laundries: "the modern hotel was both the mechanism and the product of a market society" (Berger 2011: 28). The best always had a great location, a large size, excellent service, and copious linen, and textiles and were very clean (Figure 6.2). They replaced taverns, which advertised how often the sheets were changed and what class of person had slept in them. She also observed how they served as "displays of nationalist supremacy," which is important here (Berger 2011: 5). Hotels became part of a metropolitan network in which luxury was organized for guests and "it became incumbent on the hotel to take care of anything and everything with no further effort or thought required or expected on the guest's part" (Berger 2011: 179).

In the 1880s, American hotels began to move away from very gendered spaces to more "heterosocial" ones in which women and children participated (Berger 2011: 181). Luxury shifted from a very elite model to one based more upon standardization and a broad market (Berger 2011: 181). This is why we

Figure 6.2 Room in the Waldorf-Astoria Hotel, New York, *c*.1902. George C. Boldt, photographer. Courtesy Library of Congress Prints and Photographs Division Washington, DC 20540 USA.

are still surprised by the relatively low cost and high quality of American hotels today. The hotel was compared to a theater, and it was suggested that patrons had the right to be entertained, "diverted and gay," that is free from concerns of toil and labor (Berger 2011: 185). Service areas were called "back of the house" and included vast numbers of workers. Novelists of the period capture the mood of unsettling luxury created in the new hotels. Edith Wharton wrote of a hotel encounter in *The House of Mirth* (originally 1905) thus: "The lady's [Mrs. Hatch's] habits were marked by an Oriental indolence and disorder peculiarly trying to her companion. Mrs Hatch and her friends seemed to float together outside the bounds of time and space" (2002: 223).

Hotel chain owner Statler had the idea around 1910 to build all his hotels in the same rather than regional or other styles—the preferred idiom was late eighteenth-century Adamesque—and managed nearly 8,000 rooms across America (Berger 2011: 207). He pioneered the concept of employee–guest relations in which guests were passive and passified as the service was already what they required. There was no need to ask or complain as wants were anticipated (Berger 2011: 208). Statler introduced into rooms the sewing kit, iced running water, plugs for curling tongs, a gap under the door so the paper could be slid under, bathroom heating, individual thermostats, radio receivers, bedside reading lamps, windowless bathrooms with good ventilation, back-to-back stacked bathrooms, and aligned heating systems of bath and bedroom to save space and cost. Such small luxuries continue to structure the way in which traditional luxury hotels operate; the great innovation of the owner of the first Four Seasons Hotel in the 1970s was to give the ladies hair shampoos in small bottles, which made "dressing cases" redundant. Some grand hotels in Asia today keep ossified structures such as bell boys—the liveried page boys of the Peninsula Hotels are a famous example—who were originally message boys and have been redundant for nearly 100 years since pneumatic tubes and telephones were invented. Here the matter of labor within the luxury experience— simultaneously visible and invisible—is significant. When visible it is highly codified and choreographed.

Housing and the hotel

In the late nineteenth century, an alternative to apartments was to rent rooms for an extended period of time in one of the new luxury Manhattan hotels such as the famous Chelsea Hotel (1884). Most striking in the New York building scape was the Ansonia Hotel (1904). Here was every luxury: electricity, lighting, enormous amounts of linen, message tubes, and private baths. In summer, freezing brine was pumped through the walls to cool the building. Each suite had mahogany doors and a selection of different furnishings was possible, rather like luxury "turn-key" or ready to move in apartments today (Gaines 2005: 174–77). By the late nineteenth and early twentieth centuries, such hotels, often called the "Grand hotel" of a town or city, shared similar characteristics. The ones that were most proud offered a bathroom for every room, most had grand entrance spaces, restaurants, and bars that also functioned as gathering places for civic and other functions. They were secure, with doormen and other observers ensuring security, and they generally offered expensive but guaranteed travel services ranging from tours to money changing.

Hotels in the twentieth century have run the gamut from the mass taste of motels in the 1930s and 1940s to the corporate image of large chains in the 1950s. Modern architects proposed everything from art deco visions to kitsch fantasies for hotel stays. Many such hotels themselves display photographs and memorabilia from their own pasts that point to elements of fantasy, desire, and pleasure embodied in guest experiences and stays. "Boutique hotels" were proposed by taste-makers in the 1980s in which an act of branding was reconnected with the personal taste of an individual, often quirky and idiosyncratic. We now find a reaction against too much individuality and the rise instead of designed spaces that are narrativized (heritage, colonial, safari, goût Ritz, etc.). This trend reflects practices in parts of the wider interior design sector, in which some—but not too much—individuality is favored. Various "luxuries" have always been offered by the hotel experience, whether it be a built-in radio in the 1940s, brass lamps and gilded bathroom fixtures in the 1970s and 1980s, or staff dressed to match the interior design in the 1990s.

Barefoot luxury

By the 1960s–70s the era of "barefoot luxury" arrived in Southeast Asia, opening a new set of questions about how to design for luxury travel within developing nations and tropical climates. To many of the original stakeholders, the term luxury would have been anathema, being associated with the developed world, materialism, and false values. But as early as the 1920s and 1930s, Hollywood stars, artists, and musicians had traveled by Dutch liners to new tourist destinations such as the island of Bali, then in the colonial Dutch East Indies. Many Southeast Asian hotels were linked to the activities of artists, collectors, and expatriates. The earlier travel was not considered "luxury" at the time but rather "exotic." It was connected to artistic and other bohemian elites, many being also homosexual and cosmopolitan.[4] They developed new routes into Bali such as Ubud, up in the hills, where no one went before, but where there was a royal court. This became the home of queer German artist Walter Spies who was permitted to build a pavilion on land belonging to the Ubud royal family. As the royal family needed to accommodate more visitors, they permitted more individual pavilions to be built, currently the site of the Hotel Tjamphuan. Spies' simple two-story villa is now restored and can be booked (Figure 6.3). In the 1950s–60s, Australian architects and artists who had first journeyed to Bali in the 1940s promoted the coastal fishing area at Sanur—then a village and rice paddy—as a place to stay. In order to furnish the "alternative" hotels, which are considered the first "boutique hotels" in Asia, and which were really semi-enclosed beach huts—artists such as the Australian Donald Friend devised interior designs and furnishings: "a high aesthetic applied to the rusticity of the Tandjung Sari" (Friend 1972: 11). They

Figure 6.3 Walter Spies' villa, Ubud Bali, *c.*1930, now grounds of Hotel Tjamphuan. Photo: Peter McNeil.

turned to the work of artisans—not yet "artists"—to create "local" designs and decorations (following in the footsteps of some Dutch, Javanese, and Chinese/Indonesian antique dealers). The type of approach Friend and his circle took was to not "decorate" but rather to make use of living cultural traditions to assist in furnishing the new Balinese pavilion type hotel for his Javanese business owner friends Wija Wawo-Runtu and English wife Judith. The Tandjung Sari club, for example, built a suite called the Duchess of Bedford (named after one of its regular visitors) around 1972 in which the first open-air terrazzo bathtubs in Bali were used. Friend designed the floor tiles made by local potters after Balinese textile designs. These "original" designs now cause issues with hotel maintenance if they are to be maintained rather than completely replaced, the latter being common in hotel management. The Oberoi Bali in Seminyak—also built as a private club circa 1970 and frequented by Princess Grace and Mick Jagger at the time is still extant but has been largely rebuilt. It also makes use of the "Balinese" pavilion concept promoted by Australian architect Peter Muller and his anthropologist wife Carole (Figure 6.4).[5] Such hotels used salvaged materials

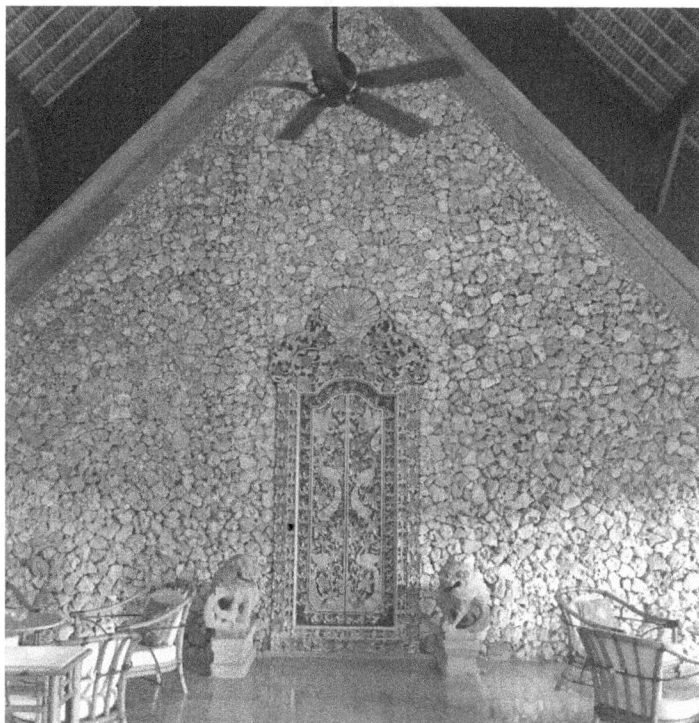

Figure 6.4 Peter Muller (architect), Oberoi Hotel, Seminyak, Bali, open-air entrance vestibule, and check-in area built of local coral rock and antique architectural fragments, 1970s, restored. Photo: Peter McNeil.

from high status dwellings and decommissioned religious structures (a society such as Bali continually remakes the sculptures and architectural elements of its many temples and offering spaces). Antique doors were set in coral stone or mud walls worked with the local idiom. At first with no air-conditioning, room service in the area meant banging on a gong (Darling 2012). The Indonesian "Jaya" Ibrahim (died 2015), who worked for fashion and boutique hotel designer Anouska Hempel in London in the 1980s, continued the tradition of combining a subdued 1930s' modernist feel with local materials and references in his revered designs for luxury hotels such as the Legian Bali.

Such hotels—now very popular—were not built according to the official Indonesian state position (Indonesia became a Republic in 1945, absorbing Bali). The Indonesian state decided to embrace intensified tourism. As well as building a new airport in Denpasar, the government constructed a large modernist "Bali Beach Hotel" (1962), which was monolithic, international, and not nearly as picturesque. Friend called it a "big boring modern many-storeyed airconditioned nightmare in the style of architecture often blamed on Le Corbusier" (Friend 2006: 9). Modernism and nation-building—official state legacies—were designed to prove the country was not backward. In Bali, official Indonesian government policy in the 1950s was to create luxury tourism around the words "Objek" [*sic*] and "Service"—but, alas for the Balinese, even spaces such as their own temples were turned by the Indonesian majority into "objects" and their cultural production—what Westerners call art, into folklorism (Picard 1997: 197). The rituals of tourism practiced today in Bali do, in fact, turn many attractions into a combination of "object" and "service."

Of particular note for the decoration of high quality hotels as well as exclusive collecting and interior decoration in the postwar period is the concept of "râtissage"—literally "combing"—used within anthropology to suggest unusual combinations of objects dislocated through time and space. Daniel J. Sherman (2004: 770) suggests that the proposition of "home" can "through either the actual or the vicarious arrangement of objects" point to themes such as "authenticity, adventure, or liberation." He points here to the concept of "association" that developed around the strategies of the decorator Andree Putman in the French publication *L'Oeil* circa 1960. Such a look was highly influential and suited the collecting mind-set of the postwar generation. For example, if you see a Buddha head mounted on a stand and sitting on a European console, next to a piece of wicker furniture, you are looking at "râtissage." At the moment, there is a cultural backlash in some parts of the world against this decontextualized practice. Friend had noticed the sacrilegious aspects of Balinese tourism in the 1970s: "the tourists . . . now dashing quite frantically with their cameras—they use them as instruments of blasphemy—add[ing] a Bosch-like aspect to the event" (Friend 1972: 74). Small souvenirs (or indeed luxury antiques) collected by tourists to decorate their homes on return now come under new ethical scrutiny. There is currently in Thailand a major movement against decontextualized use of religious imagery in hotel and other interiors. The "Keine Dekoration" (No decoration) movement in Thailand (with the support of the Thai Tourist Board) posts large billboards and internet ads reminding tourists that it is illegal to display Buddha tattooed on the body in that kingdom. The simple reason is that the body is polluted and not fit to carry a sacred image. But the movement goes much further, as it publishes examples of inappropriate practice in using reproductions of Buddha as decoration, forbidding his use in restaurants and stores, on the center of tables, in bedrooms, luxury spas, hotel lobbies, and other non-religious settings.

Generation next

There is significant generational change regarding taste and the arrangement of domestic interiors. Many of the older generation fail to acknowledge that the looks that they prefer—indeed that many of them sold—were also creations of time and place. This is particularly true of the "English country house look" of the 1980s (an amalgam of North American comfort with the cult of antiques and a filter derived from the business collaboration of British decorator John Fowler and American grandee Nancy Lancaster). Complaints are legion among the antique dealers and decorators whose business has been decimated. The style icon Iris Apfel, who ran a company in the 1980s reproducing antique textiles (Old World Weavers), noted in *Architectural Digest* in 1976: "Quality is under siege today, and I doubt whether it can survive the onslaught. Our only hope is that those of us who do care about standards will fight to keep them" ("Iris Apfel, Visual Gourmet" 2016). But the relative meaning of quality shifts over time, and vast amounts of money are still spent on luxury interiors. Shifts in global capital, the rise of cheap labor centers, reductions in tariffs, and the broader effects of neoliberalism probably contributed more to these shifts in product offerings than taste *per se*.

Houses for high net-worth individuals are now often created fully furnished. Known as "turn-key" properties, which "are ready to be lived in, complete with everything from custom furniture and curated artworks to linen on the beds. Crockery in the kitchen and towels in the bathroom. . . . Potential buyers might own several homes around the world and want one here but lack the time to design, build and fit it out from scratch" (Singer 2017). Services, including interior decoration, plugged in as modules have been proposed by the financial sector of late as the future of luxury consumption. The neoliberal agenda argues that the "confluence of technology and consumer behavior is driving an appetite for great value [that] will lead to the creation of new services" remarks Citigroups' global head of technology Jim Metzger (Adhikari 2017: 19). "Owning a valuable asset, whether it's a car or a home, is going to be a very different affair in the coming years as the concept of 'everything-as-a-service' gains further traction." Changing consumer needs "at all levels," Metzger noted, is not just for the very rich (Adhikari 2017: 19). He is correct, as we see it in Uber and Airbnb and like services.

For the high net-worth individual, essentials include absolute privacy, high quality materials, and a rather generic look in which luxury is conveyed via materiality rather than historicism. Decorators at the highest levels such as

Alidad (who decorates for many British and Middle eastern clients) and J P Molyneux (who decorates for Middle Eastern and Russian clients) continue to craft interiors with clear nods to the owner's cultural background. They might commission Moorish style screens in entrance foyers or gilded fantasies in baths, but theirs is not typical of contemporary domestic design today.

Such apartment residences are immaculately maintained to "hotel standard" in which much of the labor expended is invisible. David Brody has written a much-needed account of the hidden aspects of labor in the contemporary hotel industry. While stating how much he enjoys staying in a good hotel (they are greatly seductive spaces), he also describes hotel spaces as "some of the most obsessively designed spaces found in our neoliberal epoch" (Brody 2016: 4). Hotels to Brody are significant as they bring together material with service design. He points out that designs that appear simple or minimalistic are often much harder to clean, the beds are harder to make up, occupational injuries are high, and staff are rarely consulted about the impact of such design on their health and safety. Darker colored floors and carpets show all the dust, shower curtains are out, glass and mirrors are in: it all needs to be cleaned twice daily. Towels are rolled instead of folded, much harder work (Brody 2016: 144). Brody's contention is that the hotel experience elides labor and design itself is "fostering this illusory realm" (Brody 2016: 162). "Labor repeatedly gets asked to hide itself in a way that defers to guest satisfaction, while eliding the cumbersome and sometimes painful work required to attain the guest's approval" (Brody 2016: 20). Gardeners in luxury hotels in Bali and in Hawaii, for example, are only allowed to work once most guests have taken breakfast; they work behind screens, stop singing or whistling when guests come around corners, and labor with camouflaged bins and containers, which makes their job more laborious and difficult. The large Asian resorts have elaborate modesty screens that permit laborers to enter and exit a garden space through numerous open doorways that are hidden through the architecture of space. Such spaces allow staff to leave silently, effortlessly, and in an almost invisible fashion. At the heart of a hotel is also a hotel management team. They are rarely visible in a very good hotel unless someone leaves a door open or if you get the right angle to see into a curtained window space. The check-in or reception staff are a type of labor buffer between you the guest and the vast number of staff that work in luxury hotels. Many hotels print the numbers of staff to guest ratio which can be as high as ten to one. Many of these staff are immigrants, have college educations in order to speak the level of English required, and come from distant regions to work in cities. It makes one wonder if we have recreated the conditions of the inequitable nineteenth-century European metropolis as described by Balzac or Zola.

As we now move toward an "experience" economy less interested in traditional languages of design, how to manage the spaces of the luxury hotel becomes a central topic. City hotels that lack the "heritage" of older building forms generally rely on a generic notion of "modern luxury" to sell their brand. Others use innovative contemporary design. Moby, LA-based musician, described Zaha Hadid's floor of the Puerta American Hotel, Madrid (2005) as like "sleeping in a dumpster" (Winston 2016). He was referring to the lack of decoration, objects, conventional textures and materials, and its vision derived from three-dimensional computer modeling. An "empty" or relatively empty space is not really "empty"—it is still a set of material and symbolic signs. Residential apartments at the most exclusive addresses and price points such as One Kensington Gardens London (architect David Chipperfield) now appear like fairly beige hotel rooms so that their owners feel at ease in their multiple residences; collections are expensive to insure and difficult to maintain, anyway. Flexible homes, stays, and cars—everything as a modular service gains traction—an almost 1960s' utopian idea minus the left-wing politics.

Gentrification and its after-effects

The critic and academic Sarah Schulman paints a personal account of gentrification in the United States. She points to the loss of the "remaining mixed low-income communities . . . where longtime residents, young people, immigrants, and artists can afford to live and mix as equals" (Schulman 2012: 18). Gentrification, she argues, "is the removal of the dynamic mix that defines urbanity" (Schulman 2012: 27). In the United States it coincided with the advent of AIDS (and the loss of those tenanted rent-controlled spaces), encouraged by city tax breaks and a neoliberal agenda. Her analysis is sobering: "the literal experience of gentrification is a concrete replacement process. Physically it is an urban phenomena: the removal of communities of diverse classes, ethnicities, races, sexualities, languages, and points of view from the central neighborhoods of cities." Schulman concludes her book with a line from Jane Jacob's *Death and Life of Great American Cities* (1961): "Fix the buildings . . . but leave the inhabitants" (Schulman 2012: 179).

There are clear links to the study of gentrification and the hotel effect. Around the world as cities grow denser, low-cost housing, former light industrial buildings, and older hotels have been turned into condominium housing and luxury hotels, sometimes combined in the same building. Older housing stock in cities as different as Penang and Singapore is turned into boutique hotels, meaning local people can no longer live in what was once their "down town." Whereas the barefoot travelers wanted to meet locals, expats, drop outs, and eccentric antique dealers, luxury hotel travel today is not structured around this type of social mixing—although many hotels offer "curated" or "real experiences" that are not really so "authentic."

Today in hotels and also residences around the world, coffered ceilings that bring new air-conditioning and lighting systems into the dwelling suggest a replication of luxury high rise apartments—"mass produced aesthetics" as Schulman calls them—or the "impenetrable," "smooth and opaque surface" of contemporary design that obscures a more kinetic sense of materials and skills (Schulman 2012: 28). We are reminded here of contemporary critiques of "iPhone" aesthetics: "The eye of this new generation is trained in a different way. It's Apple—all smooth and sleek, no embellishment," remarks Frank de Biasi, a prominent New York decorator (de Biasi, 2016). These differ from "celebrations of materiality"—and the messy vitality of previous domestic environment, surely anathema to the "digital nomads" hoping to "flip" a property at a fast profit (as seen on TV) who might inhabit such a property today. I am not suggesting that contemporary schemes of the well-to-do are unsophisticated. But the market has shifted. Art fairs now have major investors. Frieze London, at which antiquities, and historical and contemporary art are shown, is underwritten by Endeavor (formerly WME-IMG), a US sport and entertainment conglomerate. Everything can be co-mingled, but in a way that would be unrecognizable to a nineteenth-century bourgeois consumer or a 1950s' or 1980s' grandee. Commenting on the London art fair "Frieze," in the art and antiques journal *Apollo* (itself tied to "Masterpiece" fair, London, at which yachts are shown next to antiques), Anna Brady remarks: "economic and political turbulence has engendered a flight to substance and created a more reflective market atmosphere in which context, juxtaposition, and dialogue are the *mots du jour*" (Brady 2016: 56).

The relative "emptiness" of a luxury contemporary interior is of course the result of enormous capital outlay and labor to keep up that appearance. It has many links to the so-called "labor saving" white-on-white interiors of the 1930s crafted by Frenchman Jean-Michel Frank and British woman Syrie Maugham, which looked simple but were really only suitable for the rich with staff, electric fires, and vacuum cleaners. The "craftivism," "stitch and bitch" groups and knitting bombs (covering trees or bridges in knitting), and other material interventions in urban space by the new generations indicate that the material world remains a contested world. *Apartmento* magazine markets itself as "an honest interiors magazine" and *Dirty Furniture* proposes alternatives to mass-produced aesthetics. Inclusion of the crafts generally, however, would be discouraged by a real estate agent in selling a luxury property today.

Room at the top

At the time of writing, the most expensive penthouse in Sydney's history is for sale at $66 million. Known as the "Boyd" penthouse it is a three-story, 2,000-square-meter apartment in the Central Business District. It contains 200 pieces of bespoke art deco style furniture and sits atop the ANZ Bank Grocon Tower (Chancellor 2018).[6] Its glass windows and enormous custom-built seating resemble the Westin Hotel in Melbourne. For purposes of selling, the only signs of inhabitation were perfume bottles in the main bathroom. In 2018, Singapore had a 2,000-square-meter apartment priced at US$100 million in the Tanjong Pagar Centre. Its price does not come close to the "reputed" £140 million for the penthouse at One Hyde Park Knightsbridge, created by the Candy Brothers CPG Group. The Candy brothers, who are very interested in decoration, have greatly contributed to the current taste for the simulation of a hotel lifestyle for the super-rich.

Domestic and touristic life blur. Consumers return from a journey and ask their designer to make their bath and bedroom resemble a hotel. Hotels—even in remote parts of developing countries such as Botswana—must carry the attributes of luxury at home, or the tourist might become disgruntled.[7] Contemporary luxury intersects with cultural tourism, the changing nature of the family and relationships, consumption of goods and services, shifting notions of authenticity and inauthenticity, within the ever accelerating pressure of tourists made possible by cheaper air travel and the growing middle-class populations of BRIC countries, particularly China. Home becomes like a hotel which looks like home.

Acknowledgments

Versions of this chapter have been presented at the Luxury Research Group "Luxury and Space" Conference in Winchester in May 2017 and at World

Luxury Destinations Conference, Bangkok, March 2018. Thanks to the editors, delegates, readers, Professor Adrian Vickers FAHA, Dr. Jesse Adams Stein, and Enya Moore for their suggestions. An interview was conducted with Aviadi Purnomo, Manager of the Tandjung Sari Hotel, July 2017.

References

Adhikari, S. (2017), "Flexible Homes Cars Part of a New Way of Thinking," *The Australian*, Financial Services Section, April 18: 19.

Berger, M. (2011), *Hotel Dreams: Luxury, Technology, and Urban Ambition in America, 1829–1929*, Baltimore: John Hopkins University Press.

Brady, A. (2016), "Preview, Frieze Masters," *Apollo*, October: 56–57.

Brody, D. (2016), *Housekeeping by Design, Hotels and Labor*, Chicago and London: University of Chicago Press.

Chancellor, J. (2018), "Room at the Top," *The Weekend Australian/Mansion Australia*, April 14–15: 18–21.

Charpy, M. (2007), "L'ordre des choses. Sur quelques traits de la culture matérielle bourgeoise parisienne, 1830–1914," *Revue d'Histoire du XIXe Siècle*, 34: 105–28.

Christie's Magazines (2000), "Collecting Issue," June–July.

Darling, D. (2012), *Tandjung Sari: A Magical Door to Bali*, Singapore: Editions Didier Millet.

De Biasi, F. (2016), Interview, "New York Social Diary," December 23. Available online at: http://www.newyorksocialdiary.com/decorator-series/2016/frank-de-biasi (accessed May 22, 2018).

Friend, D. (1972), *Donald Friend in Bali*, London and Sydney: Collins.

Friend, D. (2006), *The Diaries of Donald Friend*, vol. 4, ed. P. Hetherington, Canberra: National Library of Australia.

Gaines, S. (2005), *The Sky's the Limit: Passion and Property in Manhattan*, New York: Little, Brown.

Goldhill, S. (2015), *The Buried Life of Things: How Objects Made History in Nineteenth-Century Britain*, Cambridge: Cambridge University Press.

Hofer, M. and Scharnhorst, G. (2010), *Oscar Wilde in America: The Interviews*, Urbana and Chicago: University of Illinois Press.

"Iris Apfel, Visual Gourmet" (2016), *The Peak of Chic,* website, November 14. Available online at: http://thepeakofchic.blogspot.com.au/2016/11/iris-apfel-visual-gourmet.html (accessed May 2018).

Lim, Eng-Beng (2013), *Brown Boys and Rice Queens: Spellbinding Performance in the Asias*, New York and London: New York University Press.

Singer, M. (2017), "Luxury on Tap: Coronation Avenue, Balmoral, $20m," *The Australian*, 15th April. Available online at: https://www.theaustralian.com.au/weekend-australian-magazine/luxury-on-tap-coronation-avenue-balmoral-20m/news-story/7037179672a8e22a23af957acc651e44 (accessed 10th April 2019)

McKellar, E. (2007), "Representing the Georgian: Constructing Interiors in Early Twentieth-Century Publications, 1890–1930," *Journal of Design History*, 20 (4): 325–44.

McNeil, P. and Riello, G. (2016), *Luxury: A Rich History*, Oxford: Oxford University Press.

Picard, M. (1997), "Cultural Tourism, Nation-Building, and Regional Culture: The Making of a Balinese Identity," in M. Picard and R. E. Wood (eds.), *Tourism, Ethnicity, and the State in Asian and Pacific Societies*, 181–214, Hawai'i: Hawai'i University Press.

Picard, M. (1998), *Bali: Cultural Tourism and Touristic Culture*, Singapore: Archipelago Press.

Picard, M. and Wood, R. E., eds. (1997), *Tourism, Ethnicity, and the State in Asian and Pacific Societies*, Hawai'i: Hawai'i University Press.

Poe, E. A. (1967), "The Philosophy of Furniture," in *Selected Writings of Edgar Allan Poe, Poems, Tales, Essays and Reviews*, ed. with an intro. by D. Galloway, 414–20, Harmondsworth: Penguin. [First published *Burton's Gentleman's Magazine*, May 1840; revised for *Broadway Journal*, 1845].

Schulman, S. (2012), *The Gentrification of the Mind: Witness to a Lost Generation*, Berkeley, Los Angeles and London: University of California Press.

Sennett, R. (1998), *The Corrosion of Character: The Personal Consequences of Work in the New Capitalism*, New York and London: W.W. Norton and Company.

Sherman, D. (2004), "'Post-Colonial Chic': Fantasies of the French Interior 1957–62," *Art History*, 27 (5): 770–805.

Stammers, T. (2008), "The Bric-a-Brac of the Old Regime: Collecting and Cultural History in Post-Revolutionary France," *Society for the Study of French History*, 22 (3): 295–315.

Vickers, A. (1996), *Being Modern in Bali: Image and Change*, New Haven, CT: Yale University Press.

Wharton, E. (2002), *The House of Mirth*, Mineola, NY: Dover.

Winston, A. (2016), "Sleeping in a Dumpster More Comfortable," *Dezeen* [online magazine]. Available online at: https://www.dezeen.com/2016/09/20/moby-puerta-america-hotel-madrid-spain-zaha-hadid-dumpster-more-comfortable/ (accessed May 2018).

"The Collective": Luxury in lounge space

Samuel Austin and Adam Sharr

This chapter is about the role of luxury in the design, production, and marketing of home and community. It examines a novel housing block containing 550 dwellings, which opened in north London in April 2016. Our study of this block illustrates how individuals' sense of anchoring in the world—the means by which they imagine their place and their distinctive ideas of the real—get invested in, and developed through, the third realm of luxury.

Designed by PLP Architecture and branded "The Collective" by its developers, this block was produced out of London's hyper-gentrification. The "merely wealthy," in contemporary London, have been displaced by the global super-rich—a phenomenon most famously spatialized with so-called "iceberg" basements, excavated beneath once modest houses in desirable areas, which massively increase their size without infringing planning laws (Burrows and Knowles 2019). In this context, wealth may or may not "trickle down" (Aghion and Bolton 1997), but the miniaturization of space certainly does. "The Collective" provides the equivalent of student housing for "young professionals" priced out of both the housing market and the conventional rental market.[1] It is marketed as "a community of likeminded young people, living, working and playing under one roof" with "amazing shared spaces" (The Collective 2016). Communal spaces are provided in the block to mitigate the loss of living space. Marketing materials explain how those spaces are "designed . . . to bring young people together," ranging "from quiet places to work, themed dining rooms and a roof garden for socializing," providing "access to useful and convenient facilities such as a gym, spa and restaurant—all in your own home." Supplemented by "regular events," "such as inspirational talks, networking and film nights through to spontaneous BBQs," the developers assure prospective tenants that "there's always something to get involved in." This *Existenzminimum* is sold as though it were a youthful and luxurious private members' club. "Live somewhere you'll be excited to call home

[with] boutique interior design, beautiful shared space and luxury facilities for every member," the website exhorts. As we will show, luxury—here—is constituted as an experience: as the reassurance of belonging to a community whose members imagine themselves to share similar values and habits. It also refers to the imaginative projection of comfort, homeliness, and carefree urban sophistication, expressed through a set of knowingly familiar architectural materials and forms.

We will begin by reviewing the architectural form and marketing of "The Collective." We then compare it to the Narkomfin Communal House finished in Moscow in 1928 to designs by architects Moisei Ginzburg and Ignatii Milinis: a radical exercise in social engineering which sought to socialize previously private aspects of domestic life into the public sphere to consolidate a communist way of life (Buchli 1998). Next, we examine how the idea of luxury is constructed at "The Collective" through its shared "lounge spaces" (Austin 2012). A palette of intertextual references blends images of stylish coffee shops and bars with fashionable "Googleplex" offices, theater foyers, and pop-up shops, mixing urban imagery with homeliness to monetize consumption. We will thus examine how hyper-capitalism has produced a simulation of communist space at "The Collective," stripping out the idealism of collectivization to produce a collective of individuals, promoted using visual and marketing languages of luxury and youth to sell minimum space standards to aspirational professionals.

The Collective, London, 2016

The block sits in a local context of railway sidings and big industrial sheds. Its unpromising surroundings include an open-air bus depot, busy roundabout, canal, and small-scale terraced Victorian workers' housing. In one direction is the suburb of North Acton—now sold as an aspirational address in London—and, in the opposite direction, the Willesden Junction transport interchange. Marketing for The Collective, however, prefers to label the locality Old Oak after one of the nearby railway yards, recognizing how that name hints at reassuring virtues of nature and heritage (Mayor of London 2017; Waite 2017).

Architecturally, The Collective is organized as two blocks partially slipped past one another—one six- and one nine-stories tall—sat on a two-story podium (Figure 7.1). Residential rooms fill the floors from the second upward, with vertical circulation and shared spaces provided where the two blocks adjoin. The first floor was planned as office space, although this remains unlet at the time of writing.

Figure 7.1 "The Collective," Old Oak, London, photographed in 2017. Photo: Adam Sharr.

The Collective's 550 bedroom units are packed densely at up to 70 units per floor. Of these units, 450 were marketed initially as "Twodios," where a compact kitchenette including sink, hob, and microwave is shared between two bedrooms. Bedrooms themselves are the width of a double bed, which fills the window wall, and three times its length (Figure 7.2). In a remarkable feat of compression, the rooms manage to pack into that footprint a tiny *en suite* bathroom with WC and shower cubicle, a run of cupboards, and a small desk. The remaining units comprise a mix of tenures including sixty-three slightly larger studio units; five one-bed flats with shared connecting bathrooms and a private kitchen; four parent-and-child rooms; and two guest rooms available for hire. Prices per room (in 2018) range from £920 to £1,120 per month (approximately $1,250 to $1,500). The rent includes Wi-Fi, bills, room cleaning, bedding and linen, concierge, and the salary of two community managers who organize events for residents. A larger kitchen is provided on each floor, which tenants can book to cater for guests, with nine of these made available to the building's 500+ inhabitants. Each floor also contains one of the communal spaces that are open to all the residents of the block. By our calculations, such spaces comprise approximately 10 percent of residential floor area.

The building's forbidding exterior is finished in gray metal cladding panels and blue-gray glass planks, into which dark gray window frames have been set. An attempt has been made to break up the facades architecturally by expressing

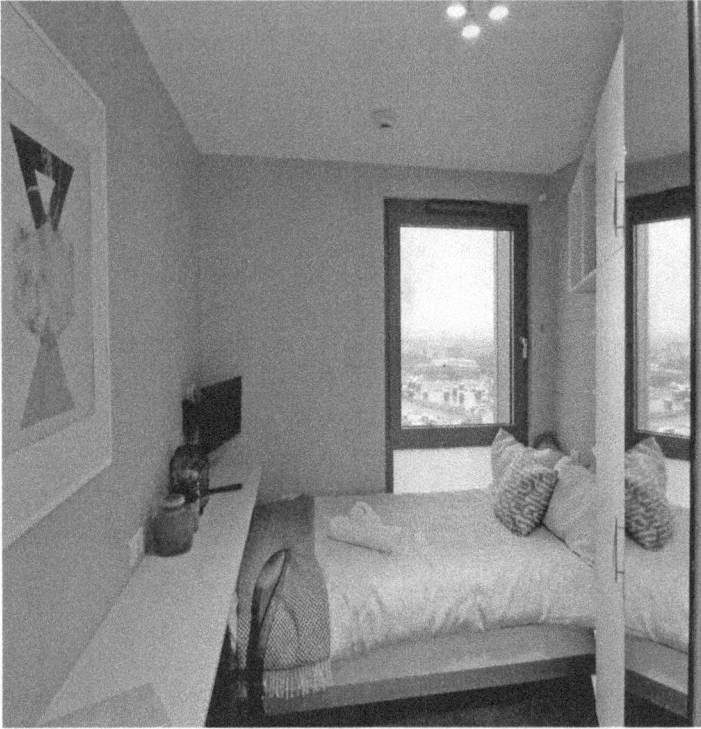

Figure 7.2 A "Twodio" bedroom, The Collective. Photo: Brandon Few.

the horizontal and vertical divisions between each unit as projecting beams and pilasters. The block's remarkably dense occupation is thus mapped across its surfaces. The toughness of the architecture externally is a foil to the building's context, answering in height the substantial bulk of nearby low-lying industrial sheds. Adjacent to the canal, one of the two blocks sails over the edge of the podium on bright red X-shaped columns, claimed as a "gesture of deference to . . . public space" by the architects (PLP Architecture 2016), to make a windy canal-side restaurant terrace that serves as one of the few external clues to the distinctively branded world within.

Another clue is the supergraphic applied around the entrance doors. Referring to London's famous "tube map" and internet connectivity diagrams—suggesting the idea of a connected, vibrant, luxurious community as mini-city—the names of the building's interior spaces are composed as a network. This emphasizes the phrases "Co-living" and "Co-working" by placing them adjacent to the junction symbols familiar from the map. Cheerful icons below, adjacent to station symbols, celebrate the branded spaces within: Spa; Secret Garden; The Common

Restaurant and Bar; Gym; Terrace; Cinema Room; Library; and Sanctuary; also exhorting a Community of Events. In the graphic language of the tube map, the line connecting these amenities terminates at The Collective. Many of the amenities listed—those located on the ground floor—are not restricted to residents. The restaurant—whose pizzas are described as "awesome" by one of the building's marketing managers—is open to the wider public, as is the supermarket, a "Simply Fresh" branded franchise. Gym membership is also for sale to all, and communal rooms grandly named "The Gallery" and "The Exchange" are available for external corporate hire.

The architectural imagery of the building and its branded projections of luxury are, however, only completed in association with the accompanying website and promotional materials. Indeed, because the turnover of tenants requires it, the block remains in a state of perpetual branding and marketing. Visitors to the front page of the site encounter first the developer's global aspirations: "We're unlocking the world's greatest cities for the creative and ambitious," it exhorts:

> Starting with London, our focus is on creating ground-breaking spaces and the greatest possible experiences within them. By doing this, we're redefining the way people can choose to live, work and play. (The Collective 2016)

These tropes of ambition, creativity, and choice pervade the site's text and imagery. The values they evoke, it is implied, constitute a culture that residents share:

> Whether you're starting a new business, building your career, pursuing a creative passion or trying to experience everything the city has to offer, we can help you focus on what you love and introduce you to a community of people on a similar journey.

The developers portray themselves not just as landlord but also as curator and custodian of a community. Indeed, they offer themselves up as fellow travelers in life. Their vocabulary of knowing companionship is presented as reassurance in the face of the alienation that has been associated with urban life since early criticisms of modernity. The site claims this:

> The greatest things often come from something as simple as a chance encounter with someone. Communal spaces are designed on each floor to bring people together: from quiet spaces you can work in through to open spaces to socialize in. Even the launderette makes doing laundry a less lonely experience.

As if to reinforce the idea of shared endeavor, the language of the site mixes its particular notion of aspiration with certain chumminess. The graphics are crisp and simple as well as colorful and amiable. Headings seek to provide reassurance: "All-in-one bill covers everything," "Cleaners every two weeks," "Small deposit," and, under a smiley-face graphic, "Someone to help 24/7." Irrespective of the substantial rent, a heading portrays the development as "A Space for Everyone." These tropes are consolidated in residents' testimonials provided at the bottom of the page. Tuulia Nummelin reassures prospective tenants that

> there's always people around to spend time with and learn from. Being influenced by people my own age from different cultural and professional backgrounds was a big reason I decided to move in.

Rita Santos adds that "Everything you could possibly need has already been thought of and provided for you—you don't need to worry about a thing." The benevolent developer, here, is a friend in troubling times, someone who thinks like you do, having already anticipated your every need as a young professional in the big city. But, as a tenant of The Collective, there is an apparent trade. You are asked not just to live in the block but also to subscribe to its values.

The themes of the website were reinforced in accompanying publicity when the building opened. The blog *Dezeen*—a design students' favorite—interviewed Reza Merchant, the London School of Economics-educated CEO of The Collective LLP who enthused about its business model. He argued that

> there has been a fundamental shift in the way people want to live. . . . Co-living appeals to millennials who are settling down later and remaining commitment free and transient for longer than any previous generation. People nowadays don't like to commit. Ultimately experiences are what people value above material possessions and co-living really embodies that. (Quoted in Mairs, 2016)

Merchant enthuses about his empathy with his tenants: "Buying a house is obviously for a lot of people still an aspiration but it's becoming less so with our generation," Reza told *Dezeen*. "Having a mortgage is a big commitment. Why have that worry when you have a super convenient offering that caters for all of your needs that doesn't commit you for a long period of time?"

Not only does the developer portray itself as reflecting and promulgating a set of ideals that it shares with its tenants, the organization also promotes itself as articulating the desires of the millennial generation. Having been priced out of both the housing and rental market is not a problem but an opening, a chance to privilege opportunity. Inability to afford a mortgage, or even rent for a conventional flat, is repackaged as luxury, as a desirable experience of freedom from commitment. In the developer's value set, ideas of aspiration, creativity, and choice are mixed with those of convenience, freedom, and comfort in a heady mix simultaneously imagined as channeling, and providing refuge from, the hyperactive market economy of the contemporary city.

A collective, Moscow 1928

While The Collective was a novel housing model in London when it was completed, it wasn't wholly original. It extended into the field of housing the WeWork co-working model promoted in New York in the late 2000s by businessmen Miguel McKelvey and Adam Neumann (Cadwalladr 2016). Whether knowingly or unknowingly on the part of its developer and architect, The Collective also recalls an architectural precedent. The Narkomfin Communal House was completed to designs by architects Moisei Ginzburg and Ignatii Milinis in 1928, intended as a prototype for widespread repetition (Figure 7.3). The building was imagined by its designers as the decisive architectural manifestation of the values of Soviet communism. It was

Figure 7.3 Living block of Narkomfin Communal House, Moscow, view from early 1930s. Courtesy of the Federal State Budget Institution of Culture, Shchusev State Architectural Museum, Moscow.

constructed at a time when the drive to industrialize the post-revolutionary Russian economy was supplemented by the Cultural Revolution seeking to expunge bourgeois thinking and restructure social life along Marxist lines.

The Narkomfin was designed for civil servants in the Ministry of Finance. The buildings were dressed in the clothing of modern architecture's so-called international style: white painted concrete walls with flat roofs and ribbon windows, appearing to hover above the ground on concrete columns. This architectural language had already become associated with a rejection of the past in favor of claims to an efficient technological future, its design sources drawn more from ocean liners and cars than the revival of classical or gothic architectural traditions. But the Narkomfin was most striking for its unusual organization. Its program, devised by a state research agency headed by Ginzburg, incorporated flats, shared cooking and dining facilities, a shared library and gymnasium, and a mechanized laundry, with a crèche with professional childcare so that women could play a fuller role in society. The flats were grouped together in a long slab connected to the separate communal block with a bridge, while the laundry and crèche were imagined as freestanding buildings in the garden. The aim was to socialize previously private aspects of domestic life into the public sphere.

Different flat types were provided. Two primary types of "transitional" flat weren't fully dependent on the communal facilities. But most interesting to the designers were twenty-four "collectivized" units for individuals or couples: compact double-height volumes addressing the shared garden, accommodating only sleeping, showers, and toilets. No kitchens were provided and living space was minimal. Residents of these flats were expected to spend most of their home lives as part of the collective, eating, relaxing, and exercising together, coalescing as a community because—it was imagined—they shared daily practicalities and social ideals.

The Narkomfin was always contradictory—never fully the communal society its champions envisaged—because of its multiple flat types. Indeed, a large private rooftop penthouse was added at a late stage specifically for the Minister of Finance, somewhat separated from the collective and contradicting the basic idea, and Ginzburg also added a bespoke, enlarged version of the "transitional" unit for himself. And, in the end, the prototype was only barely repeated because Soviet communism changed around it: while the state championed the Narkomfin in 1928, by 1930 the Stalinist authorities declared that workers preferred conventional domestic arrangements and Ginzburg was required to disown the building as an elitist intellectual experiment. Becoming neglected and poorly maintained, it was noticed again by architectural historians only in the 1990s.

On the face of it, the Narkomfin expressed a view of communist society where not only people were considered equal but individualism was also condemned as bourgeois, as a threat to the optimism and self-determination of greater society. Excepting the contradictions of those units provided for the minister and the architect, the building's conceptual diagram sought fairness and equality, where the homes of senior civil servants were the same as those of their most junior counterparts including the cleaners of the Ministry building. Units were not generous in size, nor did they represent minimum dwelling. And shared spaces were sized appropriately to their role in the complex, occupying approximately 15 percent of the total floor area.

The similarities and differences between Moscow's Narkomfin and London's The Collective are striking. Both pair living space with communal space. Both were conceived not just as housing blocks but as archetypes, as architectural expressions of social ideas. Indeed, residents of both buildings were expected to live the values that they represented.

While there may be basic similarities in the buildings' overall appearance—straightforwardly articulated slabs, flat roofs, window patterns seeking to reflect the internal layouts—their organization in plan remains significantly different. The Narkomfin articulated residential spaces and communal spaces in separate but connected buildings, planned at relatively low density around a shared garden. The Collective is planned at a much higher density and most of the shared spaces instead are located, opportunistically, in deep-plan space where the two blocks slide past each other, which—because of its distance from a window—would otherwise be unlettable. Thus, architecturally, communal spaces at The Collective remain secondary in the plan layout, mostly jammed in where floor space could not be monetized in other ways. (Beyond the ground floor spaces, the exception that proves the rule here is the compact themed kitchens, which do occupy otherwise lettable floorplate.) Indeed, the awkward shapes of many of the shared rooms, which the interior design works hard to mitigate, are a consequence of being subsidiary to money-making lettable space. Windows become such a significant commodity at The Collective that long, thin rooms stretch away from them, with daylight replaced by artificial light in bathrooms, kitchens, and corridors. In consequence, with no garden to focus on, the building produces an internalized world. The plan of the Narkomfin was symbolically centered on what was imagined to be the communal space of shared endeavor, but that of The Collective illustrates instead the dominance of the individual cells. Where one looked outward, the other largely refers inward.

These similarities and differences between The Collective and its early twentieth-century antecedent open up the question about what The Collective's architecture stands for. If the Narkomfin was an expression of communist ideals—including the contradictions already inherent in the Soviet interpretation of them in the late 1920s—what values are at work in The Collective's architecture? We will explore this question further by zooming into the building's interiors and the ways in which they seek to construct a particular kind of luxury.

Lounge space and luxury

Visitors enter The Collective through the branded entrance into the building's foyer. Immediately opposite, above the reception desk, is an illuminated sign, reminiscent of 1950s' American cinema facades, proclaiming "Honey I'm Home. The Collective Old Oak." A feature wall behind the desk is dominated by a diagonal pattern of fluorescent tubes, a contemporary take on classic neon signage. A grand piano and three antique suitcases hint that this might be the lobby of a grand hotel from the past. In the distinctive vocabulary of the building, this space is branded the Communal Lounge. Alongside the concierge desk, it offers seating, houses lockers for post and parcels, and provides access to the lifts. Its aesthetic is that of the shabby-chic warehouse café-bar, with a concrete slab floor, bare concrete columns and ceilings, dark blue brick-pattern tiles, and exposed steel air handling ducts and cabling. So-called feature light fittings are paired with velveteen sofas and traditional-looking wing-backed armchairs, with theater lamps on tripods, outsize pot plants used as space dividers, and tables in the form of supersized cassette tapes. Like elsewhere in the building, the designers have sought to combine crisp modern lines with knowingly "retro" artifacts, mixing design references from public space and domestic space, producing what can be called "lounge space."

Lounge space is a spatial type—usually a branded lining remaining conceptually independent from its host architecture—which is familiar from countless cafés, bars, nightclubs, hotels, shopping malls, motorway service areas, airport lounges, and other spaces of monetized consumption. Rarely analyzed, lounge space has become the unseen background to much contemporary Western life. Where contemporary theories of architectural space and experience have often focused on flows and speed (Koolhaas, 2002; Spencer,

2016), lounge space describes the emergence of a new kind of sedentary space within societies of increased mobility and advanced capitalism. They are spaces of itinerant occupation where rest is monetized—partly by attempting to render it luxurious.

Though lounge space gets clothed in the colors of diverse brands and located in otherwise very different kinds of building, there is a striking conformity to its patterns. A landscape of varied seating conditions is normally cocooned in a branded shell, threaded together by deliberately meandering routes. A survey of any typical café chain will reveal a range of seat forms, styles, textures, and cushioning, promising to cater for individual postures, lifestyles, and purposes, configured to accommodate a variety of social groupings. Rows of stools at high tables prop individuals in a hurry or busy working on a laptop. Sofas and club chairs arranged loosely around low tables recline those with time to relax together or to read alone. Dining chairs in twos, threes, and fours gather groups to eat or meet, offering differing degrees of formality—from padded bucket chairs with round tables for family and friends to firm upright chairs with square tables for business-like order. Even unoccupied, these constellations of chairs and tables signal sociability, comfort, and choice. Although there may actually be scant human contact, comfort is usually calibrated to ensure sufficient customer turnover, and any choice remains managed by the controlling brand. Nevertheless, lounge space mimics the many ways we make ourselves at home and share time together, inviting us in.

Surfaces and details in lounge spaces reinforce the thematic logic of homely comfort and individuality, translating them into a semi-public setting—sometimes by straightforward reproduction of architectural motifs, sometimes by caricaturing them. Walls are characteristically broken up into panels of different materials and finishes, juxtaposing concrete or brickwork, chunky timber slats, shiny ceramic tiles, and matt paint. This often cultivates the impression of a found space preceding its current use, an assemblage of domestic and post-industrial fragments knocked together, each supposedly with their own character and history. These signifiers of ambiguous longevity are layered with markers of home: skirting and dados, framed mirrors and prints, bulky canvases and stenciled graphics. Lighting and flooring communicate the organization of the space, differentiating interior "streets" from the collaged domesticity of homely nooks. Stone or "reconstituted stone" (i.e., concrete) slabs, or vinyl tiles, in muted tones mark "public" routes through "private" seating areas of grainy timber or laminate boards, the orientations of the materials never being aligned. The same logic of hard to soft, homogenized to individuated, gets reflected above: gridded spotlights over spaces of movement give way to patterns of pendant lamps over tables, clusters of supersized lampshades with sofas, and the occasional standard lamp. Waist-height planters, railings, and partitions divide larger spaces into cozier alcoves.

In terms of its historical cultural significance, lounge space might be compared to the arcades studied by Walter Benjamin (2002) and the hotel lobbies discussed by Siegfried Kracauer (1997)—or in a different way—by Fredric Jameson (1991: 37–44). For those writers, what were then new forms of public–private interior revealed changes in subjectivity and social relations under developing forms of capitalism (Rice 2007). Following this lineage, lounge space can be seen as the contemporary architectural manifestation of what has been termed the experience economy under hyper-capitalism, where commercial activity is increasingly attuned to emotional affect and the greatest added value is to be found in selling services and experiences rather than tangible artifacts; a process traced by Anna Klingmann in *Brandscapes* (2007) and, differently, by Mark Pimlott in his work on the public interior (2016). Through the increasing involvement of the private sector in providing public services, as well as pressures for those services to raise income independently, lounge space has also now spread into spaces previously free of branded shops and services, such as galleries, libraries, universities, and hospitals—increasingly taking the place of "civic" space. What sets lounge space apart from its early modern antecedents is its looseness of fit within its host architectures—its composition of recognizable fragments rearranged within the otherwise all-embracing floor and ceiling grids of shopping centers and transport interchanges, or occupying street-facing interiors of any age or style of building—and its internal layering of differences to present an image of choice.

Lounge space, then, is a proliferation of hybrid home–work–leisure spaces that operate between, and sometimes in place of, the traditionally separate buildings of house, office, pub, and club. In these collaged spaces with their apparently familiar fittings and enlivening bustle, the business meeting is apparently relaxed and domesticity apparently rendered carefree. These constellations appear to offer a form of everyday luxury as momentary rest from the stresses and motions of city life. This luxury comes about partly because its financial cost excludes: a Starbucks coffee remains an indulgence on lower incomes. Providing the opportunity to live, work, and relax in multiple spaces every day, lounge space stands for the emphasis on individual choice and self-determination in capitalist society, made enticing with a calculated caress of modest self-indulgence.

Bringing lounge space back home

The Collective's interiors fit the genealogy of lounge space. Their logic—aping tropes from contemporary spaces of leisure, retail, and work—remains reassuringly familiar. What's innovative, however, is that they bring the lounge spaces of itinerant occupation back into the home.

On The Collective's upper floors, the typical pattern of host building as a neutral background to the themed lounges extends across the floorplate. Here, the individual residential units become part of that background. The corridors are, like the private rooms, squeezed to the minimum permitted dimensions and given a generic material treatment that echoes budget hotels: lightly patterned gray carpets, two-tone gray wall paint, white skirtings and doorframes. By contrast, the shared spaces stacked in the middle of the building offer a variety of brightly decorated living spaces themed around particular activities, crossing the imagery of members' clubs and premium airport lounges with mid-range boutique hotels. Here, aesthetic resonances of hipster café, tech office, and voguish art spaces meet vibrant color accents and comic book supergraphics as popularized in the various iterations of reality television's Big Brother House. The spaces include a launderette that riffs on the traditional wall of stacked appliances alongside contemporary "chill-out" spaces; an East Asian themed spa with bamboo seats and screens, raised timber planters containing stones and cacti, tatami beds, and a glowing timber-lined sauna; and a gray-black cinema room with fitted sofa, gently stepped floor, and bright scattered beanbags facing a screen with an adjacent "sports bar." While the communal kitchen on most floors follows a standard design in the white-gray palette, those on the top two floors, where the units are larger and more expensive, become themed environments caricaturing a French Bistro, English Pub, and Japanese tea room. As in the lounge spaces described above, The Collective's loose-fit collage of homely wall effects, furniture, and lighting combines a spectrum of fashions, from retro and reclaimed, via the curved forms and inviting textures of department store designer pieces, to the clean lines of IKEA's mass-market modernism. Here, however, the palette is tuned to a younger demographic and the lounges are diversified to evoke the "reception" rooms of a large luxurious home, offering different spaces in which to spend time at rest.

The larger shared spaces repay more detailed attention. The "Secret Garden" apparently "brings the outdoors indoors" in a riff on garden space as Scandi-modern aesthetic. Blond wood shelves, filled with interior designer's *objets* become a pergola fixed across the ceiling at one end, strung with fairy lights.

Sheets of plastic foliage are glued to the walls in an echo of the green or so-called living walls found on the facades of fashionable buildings. Water gurgles from metallic spheres set in a bed of stones atop a waist-high timber planter, offering the comforting sound of an ornamental garden and the idea of fresh air it represents. A painted stone-effect counter is matched with seemingly solid "tree trunk" stools. Blockwood timber cubes for sitting are scattered over the earthy roughness of black-painted OSB board. The lack of green outdoor spaces in the development is thus replaced with the interior simulation of one, where nature is abstracted, simplified, and rendered inert as surface dressing and ornament, freed from the need for maintenance and the vagaries of weather.

In the "Games Room," a checkerboard black-and-white dimpled rubber floor offers giant games of checkers using cubic white poufs and octagonally faceted shiny black stools for pieces. Walls are themed with variations on retro game pixels and visual jokes: one is a "Tetris" relief pattern of geometrically interlocking black-and-white painted blocks; another sees a similar pattern blown up in scale, this time flat but with *trompe l'oeil* forced perspective that seems to burst forward unsettlingly; a third is occupied by supersized Space Invaders. Accessories including table football, a table tennis table, giant Jenga, a large black furry sofa, a scattering of tables—one record-shaped, others vertiginously neon-lit and internally reflective—complete a refracted, nostalgic dream of what a teenager's basement might have been for the generation before the "millennials" who comprise its intended constituency. Here lounge space's characteristic tropes of varied seating clusters, surface linings, and bold motifs stage an immersive sense of play within the usual offer of homely comfort.

According to The Collective's website, the "Library" promises a "cozy atmosphere" (Figure 7.4). It has built-in wood-veneered bookcases containing a smattering of (largely) "coffee-table" books, as well as ornaments and plastic plants. These shelves are relatively bare—so we were told on our tour of the building—to leave space for residents to add to the collection. Splayed openings in the shelves create nooks with cushioned benches. These frame not a window but another bookcase—this time of wallpaper. In the center, high-backed padded chairs and stools are loosely arranged around a coffee table of seemingly reclaimed timber boards on rebar legs and a bright yellow and white zigzagged rug. A line of large low-hanging light bulbs runs the length of each table and large timber-framed mirrors substitute for windows, reflecting more bookcase wallpaper from the opposite side of the room. With books represented as openings to knowledge and "reused" timber signaling the value of history, the

Figure 7.4 "Library," The Collective. Photo: Brandon Few.

library lounge evokes the virtues of time spent in concentrated study, set within a reassuring landscape of uncomplicated rest.

These spaces of casual knowledge, nostalgic play, and homely nature—like the apparent comforts of the café lounge—present places to relax, untroubled by chores: the promise of luxurious rest with little responsibility. The sales tour of these spaces, conducted for all prospective tenants of the building, takes an indirect route, jumping between floors, giving the impression the building is bigger than it is and that there are always more spaces to discover. Despite their sharply contrasting material and visual qualities, however, and the implication that these interiors are for different activities, residents found in these spaces tend to be doing the same thing: sitting or reclining with a laptop or mobile device, headphones in. This pose is a common signifier of privacy in public space, familiar from coffee shops and airport lounges. However, as in lounge space more broadly, luxury in The Collective's shared spaces is constituted in the *image* of difference: a series of themed seat-scapes offering different postures apparently to suit any whim or mood. If the block's lounges resonate with those of everyday consumption, they also remain linked—within the commercial logic of the development—in their architectural tactics seeking to channel the promise of luxury. The shared spaces upstairs and the publicly accessible ones on the ground floor fit the consumer economy of luxury lounging, offering pay-per-use homely supplements, pushed to an extreme by the prohibitively high cost of private space within the overheated London property market.

The shared living rooms of The Collective offer modest luxury by creating the image of a choice of restful atmospheres but remain for the most part deep-plan, internal, and windowless. Compared with the brighter, taller, more refined "adult" spaces of the ground floor, they seem a little less luxurious. The co-worker space accessed from the Communal Lounge—currently free to residents but shortly to require a supplementary subscription—is more serious, grown-up, and business-like than the "Library." Here, members can print, book private meeting rooms, and access a range of other business services, working on swivel office chairs at designer timber desks, or in plywood laptop booths surrounded by bare concrete and exposed services. The Common Restaurant and Bar offers no resident's discount for its menu of gastropub–café fare, including breakfast, brunch, grills, weekly specials, and fresh pizzas from its pizza oven, as well as freshly ground coffees, craft beers, wines, and cocktails. Its interior seat-scape of padded spindly steel stools, chairs, and sofas—in muted burgundy, brown, and racing green tones—accompanied by polished timber tables, opens onto a terrace with picnic benches, parasols, bar tables, and the canal-side view. This contrasts with the reversion-to-childhood aesthetics of the more garish themed lounges above and the barren exposure of the second-floor "roof terrace," which is a sea of concrete paving. While group yoga sessions are available in the Secret Garden upstairs, the pay-to-join gym on the ground floor offers an array of fitness machines and equipment with personal training.

This corresponds to the economic model observed by Jean Baudrillard in *The System of Objects* (1996)—also acknowledged by Verena Andermatt Conley in her chapter—where the product series from the cheaper, more basic model to the expensive, full-feature version is formulated to feed desire for the next upgrade. The youthful home of many lounges provided as standard upstairs can be supplemented with the grown-up homely city-close-at-hand available below. Through its spectrum of semi-public lounge spaces, The Collective capitalizes on changing practices of itinerant "hot-desk" living, remodeling the home as city and miniaturizing the city as home. With the apparent luxury of "free" lounges included in the rent, it attracts a pool of consumers who are used to paying to live between spaces rather than owning their own. It combines this with the offer that, when they are looking for a little extra luxury, they barely have to leave home to upgrade to the "premium" treat of dinner "out," a fully serviced office, or a more intensive workout.

Curating the community of the collective lounge

Understood as replicating spaces of the city in microcosm—the park, leisure center, library, and cinema—The Collective claims to offer spaces to "bring people together" (The Collective 2016). But its "streets" and "squares"—its corridors and shared lounges—are taken inside, secured behind the front security desk, and elevated to upper floors. The people who are brought together here remain only those vetted by the management and capable of paying the rent. One of the key selling points of the building is its promise of security and predictability, set up in opposition—in the developer's advertising—to the risks of the shared house rental sector, where the quality of spaces, services, and fellow tenants is not guaranteed (The Collective 2016). In this sense, The Collective can be read as a new form of "gated community" (a term describing secured suburban compounds that separate out their houses and residents from the city beyond). As in contemporary leisure, retail, and transport spaces, The Collective's simulated public spaces raise questions of ownership and responsibility. While its lounges seem to bring civic space inside, they also open up the home to wider scrutiny, rendering the kitchen, garden, sitting room, and study more public. Presented as belonging to The Collective as community, these spaces nevertheless remain under the control of The Collective as landlord.

Indeed, the landlord's role in forging community is not just about excluding the unruly city. During our tour of one of the themed kitchens, we were reassured that CCTV is fitted so that anyone who steals food or leaves a mess can be tracked down. The Collective as community thus relies on a form of external policing—with the ultimate sanction of expulsion—rather than a negotiated social contract between inhabitants. Where the Narkomfin sought to encourage collectiveness through the idea, made architectural, of some shared greater endeavor, The Collective forms its community of like-minded young people by marketing them the services of a higher power: the technologically supported all-seeing eye of the building manager who remains a benign background presence, until transgression occurs. As The Collective's superego or paterfamilias, the landlord establishes domestic ethics and behavioral norms, to be enforced when necessary but largely to be internalized by individuals as a form of panoptic self-governance to avoid the exposure of any misdemeanors by CCTV.

A social program is provided in the building. Club or evening events are scheduled for each day of the week. Our guide emphasized that anyone could suggest, and get help starting-up, a new club or activity. This perpetuates the impression that all residents are empowered within a self-managed building. However, any room for collective endeavor remains circumscribed by the specific branding of the spaces and the kind of leisure they prescribe. Little space exists to make or craft anything here, for example, and attempts to redesign any of the carefully branded spaces would no doubt be resisted.

In this way, The Collective reinforces the dominant subjectivity under neoliberalism, whereby freedom is asserted through the agency to choose from a range of predetermined options. Here, the curated choices offered—between different but equally prescriptive lounge spaces—also reflect a shift in economic logic from the circulation of things to the trading of services and experiences. Inhabitants of The Collective are asked to lease an environment, lifestyle, and idea of luxury with which they can identify, rather than define their own through autonomous purchases and practices. In return, there is the guarantee that this space will be maintained and curated to match their aspirational status. The Collective thus presupposes a low level of attachment to "stuff" from loungers whose identity is more likely to be defined online. For many, living in The Collective will be accompanied by a storage unit or parental attic in which the rest of accumulated life can be put on hold. "Do we have extra storage?" is one of the Frequently Asked Questions listed on the website, addressed with the short response "not at the moment unfortunately." The luxury of freedom from commitment promised by The Collective thus produces a community of minimized memories. Indeed, an attraction to some might be the possibility to leave pasts behind: the luxury of forgetting without having to rebuild afresh.

If The Collective's community—as individuals—share the opportunity to select different moods and comfort levels in communal space, it is also characterized by an assumed entrepreneurial spirit. The website depicts the lounges as a network of networking spaces, everyday settings for casual social interaction with like-minded people; like an updated version of the traditional grand country house, where the key rooms were imagined for hosting and socializing more than for everyday living. The Collective's lounges offer a suite of spaces in which young professionals can find common ground, rendering them always potentially at work while at home. Indeed, our tour seemed to double as an interview, relaxed and conversational in tone, but with questions inviting self-presentation to find out what each prospective tenant might be able to offer. This alters the reading of the shared lounges, as equipped with homely alcoves as well as CCTV, with nooks but few doors and no hidden corners. The inhabitant of The Collective's shared spaces remains always on duty and always on show, expected to account for themselves as an aspirational young professional with something to offer, ready for any demand, like the workers of the so-called gig economy. The architecture of casualness and comfort, of many ways to recline, belies this call to constant alertness where inhabitants remain defined by their choices and, in return for buying a low-commitment lifestyle, accept they must leave no trace on their surroundings.

Conclusion

Earlier, we posed the question about what the architecture of The Collective stands for. The hyper-capitalism evident in London's housing market seems at first to have produced a simulation of communist space. But the idealism of collectivization has been stripped out to form instead a collective of individuals. These are individuals united by their willing complicity in the visual and marketing languages of luxury, freedom, and youth—happy to be sold minimum space standards supplemented with a series of lounge spaces because they buy into its particular idea of luxury: as constituted in notions of reassurance, convenience, choice, modest self-indulgence, freedom from commitment, and—distinctively—a kind of homeliness in the city well understood from cafés, bars, tech offices, and hotels.

The idea of lounge space has become familiar through its formulaic, repetitive appropriation of the artifacts of home into a system, monetizing them in order to sell homeliness back to people in semi-public space, constituted as moments of pause in the increasingly transitory work patterns that follow from the demands of distributed working and the gig economy. The Collective's genius is to recognize that lounge space has *itself* now become a reassuringly comforting set of spatial tropes which are themselves capable of further monetization. And its developers have done that by reinserting lounge space back into the home. The familiar interior design tropes are used to theme a few shared rooms to supplement dwelling units of absolute minimum size in order to rent those units at a premium. Domesticity reformulated for sale in the city gets cleverly repackaged as a new way to further monetize the imagery of home.

The spatial configurations of The Collective, and its lounge spaces in particular, illustrate evident parallels with the changing economies and practices of city life. Just as the Narkomfin set out a particular set of relations between the individual, society, culture, and capital, so does The Collective. As the average size of urban dwelling units has shrunk, so the number of cafés, eateries, and bars has increased (IbisWorld, 2017).[2] In part, this follows a broader shift in the post-industrial, networked economy, where space is monetized to sell branded experiences rather than products that might be more cheaply and conveniently purchased online. For an increasingly precarious and self-employed workforce with increasingly smaller homes, these spaces also function, for the price of a coffee, as workspaces or meeting venues. Luxury, here, involves the recompression of time and space for the presentee-ist aspirational young professional and the assurance of a certain kind of familiarity within the more varied marketplace beyond. This effective outsourcing of living and working space secures a constant subscription for activities that were previously understood to exist within the overheads of housing or employment, or within the public realm, in the library or park, or leisure center. The Collective's branded world of luxury, convenience, and choice stands for these new norms of urban life, facilitating a kind of domestic nomadism and bringing it back from the city to the home. The result is a building inseparable from the distinctive idea of self that it promotes and enables. The Collective constructs a fantasy which distinctively unpicks and recombines ideas of home and city, community and individual, freedom and productivity, privacy and public-ness, and comfort and urban grit, melding imagined urban spaces with physically existing spaces to curate an idea of luxury that enables the sale of *Existenzminimum* at a premium.

References

Aghion, P. and Bolton, P. (1997), "A Theory of Trickle-Down Growth and Development," *Review of Economic Studies*, 64 (2): 151–72.

Austin, S. (2012), "Lounge Space: The Home, The City and The Service Area," in A. Sharr (ed.), *Reading Architecture and Culture: Researching Buildings, Spaces and Documents*, 106–20, London: Routledge.

Baudrillard, J. (1996), *The System of Objects*, translated by J. Benedict, London: Verso [especially "Models and Series," pp. 137–55].

Benjamin, W. (2002), *The Arcades Project*, translated by Howard Eiland and Kevin McLaughlin, New York: Bellknap Press [Written between 1925 and 1940 and first published in 1982].

Buchli, V. (1998), "Moisei Ginzburg's Narkomfin Communal House in Moscow: Contesting the Social and Material World," *Journal of the Society of Architectural Historians*, 58 (2): 160–81.

Burrows, R. and Knowles, C. (2019), "The 'Haves' and the 'Have Yachts': Socio-Spatial Struggles in London between the 'Merely Wealthy' and the 'Super-Rich'," *Cultural Politics*, 15 (1): 72–87.

Cadwalladr, C. (2016), "WeWork: They've Transformed the Office, Now It's Time for Your Home," *The Guardian*, January 11. Available online at: https://www.theguardian.com/global/2016/jan/11/wework-transforming-office-life-and-home-life-carole-cadwalladr (accessed May 8, 2017).

Collective, The (2016), "A New Way to Live in London." Available online at: https://www.thecollective.co.uk/coliving (accessed October 20, 2016).

IbisWorld (2017), "Cafes and Coffee Shops in the UK: Market Research Report." Available online at: https://www.ibisworld.co.uk/market-research/cafes-coffee-shops.html (accessed May 13, 2017).

Jameson, F. (1991), *Postmodernism, or, the Cultural Logic of Late Capitalism*, Durham, NC: Duke University Press.

Klingmann, A. (2007), *Brandscapes: Architecture in the Experience Economy*, Cambridge, MA: MIT Press.

Koolhaas, R. (2002), "Junkspace," *October*, 100 (Spring): 175–90.

Kracauer, S. (1997), "The Hotel Lobby," in Neil Leach (ed.), *Rethinking Architecture: A Reader in Cultural Theory*, 51–57, Abingdon: Routledge.

Mairs, J. (2016), "'In the Future We Will all Be Homeless' Says Co-living Entrepreneur," *Dezeen*, July 15. Available online at: https://www.dezeen.com/tag/the-collective/ (accessed May 8, 2017).

Mayor of London (2017), "Old Oak and Park Royal Development Corporation." Available online at: https://www.london.gov.uk/about-us/organisations-we-work/old-oak-and-park-royal-development-corporation-opdc (accessed May 13, 2017).

Pimlott, M. (2016), *The Public Interior as Idea and Project*, Heijningen: Jap Sam Books.

PLP Architecture (2016), PLP Architecture. Accessed online: http://www.plparchitecture.com (accessed May 8, 2017).

Rice, C. (2007), *The Emergence of the Interior: Architecture, Modernity, Domesticity*, Abingdon: Routledge.

Spencer, D. (2016), *The Architecture of Neoliberalism: How Contemporary Architecture Became an Instrument of Control and Compliance*, London: Bloomsbury.

Waite, R. (2017), "All-star Team Beats Heavyweights to Land Old Oak Common Jackpot," *The Architects' Journal*, May 12. https://www.architectsjournal.co.uk/news/all-star-team-beats-heavyweights-to-land-old-oak-common-jackpot/10019879.article

"The third realm of luxury" as I experienced it in the legacies of Getty and the Rockefellers: Elite enclosure, "as far as the eye can see . . ."[1]

George E. Marcus

The study of luxury has most commonly and productively been associated with key concepts like conspicuous consumption, status rivalry, distinction, sumptuary goods, and specialized markets that all concern the complex relations of social classes, of elites to non-elites, within nation-states or transnationally. Here I am concerned rather with one particular form of luxury consumption, themed as "the third realm of luxury" in this volume, which deals seemingly with the most enclosed condition of elite life, which appeals to fantasy, sometimes eccentricity, but defines immersion in an environment that sets a limit on and horizon of experience. This is the personal space constituted by the special dwellings, and more importantly for me, environments, that elites create for themselves, or in the case of dynastic or notable families, find themselves bequeathed. It is how elites fit into privileged enclosures, and particularly how they design and transact the limit or borders of the latter. The limit of what can be seen or noticed is the guide to such design. Whatever the effect of enclosure that they create for themselves, it very much depends on the limit, border, or horizon of such space that is crucial—how they can feel immersed in an opaque or translucent bubble, which depends on a kind of seeing in the distance—literally "as far as their eyes can see"—a limit on looking in their surrounds that only confirms a particular reality. This is luxury, in the sense of being able to construct and sustain such an environment, or to commission that it be made and maintained, and an experienced luxury of reflexive isolation according to one's taste if such an experience can be achieved.

During a career of studying dynastic legacies and institutions, as well as passing through them circumstantially as an academic beneficiary of their philanthropic largesse (in the form of conferences, meetings, and research sojourns), I have repeatedly found myself in such luxurious enclosures and domains with a curiosity for how they are cultivated as such by their creators or beneficiaries. This is perhaps the professional preserve of the architect, or the landscape architect, who, in connecting with patrons and their visions, negotiates and designs on commission such enclosures. My interest here is somewhat more specific. I will be concerned with what defines the limit or horizons of such enclosures from the point of view of those who dwell within them. Are they finally barriers or media through which subjects deal with unseen, but known agencies mimetically at the line of constructed sight in emplacement? Elites *know* there is a complex world of interests beyond and operate in it as well, but still they have the privilege and capacity to see only what they design to see, to the edge of everyday perception.

Such carefully constructed places only work as enclosures if those who dwell there cannot see beyond them. They live every day in constructed landscapes with controlled horizons. Whether this means total, willed isolation or a less direct and more mimetic relation to unseen social relations is a key question of my particular inquiry into this "third realm" of luxury.[2]

My most sustained experience of and exposure to this character of luxurious enclosure, or emplacement, emerged in a sustained project in Portugal during the late 1990s that I conducted in partnership with a nobleman (now deceased), Fernando Mascarenhas, the Marques of Fronteira and Alorna (see Marcus and Mascarenhas 2005), whose understanding of his experience was very much shaped by the enclosure of place—an elaborate palace in a neighborhood of Lisbon—to which he became devoted in his adult life. Our most productive moments of collaboration occurred outdoors on the porches of the palace overlooking its gardens, statues, and tile work; working inside the house struck, I observed a different tone or mood in our work. This difference became diagnostic for me of the characteristics of elite enclosure. I have dealt with this case in more detail elsewhere and will instead develop here two other cases of the same phenomenon of privileged enclosure that I have encountered in the United States: namely, a period (1988–89) as a fellow at the recently established Getty Trust in Los Angeles, then dispersed in a number of West LA business tower locations, but focused on the established Museum in Malibu, a replica of a Herculaneum villa that J. Paul Getty, enclosed hermetically in the English estate, Sutton Place, had built from afar, but never visited. The art world expert inhabitants of this villa were enclosed in the materialization of the far-off imaginary of an infamous billionaire, who had co-written about his imagined life as a Roman aristocrat living in such an estate. It was for the heirs to the Getty fortune—the managers and experts who occupied and administered the Getty Trust—to think of a successor to Getty's earlier odd projects of enclosure in the southern California landscape.

And then, I turn to my attendance at a conference in 2002 at the Rockefeller Pocantico estate, centered on the house called Kykuit, near Sleepy Hollow, New York. This, too, is a case of elite enclosure and the dynamics of perceived limits as enclosure—what the eye (my eye, the patron's eye, and those of other habitués) could see at a horizon.

The key concept in treating subjectivity that I will be evoking in this chapter is emplacement—rather than embodiment, which is a more common mode of conceiving the subject in ethnographic research.[3] This is a distinction that I owe to James Faubion in an intriguing case study of Fernando Mascarenhas, the Marques of Fronteira, in his book, *The Anthropology of Ethics* (2011). In the project that I developed with Fernando, at one stage I invited Faubion in, and we all worked together at the Palace of Fronteira for a few weeks. From that period, Faubion produced a brilliant study of Fernando under the rubric of "an ethics of composure," the title of his chapter on him. How Fernando practices an ethical self, Faubion notices, is based largely on a discourse of attuning himself to the places that enclose him—the palace, and especially its exteriors and gardens, as well as a rural estate of cork groves in the Alentejo. Deeply involved in restoration and a curator of Fronteira's magnificent tilework, Fernando manifests a frame of reference in many of his conversations to what he sees in his surround. These observations are like the spiritual exercises that Pierre Hadot describes in *Philosophy as a Way of Life* (1995).

While Bachelard's *The Poetics of Space* (2014) is the theoretical foundation for the kind of elite phenomenology that I am addressing in this chapter, I have found one side of Michel de Certeau's classic distinction between "strategies" and "tactics" in the practice of everyday life (1984), that is, his cogent thoughts on "strategies" (the side of the distinction that theorizes the experience of the everyday for the elite and powerful, rather than the "tactical" deceptions of the dominated) most specifically relevant for the "seeing" of those enclosed by their own luxury designs, but who still have functions, concerns, interests, and curiosities in what lay beyond their enclosures. For de Certeau, strategies are the techniques of the empowered: "I call a 'strategy' the calculus of force-relationships, which becomes possible when a subject of will and power (a proprietor, an enterprise, a city, a scientific institution) can be isolated from an 'environment.' A strategy assumes a place that can be circumscribed as proper"

(1984: xix). He elaborates further on this proposition, which captures the effect of luxury enclosure without probing its consequences for experience: "The 'proper' is a triumph of place over time. . . . It is also a mastery of places through sight. . . . It would be legitimate to define the power of knowledge by this ability to transform the uncertainties of history into readable spaces" (1984: xix).

However, the capacity to indulge the luxury, as everyday experience, of seeing only what pleases one, or even of allowing one to problematize the world in a way that indulges one's fantasies, pleasures, principles, and beliefs, is never "ironclad." "Alterity," difference that will not be denied, is always somewhat perceptible at the limits of enclosure, where those who have the luxury of determining such enclosure experience perceptions of such difference actively or passively. It is here in this chapter that I evoke Michael Taussig's work on mimesis and alterity (1992), inspired by Walter Benjamin. This mimetic engagement results in what might be understood as the stuff of "eccentricity," what marks them (the luxuriously enclosed) as different from "you" and "me." Though reflexively, in a postscript to this chapter, through a personal anecdote, I am not satisfied to let the effects on experience within spaces of luxurious enclosure rest with the strangeness of those in the markedly powerful, distanced, and privileged classes. I also want to extend my argument to those, like me, in the professional middle classes, who also enjoy and are challenged by the achievement of living within a luxuriant enclave where the horizon as perceived poses phenomenological puzzles of class standing.

Before proceeding, I want also to set the scene further for the ultimate final stage of my argument (concerning luxurious enclosure becoming a possibility of mass consumption by the marketing of immersive technologies and games, currently as entertainment, or in the name of education) by citing my discovery of an essay, a *récit*, by Count Xavier de Maistre, published in 1794, on his behalf by his older brother, the infamous Joseph de Maistre. My discovery of it led me to the development of the long simmering ideas in this chapter from previous research experiences in elite enclosures. It is entitled *Voyage Around My Room* (de Maistre 2016) and was a popular success (encouraging de Maistre into a further literary career of less notice). This work eminently performs emplacement as subjectivity written elaborately in terms of the luxury of enclosure. Only that it is a miniaturization of the grandeur of elite enclosure design (see Stewart [1984] to make a connection with the contemporary popular sentiments associated with the affective power of immersive technologies).

In 1790, de Maistre, a twenty-seven-year-old Savoyard officer, stationed in Turin, fought a duel and was put under house arrest for forty-two days, during which he wrote this experimental account of a world of imagined travel within the limited horizon of favored objects, paintings, and furniture. As he says, "Indeed is there anyone so wretched, so forlorn as not to have some sort of garret in which to withdraw and hide from the world? For such is all that is required for travel" (2016: 7). For de Maistre, the room became the horizon of experience and created in miniature an environment of luxury. Travel could mean an experience of the broader world in actual enclosure and confinement—by mimesis, a core theme of symbolic (and real!) transaction in Michael Taussig's writing (1992). De Maistre's mimesis is making relations in restricted space and its limits. This is what I argue is being done at the normal scale of human action in more ambiguous and luxuriant creations of place as enclosure, as in the cases presented below, that symbolically and otherwise communicate with a larger unseen world beyond the horizon and confines of luxury enclosure—at the limit of "as far as the eye can see" from within them.

De Maistre's is a work of elite eccentricity that evokes for me a favorite personal essay of mine, which I wrote in the 1990s, on eccentricity as a form of creative and critical self-making within notable families that are in decline (Marcus 1995). I argue for a kind of social and class critique embedded in the habits and practices of some notable eccentrics against the now tarnished "character" affirming discourse defining of upper classes. I aimed for a familiarization of the oddity and exotic-ness with which behavior labeled as eccentric is conventionally associated. Most relevant here, I understood eccentricity to be related to the distinctive styles of emplacement of elites in the sort of luxury enclosures that they have designed for themselves or found to dwell within. Most interesting to me then were such denizens of the luxuriously self-enclosed who exhibited eccentric habits of thought and action, but without appearing clinically odd, disturbed, or mad. Quite a few of the elite subjects I have known would fit this criterion of normal eccentricity—it is, for example, the style of self-fashioning cultivated by the Count de Maistre's writing of his *récit*.

My argument was that such eccentrics were engaged with the limits of their enclosed worlds, not in an attempt to see beyond the horizon of luxury enclosure "which is as far as the eye could see," but to create mimetic processes at the limit or horizon in relation to unseen agencies that were nonetheless to be engaged in conditions of splendid enclosure. Here (and then) I made use of Michael Taussig's above noted very interesting thinking about mimesis and alterity (1992). The limit or horizon of elite enclosure is susceptible to thought experiment, spiritual exercise, and so on, as a way of mimetically seeing and acting beyond it. I conceived of eccentricity in this context as a means of embedded cultural critique in the process of elite self-emplacement in the generally luxurious enclosed proximate worlds that have been made for them or that they have commissioned for themselves through class institutions or notable family traditions and identities.[4]

De Maistre meets his confinement by drawing on his luxury-inflected class resources to create a micro-world. Mention of this work here is suggestive of where this chapter concludes as well. To foreshadow, not with elite luxury enclosure, of the major exemplary cases explored below, but in the proliferation of media technologies that has made, and will make further, such enclosure a luxury that mass consumers already are, and will be able to afford, as these technologies develop: namely, virtual reality enablers, games, and larger scale immersive technologies that shape the experience of spectacles and their crowds in theater, concerts, theme parks, and museums (see Lukas 2012, 2016). As with the opening of markets for luxury goods for broader, if not mass consumption, so the challenges of luxurious enclosure will spread to larger populations as de Maistre's essay, rooted in eccentric elite experiment, registers in its address not to elites, but to a more general reader.

Two exhibits of moments of enclosed privileged seeing at variable horizons

Exhibit 1: The Getty Trust and the Getty Villa, Los Angeles, and the hilltop Getty Center to come, 1988–89

I spent a year, 1988–89, as a resident scholar at the Getty Center in Santa Monica, then situated on four upper floors of a tall bank building near the Pacific Ocean. This was just four years after the Getty Trust had been established by J. Paul Getty's will as his major beneficiary. At that time, the Getty Trust was keeping a low profile on the urbanscape of Los Angeles, its major operations divided and situated rather anonymously in two tall office buildings and some warehouses. The Getty scholars were housed in Santa Monica in a nearby Raymond Chandleresque apartment house that had the features of a Mediterranean villa. At the time I was there, the Getty Trust was devoted to its art world and art market reputation, concerned about being taken seriously as a force, especially in European art markets and museums—this was its imagined and ever-present horizon of luxurious elite enclosure and emplacement. During my stay, on a monthly basis, the Getty was using its wealth to acquire whatever became available on the international market, or at auction, of classic and modern European painting at exorbitant prices. My fellow scholars, except for one, were leading figures in European art history and museum curation. Very little interest was shown in local artists or the kinds of contemporary concerns of southern Californian urban life that drove them.

The Getty has since gone through considerable changes, especially after the Rodney King insurrection of the early 1990s, some scandals about fake and stolen art in J. Paul's originary Greek and Roman collection, and the building and opening of the extraordinary Getty Center complex, designed by the architect Richard Meier, on the top of a prominence in the exclusive Brentwood section of Los Angeles. But when I was there, it was a curious, eccentric organization without a real home for its Trust operations and ambitions. It was not being emplaced by enclosure so much as operating with a minimal profile, hiding in plain sight. European art worlds were its horizons then marked by the origins of the visitors who worked in its anonymous locations. The urbanscape of Los Angeles in which it was immersed was then entirely incidental and coincidental (see my papers on the Getty Trust during its early existence from my vantage point as a visiting and pampered scholar, acquisitioned for a year, but with a career ethnographic interest in dynastic legacies—Marcus 1990, 1996, 2002).

The one notable exception to this anonymity was the Getty Museum itself—displaying then J. Paul Getty's personal collection of Greek and Roman art, as well as of baroque furniture—but rapidly acquiring Renoirs, Van Goghs, and other works of the modernist canon as they became available at auction. The Getty's iconic existence inhered in the eccentricities and beauty of the Getty Museum accessed through a poorly marked drive in Malibu off the Pacific Coast highway. The museum, pre-dating the Trust and displaying J. Paul Getty's art collection, was housed in an exact replica of an ancient Roman villa in Herculaneum. J. Paul Getty, who dwelt in an English manor house, had this villa built from afar. He never visited it, yet it captured his imagination. He coauthored, or had ghostwritten, a book on this villa in which he imagined himself living within it in ancient times. It constituted a sort of vision in his mind's eye of the horizon of enclosure (much like the exercise of the imagination in the Count de Maistre's *récit*). Its material reality arose in the Malibu site. As a member and accessioned scholar of the Getty Trust, I visited the Malibu museum several times that year, once for a memorable annual Christmas party and several times to attend lectures given by its scholarly/connoisseur director about the latest acquisitions to the Getty collections on the European art market. The Malibu museum was a luxury construct that created a horizon of enclosure and eccentric elite emplacement—in this case transferred by the will and imagination of its creator to others who served his fantasy even after his death.

On the ground, the Trust scholars, curators, and administrators were left to account for the oddities of the Getty Museum. It had visitors, but a visitor had to have reservations to go there. Once there, a visitor would have a sense of being inside a privileged person's enclosure. It was no different for the scholars who had access. Actually, the eccentric emplacement of the museum in which any visitor would become immersed conformed not to the will of its creator, but to the difficult-to-meet unwritten rules of privileged dwelling that determine the form of prestigious, affluent real estate along the coast and in the hills around Los Angeles. Not being seen is the basic principle. Owners of such properties wanted vistas for themselves, but they did not want to see or be seen by other properties. Many lawsuits arise from the frequent violation of these difficult to achieve rules. The Getty Museum met them—except for the traffic in visitors for which it agreed to the stringent reservation system.

Indeed, these rules of luxury dwelling in Los Angeles arose again in connection with the other major project that was in active planning during the year when I was in residence. The architect Richard Meier was commissioned to design and build the Getty Center complex, and he was in the early stages of planning this defining project of the Getty's future when I was in residence. He was working out of his own temporary offices in Westwood near the UCLA campus. The Getty complex in all of its magnificence opened in the early 1990s, under far different management than the Getty Trust and Center had when I was a resident scholar. The Brentwood complex rapidly became one of the great attractions of Los Angeles, and it has more than come to fulfill the role of civic patron. The story of the coming into being of this vision in transforming its building and landscaping design into material reality has been told many times by now, not least, in the account of Richard Meier himself (1997). To follow the thread of argument of this chapter, I am most interested here in merely noting Meier's reported encounter with the rules and politics of building amid other privileged dwellers emplacing themselves in luxury enclosures. As with the siting of the Getty, Meier found himself facing the rules of seeing, but not being seen in the construction of luxury enclosures in affluent terrains of dwelling in Los Angeles. Brentwood is one of the most affluent. When the scholars met with him during my year at the Getty, he reported with exasperation and disbelief that he had to make over 200 changes in his planning for the new Getty Center, based on negotiations with watchful neighbors. And the negotiations were not over at the time we met with him. No dweller in the vicinity of the new complex wanted to see any part of it from their property. Actually, in pursuing its own ambition for landscaping, as with the Malibu museum, it was to the Getty's advantage not to have any of its neighbors visible from the grand vistas and horizons that it eventually achieved. Somehow, it was worked out.

I did not follow the story after my departure (except to read Meier's account), but I have visited the new Getty complex since its establishment in Brentwood. The Getty Center accessed only by a funicular is difficult to see from below, but from its own vantage points it provides the most spectacular views of Los Angeles and beyond. The effects of changing sunlight on the travertine surfaces radically affect and direct a kind of continual staged light show in shaping the depth and scope of the horizon or limit of "what the eye can see." So the Getty has achieved an architectural existence of enclosure in a very tightly regulated residential culture, which is now invisible to it, in favor of what seems a boundless horizon, one that miniaturizes the smoggy cityscape of Los Angeles for something more magnificent, caught in the sun's daily reflection off the travertine surfaces that Meier installed. My self-conscious evocation here captures the achieved grandeur of the style—only it is unclear who on the inside of the Getty is emplaced by this creation. The answer is perhaps no one in particular, or everyone who visits. It is a kind of emplacement of grandeur, a definition of horizon, an effect that is experienced by anyone who visits. It suggests comparison with the spectacular immersion that media technology offers today on a mass basis, here achieved by the means and skills that have classically produced luxury enclosure and fantasy horizons, as far as the eye can see, for elite patrons and clients. The average visitor, ennobled by her visit, or the returning, former Getty scholar becomes the simulacrum of the latter.

Exhibit 2: Kykuit and Pocantico, the Rockefeller Estate, Sleepy Hollow New York, 2002

In 2002, I attended a three-day conference at the Pocantico Center on the estate of the Rockefeller family. It was organized by an MIT professor, who turned out to be married to a daughter of David Rockefeller (an economics professor and attendee at the conference, who went under a different name), and included a diverse array of academics charged with thinking together about different modes of imaging the globe, using the then latest information and media technologies. For me, it was an unusual and uncertain conference participation. I was much more interested in the landscape that surrounded me. Rockefeller family members still lived on the estate, but they were situated carefully out of view of the conference center. Sharing that cultivated space for the three days, I was very interested then in what they could see, what their sculpted views were—the horizons that we could share with them, though they and their residences were invisible to us. Clearly the sacred family sites of the estate were now given over to curation and heritage specialists. We stayed in the old carriage house and had access to the family mansion, named Kykuit, a Dutch word meaning "lookout." The arrangement of art collections, with an eccentric mark (e.g., the family golf course was also the site of display of an array of modern sculptures) conveyed a history of elite quirkiness, rather than cultivated distinction (that was for those who strived!). Did this effect originate with the family, their advisers, or the curators? Or a collaboration among them? As pioneers in the modern administration of dynastic wealth, from cradle to grave and beyond, the Rockefellers have posed such difficult questions for scholars to disentangle (see especially Hall 1992).

At the time of my visit, I had even then been interested *de facto* in the questions of elite luxury enclosure (following upon my project in Portugal), how views of the horizon—as far as the eye could see—were sculpted. It was the one characteristic of the site that the visitor might share with family residents who stayed in the carefully enclosed locations on estate now given over to more public uses. Obviously, given the naming of the family mansion ("lookout") the horizon views were, and continue to be, of key importance in constituting this site for dwelling. I eventually learned that the estate had bought up or leased all of the contiguous land as far as the eye could see for preferred landscaping. Indeed, behind the forested growths of the hills beyond is the village of Sleepy Hollow, New York, famous as the setting of a well-known Washington Irving story, completely obscured by Rockefeller landscape artifice. From the Pocantico estate, nothing of that community or any other dwelling could be seen through the screen of forested hills. Not part of the estate, the vistas that the surrounding hills composed were something that the Rockefellers cultivated as a luxury form of enclosure. In creating beautifully green forested horizons, they emplace themselves alone among others in the surround of their estate, as far as the eye can see.

On another occasion, I stayed nearby in another conference location at Tarrytown, New York. While nicely landscaped in its own compound, there was no attention to sculpting the horizon and no question that we remained embedded in suburban America, which in that vicinity (the same vicinity as the Pocantico estate) had become quite gritty and urbanized over the years. The Rockefeller estate was as if in another world of its own sculpted enclosure. The

Rockefellers were alone and emplaced, even though they had constant visitors on site, in a world, a horizon of their own design. Enclosure opened a natural world on the "as far as the eye could see," obscuring what has happened to the once quaint villages, now communities of suburbanites and commuters, failing to keep the urban sprawl at bay. In contrast, for a moment I shared that Rockefeller's difference in dwelling through their achievement of meticulous isolation, enclosure through the effect of a pleasing nature all around, as far as the eye can see, as if there were nothing else beyond. But of course, from the conference center and staying in the old carriage house, I could see nothing of them within, either—except when they chose to appear!

Envoi

The democratization of the capacity to experience "the third realm of luxury" as elite enclosure in the present, through the contemporary mass distribution of new(er) media: The development of virtual reality apparatuses, game technologies, and the taste for immersive spectacles in theme parks, museums, and entertainment

In these media developments for mass consumption, what we are seeing is the emergence of what was largely an elite experience of managing enclosure, as increasingly experiences of everyday life on a mass and global scale through immersive entertainments and pastimes at least initially. This is hardly, however, a phenomenon of conspicuous consumption, the prestige of distinction, or the accumulation of symbolic capital which have defined and been defined by the circulation of, and markets in, luxury goods moving from elites to the privileged, aspiring sectors of masses. Rather an eccentric but core existential and private problem of elites as I have defined it (think of Count de Maistre's eighteenth-century *récit* as iconic, but a condition that is also reflected in each case as contending with the horizons of enclosed existence) has become an existential problem (or indulgence, for now?) of mass consumers (especially observed as youth cultures) generally as new affordable media technologies define emplacement, as well as embodiment, for those many who entertain and occupy themselves in more thoroughly enclosed and immersive ways, incorporating public cultural spectacles, as well as private pastimes.

In light of this separate, parallel trend in immersion and enclosure in the realm of mass entertainment raising the specter of clinical problems associated with eccentricity—obsession, addiction, detachment, alienation—the management side of elite enclosure and emplacement, described in this chapter, might be both instructive and cautionary. Without the prestige and resources (the luxury, in a word) through which elite emplacement has been achieved in the cases that I have reviewed, the situation of enclosure is something to be endured and resisted by applying the imagination to limits, borders, and horizons—the line of "as far as the eye can see"—for which I employed in this chapter the concept of mimesis, as explored by Taussig at the horizons of relations with others, as the state of alterity.

So, while technology driven, what we are seeing is the experience of carefully crafted, curated luxury experiences of elites becoming independently a mass consumer phenomenon. The latter has little to do with emulation or prestige, but rather with the development of technologies that make enclosure, emplacement (and the key term of experience) a dominant trend, initially, in consumer entertainment markets. In such a development, the elite versions of enclosure, based in commitments to old houses, estates, and projects, appear even more eccentric than they often are. Still the horizon question is common to both: What can be enclosed, bounded, and observed? What breaks through in what experiences of mimesis? The elite form was never reality denying, but just a coping with the existential problems posed by a condition of privileged enclosure. Can consumer responses to similar effects of the mass distribution of new media technologies, requiring emplacement and enclosure, do the same, or better?[5]

Postscript: "University Hills—the nation's foremost on-campus community"

As both a supplement to and personal reflection on the concerns of this chapter, I provide some comments on my own ambivalent experience of this luxury in dwelling of privileged emplacement and enclosure. They arise from my living in a version of the coastal southern Californian gated community of affluence. It is afforded me by residence and ownership of a property in the University Hills (UH) development of the University of California, Irvine, where I am faculty. It is a luxury residential enclave that derives in style from the history of Irvine as a planned community for which the university, founded in 1965, was to have been a center and stimulus. This development, as part of the campus of UCI, is on ranchland owned by the Irvine Company and leased on a long-term basis to UC. Most of the housing (with a few notable exceptions, e.g., the chancellor's house and grounds) has been developed as tracts, but the landscaping has been carefully sculpted as a luxury amenity (luxury being a self-conscious category and goal by those who have developed it as a commodity/industry on this landscape; there are no gates in this community, but it is enclosed by the campus in the same way as other developments in and around Irvine and Newport Beach are "gated"). UH is thus an enclave whose mostly faculty denizens live in comfortable alienation from it. As a noted scholar in critical theory, and longtime denizen of UH, observes about the state of comfortable alienation of the residents, "Everyone complains, but no one is unhappy."

Despite the dull uniformity of the housing models, there is a carefully designed landscape of parks, vistas, and views. This is luxury as the horizon designed for enclosure. The aesthetics of situated horizons is a key amenity of living in UH for its residents, which each is bound to notice to varying degrees. Given the horizon, "as far as the eye can see" focus of this chapter, I am particularly interested in noting the latter as a condition of everyday life in UH—of living in a privileged and luxuriant landscape of someone else's making—and how it might differ from similar seeing, noticing, envisioning as an eccentric and cultivated privilege and luxury of being enclosed and emplaced at the Getty, or Kykuit. I can best evoke the perceptual ambivalence for me personally of living in this privileged and sculpted landscape by something I notice frequently in experiencing two of the most striking vistas that this development offers daily strollers such as myself. One vista on a hill a few hundred feet from my house is a carefully designed viewing point that allows one to look out over the mountain-framed interior of Irvine and other inland communities. This landscape is very often obscured by a thick smog, relieved only by rare days when the mountain range is clearly in view. When I see the rather alarming smog cover inland, I look up at our own very blue sky above and behind me that defines the nearby coastal contrasting climate of beautiful skies always, except for a few gray days of marine layer. I wonder ambiguously whether we are part of that interior, or of the coast, and that maybe I just can't see the smog that in fact engulfs us. It is indeed a kind of status anxiety. But I always reassure myself that we are part of the privileged zone of coastal climate. It is a reinforcing, daily experienced, psychological and sociologically confirming "luxury" effect of a distinctive sort that the view inland, "as far as the eye can see," combined with a view above and then reverse toward the coast achieves for me, at least as a resident of UH. We may be on the border, but we are part of the latter and not the former. I then confirm and affirm this status effect by walking a half-mile to the bluffs and ecological reserve that border the chancellor's house with its own manicured grounds. There, the other major vista in UH faces the coast about ten miles away. It approximates what those who live there see: brilliant, colorful skies touching the ocean. It overwhelms the slight indications of inland view, and while that coastal line too may be affected by smog and urban ecology, it provides visually the sort of unconflicted horizon and limit of viewing comparable to the states of luxury enclosure that those I have described in this chapter have created and maintain for themselves in their vision as well as in their mundane housekeeping. As with them, the horizon remains finally ambiguous—effects are created by viewing and explicit design, but exactly whether UH is coastal (privileged) or inland (not) despite crafted vistas remains ambiguous and relational along the border as UH is. House and grounds keeping in the privileged sites of luxury emplacement and enclosure has its own fascinating versions of this ambiguity of the UH horizon.

References

Bachelard, G. (2014), *The Poetics of Space*, New York: Penguin.

De Certeau, M. (1984), *The Practice of Everyday Life*, Berkeley: University of California Press.

Faubion, J. (2011), "An Ethics of Composure," in *An Anthropology of Ethics*, 119–202, Cambridge: Cambridge University Press.

Feld, S. and Basso, K., eds. (1996), *Senses of Place*, Santa Fe: School for American Research Press.

Hadot, P. (1995), *Philosophy as a Way of Life*, London: Blackwell.

Hall, P. D. (1992), "The Empty Tomb: The Making of Dynastic Identity," in G. E. Marcus and P. D. Hall (eds.), *Lives in Trust*, 255–348, Boulder, CO: Westview Press.

Ingold, T. (2011), *Being Alive: Essays on Movement, Knowledge and Description*, London: Routledge.

Lukas, S. (2012), *The Immersive Worlds Handbook: Designing Theme Parks and Consumer Spaces*, Los Angeles: Focal Press.

Lukas, S. (2016), *A Reader in Themed and Immersive Spaces*, Pittsburgh: ETC Press.

de Maistre, X. (2016), *Voyage Around My Room*, translated by Stephen Sartarelli, New York: A New Directions Book.

Marcus, G. E. (1990), "The Production of European High Culture in Los Angeles: The J. Paul Getty Trust as Artificial Curiosity," *Cultural Anthropology*, 5 (3): 314–30.

Marcus, G. E. (1995), "On Eccentricity," in D. Battaglia (ed.), *Rhetorics of Self-Making*, 35–48, Berkeley: University of California Press.

Marcus, G. E. (1996), "Middle Brow to High Brow at the J. Paul Getty Trust of Los Angeles," in Elizabeth Bakewell and Brenda Bright (eds.), *Looking High and Low: Art and Cultural Identity*, 173–98, Tucson: University of Arizona Press.

Marcus, G. E. (2002) "The J. Paul Getty Trust of Los Angeles, Made-Over: A Visionary Institution In(to) Perpetuity," *Folk*, 44: 19–35.

Marcus, G. E. and Mascarenhas, F. (2005), *Ocasiao: The Marquis and the Anthropologist, A Collaboration*, Baltimore: AltaMira.

Mason, Z. (2017), *Void Star*, New York: Farrar, Strauss, and Giroux

Meier, R. (1997), *Building the Getty*, New York: Alfred A. Knopf.

Stewart, S. (1984), *On Longing: Narratives of the Miniature, the Gigantic, the Souvenir, the Collection*, Baltimore: Johns Hopkins University Press.

Taussig, M. (1992) *Mimesis and Alterity*, New York: Routledge.

Tsing, A. (2015), *The Mushroom at the End of the World: On the Possibility of Life in Capitalist Ruins*, Princeton, NJ: Princeton University Press.

Secret spaces of luxury:
Ignorance, free ports, and art

Joanne Roberts

Introduction

Luxury is often associated with conspicuous consumption (Veblen 1899), such that a lavish lifestyle, replete with expensive products and services of the highest quality, demonstrates one's economic wealth and position in society. Though, in an age when the consumption of luxury is becoming ever more democratized owing to its often-standardized production, we are witnessing the rise of inconspicuous consumption of luxury goods and services. This may take the form of what has been referred to as "stealth luxury" (Faiers 2016). Such luxury consumption is only recognized by those who are party to relatively restricted knowledge, which allows them to distinguish between, for instance, a Wal-Mart white T-shirt costing $9 and a Dior Homme white T-shirt priced at $480. Luxury of this type may be included in what I refer to as secret luxury. However, secret luxury goes beyond the inconspicuous yet public consumption of expensive goods and services. This chapter will explore a particular form of secret luxury, one that is dependent upon certain places that provide private spaces for the surreptitious consumption of luxury. These spaces range from safe-deposit boxes and private jets and yachts to secluded private islands and the secure storage facilities housed in free ports in locations such as Luxembourg, Switzerland, and Singapore. Knowledge about these secret spaces of luxury is largely confined to those who have the resources to access them, while others who remain, at most, barely aware of such places can only imagine what they hold. Indeed, many remain completely ignorant of such places. The presence of secret spaces of luxury generates and perpetuates ignorance while simultaneously providing subjects for popular fiction, for instance, the villain in James Bond films often resides on a private island or secluded estate in magnificent surroundings. Accordingly, an ignorance perspective (Roberts 2013, 2018) is adopted to investigate secret spaces of luxury with the aim of evaluating their wider societal consequences. Specific attention will be given to free ports as secret spaces of luxury. Originally facilities for the storage of goods in transit, today, free ports are increasingly used by the world's super-rich[1] to store their investments in luxury goods ranging from works of art and fine wine to jewelry and classic cars (*The Economist* 2013). Through an exploration of free ports and art this chapter will address the following questions: Who uses these secret spaces of luxury and why? How do such spaces facilitate secrecy? How does the ownership of real luxury goods in a physical storage facility, rarely visited by the owner, facilitate the imagined experience of distanciated possession? What are the implications of the ignorance that such secret spaces generate for society?

The chapter begins by elaborating the nature of ignorance and identifies secrecy as a form of ignorance arising from the suppression of knowledge, before moving to a consideration of the relationship between luxury and secret spaces. This is followed by a discussion of the free port as an example of a secret space. Through the way free ports are used to store real luxury goods, including fine art, and the secrecy that they afford, imaginary qualities are given to the luxuries they hold. The real and imagined dimensions of fine art stored in free ports are then explored[2] and the implications of free ports as secret spaces of luxury for the ownership of works of art and for society are considered. Finally, brief conclusions are drawn.

Ignorance and secrecy

Ignorance and the unknown are important features of luxury as I have discussed elsewhere (Roberts 2018). For instance, a key characteristic of luxury recognized by academic researchers and consultants alike is "aura," which is often associated with quality, cultural heritage, creativity, craftsmanship, and the highest level of service (Frontier Economics 2014: 6); but aura defies precise definition because it includes ambiguities and unknowns. In a sense, it is in these unknown qualities that the mystery and attraction of luxury often rests. Hence, I situate my examination of the secret spaces of luxury in the field of ignorance studies (Gross 2010; Roberts 2013; McGoey 2014; Gross and McGoey 2015; *inter alia*). Ignorance is typically defined as a lack of knowledge or information (*OED* 2003: 862). Related to ignorance is the condition of being ignorant, that is, of lacking knowledge. To be ignorant is also associated with being rude, discourteous, or stupid. A person with no knowledge may be referred to as an ignoramus (Roberts and Armitage 2008). Moreover, to ignore refers to a failure or refusal to notice something or someone. Ignorance is then defined in relation to either the absence of, or the failure to understand, or refusal to recognize, knowledge. Ignorance must therefore be understood in relation to knowledge. Importantly, ignorance, like knowledge, is socially constructed (Smithson 1989).

From an earlier extensive review of literature on the nature of ignorance, I identified the following three key sources of ignorance (Roberts 2013: 219):

1. ignorance arising from the absence of knowledge: unknown unknowns and known unknowns;
2. ignorance about knowledge: knowable known unknowns, unknown knowns, and errors;
3. ignorance from the suppression of knowledge: taboos, denials, secrecy, and privacy.

All three of these sources of ignorance are of relevance to the promotion and consumption of luxury (Roberts 2018). However, it is the last of these three that is central to the understanding of secret spaces of luxury developed in this chapter. The conscious suppression of knowledge by either individuals or organizations, including business corporations and government bodies (Galison 2004; Proctor 2008), gives rise to ignorance from secrecy. Ignorance arises for individuals and organizations when they are subject to the secrecy of others. Certain types of secrets may be socially sanctioned, such as those arising from the individual's right to privacy. For this reason, ignorance can also be identified with privacy—the ability of an individual or group of individuals to restrict access to, or information about, themselves. Unlike secrecy, privacy is multilateral in nature (Roberts 2013). This is because the right to privacy is enshrined in the laws of many countries and in supranational declarations, including the United Nation's Universal Declaration of Human Rights. Social and cultural practices also determine patterns of privacy. Giving someone his or her own privacy may be seen as polite in certain cultures and may lead to individuals suppressing their own curiosity and therefore knowledge of the lives of others. In this sense, privacy can create knowable known unknowns: we choose not to know something about someone. Moreover, the preservation of privacy may require the creation of taboos or denials: there are certain things that we should not know or that we cannot acknowledge.

Ignorance arising from the suppression of knowledge, through secrecy and privacy, is clearly socially constructed, and it varies according to social and cultural norms. Indeed, the ability to suppress knowledge through secrecy and privacy is continually challenged by societal and technological forces. For instance, the website WikiLeaks, through the acts of its contributors, has become renowned for the disclosure of state secrets, while the activity of members of social media sites like Twitter are challenging the enforcement of privacy laws (Preston 2011).

Luxury and secret spaces

In today's world of big data, digital communications, and easily accessible surveillance technologies, maintaining privacy by keeping information about one's activities, families, friends, and possessions secret may be regarded as a luxury, or even an unattainable luxury (KnightFrank 2017). This is because through our use of social media, payment cards, and mobile telephones, which accompany us almost everywhere, our social interactions, each economic transaction that we complete, and every movement that we make can be traced (Mayer-Schönberger and Cukier 2013). Additionally, an array of technologies, including drones and other surveillance technologies, is available for those keen to learn through legal or illegal means about the activities of individuals. For example, businesses can monitor social media and analyze sociocultural habits and purchasing trends in order to precision target advertising, and governments are able to observe political and social behavior to identify potential terrorist tendencies as well as scrutinizing income-generating activities to ensure that individual citizens pay their full tax liabilities. Moreover, access to such technologies allows criminals to identify opportunities to fraudulently exploit information about individuals, and it permits unscrupulous journalists, looking for their next scoop, to access information about the private lives of, for instance, celebrities, politicians, members of royal families, or those already in the news due to their success or misfortune. Simultaneously, CCTV cameras ensure that in the streets of towns and cities, as well as in public and private buildings, including stores and hotels, our movements are tracked. Of course, in an era of social networks, many individuals are willing to share an enormous amount of information with people they barely know and the public at large. Keeping one's identity, location, and daily routine private requires not only vigilance in relation to those with whom one interacts and how one engages with others but also the resources to employ others to act on one's behalf. In the contemporary era, privacy requires the purposeful mobilization of secrecy.

Unsurprisingly, then, the secret or inconspicuous consumption of luxury is a growing trend, and one that has been promoted by the period of austerity in the Western world, following the 2008 global financial crisis. While most people in the economically advanced nations have experienced declining incomes in real terms since 2008, the super-rich, having benefited from investment opportunities, have seen their wealth increase. Yet, the subsequent rise in inequality since 2008 (Dorling 2014; Piketty 2014) has increased fears among the super-rich of a backlash and of crime. Flaunting luxury can be viewed as not only in bad taste but also dangerous. The armed robbery in Paris of the reality television star Kim Kardashian West in October 2016 is one of many examples of the wealthy being targets of crime (Willsher 2016). While it is possible to criticize the wealthy for drawing attention to their luxury lifestyle, including displaying jewels worth millions of dollars on social media, where the person involved depends on their wealthy image for their celebrity and financial success, displaying their life of extravagance and opulence is a key part of maintaining and expanding their income. However, as Karl Lagerfeld commented in reaction to the robbery:

> I don't understand why she was in a hotel with no security. If you're that famous and you put all your jewellery on the internet then you go to a hotel where nobody can come near to the room. . . . You cannot display your wealth and then be surprised that some people want to share it with you. (Quoted in Samuel and Allen 2016)

The key point here is not so much that the victim of the robbery was wealthy or indeed flaunting their wealth, but that Kim Kardashian West was staying in the wrong hotel. The right hotel would have afforded her the appropriate level of security, and, thus, acted as a secret space to protect her from the reach of armed robbers.

The super-rich need safe, secure locations to live and visit. They need secret spaces and places that can offer them privacy. Additionally, they need safe locations to hold their expensive assets. Given the contemporary environment of easily accessible technologies of surveillance, safety necessitates a high degree of secrecy. Consequently, many wealthy people live in exclusive gated communities, private estates, or town houses and apartments in enclaves reserved for the super-rich, like Mayfair or Knightsbridge in London, where they are protected by twenty-four-hour security services. The super-rich holiday at exclusive hotels, private islands, or aboard super yachts inaccessible to all but a select and vetted few whose job it is to serve and protect them. With private jets, helicopters, and super yachts the super-rich can traverse the globe with relative ease behind a veil of privacy afforded by their independent transportation arrangements. In this way, their lives and consumption activities are hidden from the public's gaze and from the intrusion of criminal activity. Privacy and security are constant and growing concerns for the super-rich.

As a result, there is a growing demand from the super-rich for security consultancy and services (Arlidge 2015). Security systems are designed to provide physical safety for family members from kidnapping and harm as well as to protect tangible and intangible assets. Such systems include fingerprint-activated locks and programmable staff keys, which can limit staff access to areas in the home; vinyl polymer coatings that make windows blast-resistant; safe rooms with steel door and strengthened walls and fast-acting security shutters that can block off key rooms; high value collectibles can be fitted with mobility sensors that alert security to their unexpected movement, and unique DNA solution coatings can ensure their identification; a stolen asset register alerts dealers, auction houses, and police in the event of a theft; and, safes have two codes—one for normal use, the other for when the owner is being forced to open it, which when used alerts the police (Wingfield 2010; Arlidge 2015; Cox 2016).

In addition to the physical security of persons and possessions, the super-rich are also concerned to secure their wealth, and this requires privacy and secrecy in relation to banking, investments, tax issues, and inheritance planning. Importantly, privacy may offer strategically important secrecy in relation to the commercial or investment activities of the super-rich. One way of protecting and securing wealth is to hold a diversified portfolio of assets. Given the historically low levels of interest since 2008 together with higher levels of economic uncertainty, holding wealth in forms other than familiar financial instruments has become increasingly popular (*The Economist* 2013). There is, then, a growth in the use of luxury cars, fine wines, and fine art as investment assets. Nevertheless, holding wealth in such forms presents significant security issues. This is because there are limits to the tangible goods that family homes and additional residences can hold. Moreover, just as securing wealth requires the diversification of assets, the protection of one's tangible assets can be enhanced by using multiple locations for storage to take account of potential dangers arising from natural disasters, including floods, fires, and earthquakes, and the risks resulting from terrorism and political upheavals. Hence, the diversification of wealth portfolios such that they include luxury goods like classic cars, fine wine, jewels, and works of fine art accounts for the increasing demand for secret storage spaces. This demand has contributed to a growth in the number of free ports with specialist storage facilities to accommodate such items. Consequently, attention now turns to the nature of the free port.

Free ports as secret spaces

Free ports offer places to store precious items safely and securely, with the appropriate level of care. But free ports are more than storage facilities because they offer further advantages arising from their legal status and the anonymity that they allow. According to UNESCO (2016: 2):

> Free ports are tax-free warehouses that were initially created to store raw materials and, later, to hold manufactured goods for a short period of time before their transportation, transit and reshipment.
>
> The "free" aspect of free ports refers to the suspension of Customs duties and taxes. Today, goods may be kept there for an unlimited period of time and at minimal expense. While goods are stored at free ports, owners pay no import taxes or duties until the goods reach their final destination. If the good is sold at the free port, the owner pays no transaction tax either.
>
> This system allows collectors and galleries to store unlimited quantities of cultural objects without paying VAT and Customs duties.

Indeed, in many nations, the storing of goods or artifacts only requires a declaration of the nature of the asset and the name of the depositor, but not the name of the owner of the object (UNESCO 2016: 2).

The first free port was founded in Geneva in 1854. The facilities in Geneva have expanded over the years such that they now include high security storage with sophisticated surveillance and climate control systems together with private showrooms. Driven by the growth in wealth and the resultant increase in demand for facilities to store high value goods, since 2010 there has been a significant expansion in the number and geographical spread of free ports specializing in the storage of fine art and other luxury collectibles (see Table 9.1). This expansion also reflects the growth and globalization of the luxury market, including the art market, which has been bolstered by the rise in demand from emerging countries especially China (McAndrew 2017).

The free ports in Luxembourg and Singapore are permitted, under national regulations, to allow the owners of works of art to remove them temporarily for local exhibition without incurring the tax costs that would normally arise when moving assets from free ports. In this way, local cultural industries are supported

Table 9.1 Free ports specializing in the storage of fine art and other luxury collectibles

Location	Date of establishment
Geneva, Switzerland	1854
Singapore, Singapore	2010
Monaco, Monaco	2013
Luxembourg, Luxembourg	2014
Beijing, China	2014
Delaware, USA	2015
Shanghai, China	2017
New York, USA	2018

Source: Compiled from Ditzig, Lynch, and Ding (2016: 184), Geneva Freeport and
  Warehouses Ltd (http://geneva-freeports.ch/en/ [accessed May 6, 2018]), SMT
  Fine Art (https://www.smt.mc/en/smt-fine-art/monaco-freeport/ [accessed May
  6, 2018]), and ARCIS (http://www.arcisartstorage.com/news/ [accessed May 6,
  2018]).

by the exhibitions that result from the presence of the free port. At the same time, owners of art can get the pleasure and benefits of exhibiting their art, while also maintaining the free port tax advantages. Making use of such opportunities to show art may be more than a philanthropic act as the inclusion of works in exhibitions can contribute to a strategy designed to increase the value of an art portfolio (Thompson 2008).

Free port storage facilities take the form of anonymous buildings. They are generally located close to airports for the convenient receipt of goods and visitors wishing to view their own stored items or to peruse items on sale. Such buildings are inaccessible to the public at large, who are often unaware of their role as locations for the storage of high value goods. Free ports offer high levels of security and privacy. The short-term use of free ports may result from situations when items are in transit or waiting for their final destination to be prepared. For example, museums may use free ports to hold securely exhibitions that are in transit between venues or as additional storage space. The long-term use of free ports may be associated with the storage of items held as investments.

The companies that manage the space within free ports and deliver specialized logistics and storage services are known for their discretion. For the owners of luxury goods deposited in a free port, a further layer of secrecy can be added through the use of an offshore shell company, which gives anonymity to the ultimate owner of the objects stored. Once luxury goods are placed in the secure storage facilities of the free port, owners can be sure of their safety. Of course, there are costs involved, for instance, Maertens (2013) reports that prices range from 250 to 700 euros per square meter per annum. In addition, holding tangible assets incurs insurance costs. Nevertheless, in 2013, the Geneva free port was estimated to have held around 1.2 million artifacts, and approximately 3 million bottles of vintage wine and several tonnes of gold bars (Maertens 2013).

One of the most notable companies offering free port services is Fine Art Logistics Natural Le Coultre, which was established over 150 years ago.[3] This company provides expert advice and solutions in the area of fine art logistics to a select global group of museums, galleries, and collectors through its headquarters in Geneva and its sister companies in Singapore and Luxembourg. In total, Natural Le Coultre manages over 30,000 square meters of fine art storage worldwide, and thereby claims that it contributes to the protection and maintenance of the cultural heritage of humanity. Its warehouse located at LE FREEPORT Luxembourg, which is the highest rated maximum-security vault in Europe, was launched in September 2014. This facility has over 13,000 square meters of fully climate- and humidity-controlled storage space for fine art, four fine wine cellars, and dedicated storage rooms for classic cars and precious metals. Additionally, the company's clients have access to a scientific laboratory and a restoration workshop as well as eight showrooms and an impressive lobby for events, private exhibitions, and the purchase and sale of fine art.

Clearly, free port facilities go beyond the provision of mere storage space. Free ports have become one-stop shops for the management and secure storage of collections of art and other high value possessions, providing all the services required to keep such goods in pristine condition. Furthermore, galleries and art advisers have offices in free ports where clients can view, buy, and sell art. So, let us now turn to the relationship between art and the free port.

Transforming art in real places to assets in imaginary secret spaces

Fine art refers to the expression or application of human creative skill and imagination, typically in a visual form such as painting or sculpture, producing works to be appreciated primarily for their aesthetic or emotional power. In this sense, for art to fulfill its purpose, it must be experienced and generate meaning through being exposed to human perception (Klamer 1996a). As Arjo Klamer (1996b: 21) notes, "Art exists not in the physical form of a painting or a performance but in the moment of wonderment, of the question mark that the physical form evokes in our minds." So, from this perspective, art has value beyond measure and therefore cannot be equated with a monetary sum. Yet, art can also function as an object of conspicuous consumption, as an investment, as decoration, or as a combination of these forms.

Art provides enjoyment in and of itself, but as a form of conspicuous consumption (Veblen 1899) it provides a means of signaling one's wealth to others. Fine art is a luxury good, and its collection is a pastime of many of the super-rich who use art to signal status and to adorn the entrance halls and walls of their multiple residences. As the super-rich have grown in number and wealth, so too has the demand for art. It is a demand that is evidenced by the size of the global art market, which achieved total sales of $56.6 billion in 2016 (McAndrew 2017: 26–27). Indeed, art is among the top interests and passions of the world's billionaires. As Wealth-X (2016) reports, art was the third most popular "passion/interest/hobby" in 2014, with 28.7 percent of billionaires surveyed referring to it, after philanthropy (56.3 percent) and travel (31 percent).

Although art may provide a source of pleasure and prestige, it is also an investment asset. In recent years, art has become one of a number of assets held by the wealthy as a means of diversifying their investment portfolios (Thompson 2008). However, whether art is a sound investment when compared to other assets is debatable (Baumol 1986; Gerlis 2014). Nevertheless, there are tax advantages to be gained from holding art rather than cash, including inheritance planning benefits. Art can be a safe haven in periods of economic uncertainty and a means of storing and moving wealth. So, for instance, although art sales declined sharply in the aftermath of the 2008 global financial crisis, the art market recovered quicker than the economy as a whole (McAndrew 2017). Still, the art market is tied to the wider economic context, particularly in relation to those factors affecting the growth and distribution of private wealth. Slowing economic growth, and continuing political uncertainty in the global economy, influenced the art market in 2016 and was reflected in cautious buying and selling in some areas (McAndrew 2017: 26–27). Even so, with the increasing numbers of wealthy people across the globe, supported by growth in the emerging markets, the demand for art is likely to increase in the longer term.

According to the Mei Moses World All Art Index, a leading barometer of art returns, as an investment fine art provides a return comparable to that achieved through an investment in the FT all share index and certain categories of art display even higher returns.[4] In particular, the Mei Moses Post-War and Contemporary Art Index has outperformed the FT all share index and the S&P

500 total return index over the past twenty years (Deloitte and ArtTactics 2016: 107). Nonetheless, when considering art as an investment, the cost of keeping it securely and preserving it in pristine condition as well as insuring it against damage or loss must be taken into account (Baumol 1986).

Hence, it is hardly surprising that the growth in the market transactions of artworks has led to a rise in the use of free ports as a location to store art while in transit and increasingly for longer periods of time. Indeed, as collectors accumulate increasing quantities of art, it may be necessary to look for storage beyond their multiple residences. Consequently, there is a demand for safe places to store such goods when they are not on display in homes and to reduce risk by ensuring the geographical dispersion of such assets. Moreover, items purchased as investments rather than for display also require safe storage.

As assets, works of art are not liquid but they can be used as security for borrowed funds. Indeed, storing works of art in free ports makes it easier to use them as collateral for loans (Deloitte and ArtTactics 2014: 88). As art becomes a financial instrument, like bonds, stocks, and shares, its tangibility for the owner becomes secondary to its imagined symbolic value. Art can be stored away in free ports like money in the bank and rarely withdrawn.

Importantly, when art is stored as an investment asset, its nature and relation to its owner changes. A real luxury good transforms from being a tangible object that has some perceptual impact on the owner's existence into an abstraction: an abstraction that is disconnected from the everyday life of the owner through its incorporation into a set of financial assets. Art's tangibility is neutralized in the secret spaces of the strong rooms and vaults of the free port. It moves from the real places of owner's lives to the imagined spaces of the abstract world of financial asset. Hidden out of sight, works of art cease to produce moments of wonderment in a viewer. As a result, the value of such art is no longer beyond measure, and individual works of art lose their uniqueness and become homogenized as a set of financial assets. Taking on the characteristics of a financial instrument, art's only solidity becomes its value listed on a balance sheet. Consequently, just as the ownership of stocks and shares can be transferred in the abstract world of electronic financial markets, the ownership of art may change easily from individuals to companies and arts-based investment funds, without the need for the work to be physically moved from its free port location. Indeed, free ports do have showrooms, to allow owners the opportunity to reconnect with, and maintain distanciated possession of, their luxury goods. But these facilities are just as likely to be used for inspections, valuations, and sales of the items in storage.

Free ports as secret spaces of luxury: The social implications

The use of free ports as secret spaces for the storage of luxury goods, including works of art, has a number of social implications. The first of these arises from the secrecy that free ports afford to clients in terms of discretion and privacy, which is further enhanced when works of art are owned through offshore shell companies. Moreover, owners benefit by establishing a shell company in the most favorable tax location, namely tax havens like the British Virgin Islands. For some, this provides a further layer of secrecy; for others, it is a way to legally avoid tax or to structure inheritance planning; and for yet others, it is a means to distance themselves from illegal activity, including tax evasion, money laundering, and fraud. Legal advisers providing services to establish such offshore shell companies include the now notorious Mossack Fonseca & Co., a Panamanian law firm and corporate service provider founded in 1977, which was once the world's fourth biggest provider of offshore services. This company was largely unknown until the widespread reporting of the leaked Panama Papers in 2016 (Obermayer and Obermaier 2016), which exposed its role in tax evasion schemes and other dubious activities. In March 2018, Mossack Fonseca & Co. announced that it was shutting down, because of the economic and reputational damage caused by the disclosure of its role in global tax evasion (Slawson 2018). Importantly, unlike the market for financial assets, such as equities, the art market is not subject to direct regulation (Thompson 2008). As such, it is vulnerable to abuse, including money laundering, tax evasion, trading on inside information, and price manipulation (Gapper and Aspden 2015).

Consequently, free ports and the logistical, legal, and financial services that support their activities are actively engaged in the suppression of knowledge and the construction of ignorance through secrecy. While this secrecy may be created to give the free port's clients anonymity and privacy, it is open to abuse by criminals and produces ignorance at a societal level. Critics have raised concerns that free ports could be used to hide illegally acquired assets, to launder money, or evade tax. The use of free ports to store illegally acquired and trafficked goods is evidenced by the recent case of the Swiss authorities seizing artifacts looted from Syria's ancient Semitic city of Palmyra after they were discovered in the Geneva free port (Agerholm 2016). Moreover, given the unregulated nature of the art market, it is possible to buy something for half a million US dollars without the need for one's identification to be verified. Most art is highly portable and easily shipped across borders and, since its value can be difficult for a non-expert to assess, it provides a vehicle for moving funds across borders and for money laundering. The former Brazilian banker Edemar Cid Ferreira, who was convicted of money laundering and bank fraud, stored millions of dollars in art works, including the $8 million painting titled *Hannibal* by Jean-Michel Basquiat, which was smuggled into the United States with a customs form saying it was worth $100 (O'Murchu 2015). Such examples undermine the protests of art market intermediaries and the operators of free ports who reject the view that such dubious activities provide a case for the regulation of art markets. Their counter-argument is that customs officers in the various jurisdictions have access to inventory data of what is stored in the free ports. However, for most free ports, information on beneficial ownership is not captured (FT.com 2017). As a result, the ignorance facilitated by free ports may encourage illegal activities, with negative consequences for victims of the theft of high value goods whether these are members of the super-rich, private or state museums, or countries whose national treasures have been plundered in times of conflict.

The second social implication of free ports as secret spaces of luxury derives from the tax avoidance and evasion they facilitate. This is detrimental to society because it reduces the tax revenue available for public services, further undermining the quality of life of those individuals reliant on state support. Moreover, the secrecy afforded by free ports ensures that the public at large remains ignorant of the true wealth of the super-rich. In addition to preventing governments from collecting tax, this ignorance supports the growing income and wealth inequality that has characterized the global economy, and particularly the UK and US economies, since the 1980s (Dorling 2014; Piketty 2014). Ultimately, the continued growth of inequality has consequences for the governance and stability of democracies (Piketty 2014). It also raises moral questions concerning the consumption of luxuries by the super-rich (Roberts 2019). So, when companies like Fine Art Logistics Natural Le Coultre claim that they "contribute each day to protect and maintain the cultural heritage of humanity,"[5] it is important to note that they do this for a select few not for humanity as a whole.

A third social implication of the use of free ports as secret spaces of luxury is that through their role supporting the use of art as a financial asset, they deprive growing proportions of humanity of access to cultural artifacts in the present day. Society becomes culturally impoverished through the ignorance that the secrecy and privacy facilitated by free ports create. We remain ignorant of the vast quantities of cultural artifacts that are hidden away in the secret spaces of free ports. Opportunities for creativity resulting from exposure to, and engagement with, such items are lost, with implications for the future development of knowledge. The study of works of art and cultural artifacts is limited by what is available and known. In addition, the ownership of such items is difficult to trace and potentially works of national significance may be moved offshore and disappear into a free port storage facility without adequate notice being given to cultural institutions or national authorities. Importantly, artifacts that could enrich culture remain out of view. By providing clients with privacy through secrecy free ports are complicit in the generation of ignorance for society.

Finally, the suppression of knowledge by free ports ensures that what is held in these real places scattered across the globe, remains unknown to the majority. Free ports become mysterious entities that can only be imagined by those who have no experience of their use. Moreover, they become globally networked imagined spaces characterized by high security vaults and riches beyond imagination. For many people, these secret spaces of luxury remain either unknown or purely imagined. While for those individuals using free ports to store their luxury artifacts the free port becomes a third realm of luxury, a place that is simultaneously real and imagined.

Conclusion

This chapter has utilized an ignorance perspective to explore the phenomenon of the free port as a secret space of luxury. It has brought to light the connections between art, ignorance, and the real place of the free port, which, by virtue of its nature, becomes an imaginary space for many of those using the services of the free port and for those who have little knowledge of the facility. Yet, as with other imaginary spaces, some of which are discussed in other chapters of this book, the imaginary does depend on a real manifestation of tangible works of art that are stored in the real place of the free port.

Importantly, when art is hidden from view and held in free ports as an investment asset, it loses its real and fundamental purpose for the individual and for society. To fulfill its purpose art must be experienced and exposed to human perception. So, the storage of art in free ports not only diminishes the quality of art available to the general public but also the fundamental cultural role of art is challenged. No longer appreciated for its aesthetic or emotional power, but for its financial value alone, art's fundamental value is neutralized, and it loses its true purpose. Through the use of free ports, cultural knowledge is thereby diminished together with the creativity it inspires. In this way, the secrecy free ports provide for a select few perpetuates ignorance for society as a whole.

References

Agerholm, H. (2016), "Stolen Artifacts from Palmyra and Yemen Seized in Geneva: Relics Date Back to Third and Fourth Centuries," *The Independent*, December 4. Available at: http://www.independent.co.uk/news/world/europe/stolen-artifacts-palmyra-yemen-geneva-enesco-switzerland-a7454001.html (accessed May 7, 2018).

Arlidge, J. (2015), "The Paranoid World of London's Super-Rich: DNA-Laced Security Mist and Superyacht Getaway Submarines," *Evening Standard*, October 22. Available at: http://www.standard.co.uk/lifestyle/esmagazine/the-paranoid-world-of-londons-superrich-dnalaced-security-mist-and-nuclearproof-panic-rooms-a3096491.html (accessed May 7, 2018).

Baumol, W. J. (1986), "Unnatural Value: Or Art Investment as Floating Crap Game," *The American Economic Review*, 76 (2), Papers and Proceedings of the Ninety-Eighth Annual Meeting of the American Economic Association (May), 10–14.

Boucher, B. (2016), "See What Experts Have to Say About Sotheby's Acquisition of the Mei Moses Art Indices," *artnet News*, October 29. Available at: https://news.artnet.com/market/sothebys-acquisition-mei-moses-art-indices-725648 (accessed May 6, 2018).

Capgemini (2017), *The Wealth Report 2017*, Capgemini. Available at: http://www.worldwealthreport.com/ (accessed April 30, 2018).

Cox, H. (2016), "Safe as Houses: How the Super-Rich Make Their Homes Super-Secure," September 7, *Financial Times* (FT.com). Available at: https://www.ft.com/content/069be746-6f92-11e6-a0c9-1365ce54b926 (accessed May 29, 2017).

Deloitte and ArtTactics (2014), *Art & Finance Report 2014*, Deloitte Luxembourg and ArtTactic. Available at: https://www2.deloitte.com/content/dam/Deloitte/es/Documents/acerca-de-deloitte/Deloitte-ES-Opera_Europa_Deloitte_Art_Finance_Report2014.pdf (accessed April 17, 2017).

Deloitte and ArtTactics (2016), *Art & Finance Report 2016*, 4th edition, Deloitte Luxembourg and ArtTactic. Available at: https://www2.deloitte.com/content/dam/Deloitte/lu/Documents/financial-services/artandfinance/lu-en-artandfinancereport-21042016.pdf (accessed April 16, 2017).

Ditzig, K. Lynch, R. and Ding, D. (2016), "Dynamic Global Infrastructure: The Freeport as Value Chain," *Finance and Society*, 2 (2): 180–88. Available at: http://financeandsociety.ed.ac.uk/issue/view/139 (accessed April 17, 2017).

Dorling, D. (2014), *Inequality and the 1%*, London and New York: Verso.

Economist, The (2013), "Freeports: Über-warehouses for the Ultra-rich," *The Economist*, November 23. Available at: http://www.economist.com/node/21590353/print (accessed July 30, 2018).

Faiers, J. (2016), "Sartorial Connoisseurship, the T-Shirt and the Interrogation of Luxury," in J. Armitage and J. Roberts (eds.), *Critical Luxury Studies*, 177–98, Edinburgh: Edinburgh University Press.

Frontier Economics (2014), *The Contribution of the High-End Cultural and Creative Industries to the European Economy*, report prepared for European Cultural and Creative Industries Alliance (ECCIA), November 2014. Available at: https://www.eccia.eu/assets/activities/files/2014%2011%2027_FINAL_Frontier%20Economics%20report%20prepared%20for%20ECCIA.pdf (accessed July 5, 2018).

FT.com (2017), Lexicon: Freeport, *Financial Times*. Available at: http://lexicon.ft.com / Term?term=Freeport (accessed April 16, 2017).

Galison, P. (2004), "Removing Knowledge," *Critical Inquiry*, 31 (Autumn): 229–43.

Gapper, J. and Aspden, P. (2015), "Davos 2015: Nouriel Roubini Says Art Market Needs Regulation," *FT.com*, January 22. Available at: https://www.ft.com/content/992dcf86-a250–11e4-aba2–00144feab7de (accessed April 16, 2017).

Gerlis, M. (2014), *Art as an Investment? A Survey of Comparative Assets*, Farnham, Surrey: Lund Humphries.

Gross, M. (2010), *Ignorance and Surprise: Science, Society, and Ecological Design*, Cambridge, MA: MIT Press.

Gross, M. and McGoey, L., eds. (2015), *Routledge International Handbook of Ignorance Studies*, London: Routledge.

Klamer, A. (1996a), "Introduction," in A. Klamer, *The Value of Culture: On the Relationship Between Economics and Arts*, 7–12, Amsterdam: Amsterdam University Press.

Klamer, A. (1996b), "The Value of Culture," in A. Klamer, *The Value of Culture: On the Relationship Between Economics and Arts*, 13–28, Amsterdam: Amsterdam University Press.

KnightFrank (2017), *The Wealth Report: The Global Perspective on Prime Property and Wealth*, 11th edition. Available at: KnightFrank.Com/WealthReport (accessed May 29, 2017).

Maertens, M. (2013), "Dans le secret des Ports Francs," *Connaissances des Arts*, January 16. Available at: https://www.connaissancedesarts.com/marche-de-lart/dans-le-secret-des-ports-francs-11136/ (accessed May 7, 2018).

Mayer-Schönberger, V. and Cukier, K. (2013), *Big Data: A Revolution That Will Transform How We Live, Work and Think*, London: John Murray Publishers.

McAndrew, C. (2017), *The Art Market 2017*, An Art Basel and UBS Report, Basel, Switzerland. Available at: https://d33ipftjqrd91.cloudfront.net/asset/cms/Art_Basel_and_UBS_The_Art_Market_2017.pdf (accessed May 7, 2018).

McGoey, L. (2014), *An Introduction to the Sociology of Ignorance: Essays on the Limits of Knowing*, London: Routledge.

Obermayer, B. and Obermaier, F. (2016), *The Panama Papers: Breaking the Story of How the Rich & Powerful Hide Their Money*, London: One World.

OED (2003), *Oxford English Dictionary*, Oxford: Oxford University Press.

O'Murchu, C. (2015), "Art: A Market Laid Bare," *Financial Times*, April 7, Ft.com. Available at: https://www.ft.com/content/a91a1608-d887–11e4–8a23–00144feab7de (accessed May 7, 2018).

Piketty, T. (2014), *Capital in the Twenty-First Century*, Cambridge, MA: Harvard University Press.

Preston, P. (2011), "Twitter and WikiLeaks Have Made a Mockery of the Courts: A Showdown between the Law and Common Sense Is Brewing as a Footballer Takes Legal Action Over Twitter's Injunction Breach," *The Observer*, May 22, 28. Available at: https://www.theguardian.com/media/2011/may/22/twitter-wikileaks-mockery-of-the-courts (accessed May 7, 2018).

Proctor, R. N. (2008), "Agnotology: A Missing Term to Describe the Cultural Production of Ignorance (and Its Study)," in R. N. Proctor and L. Schiebinger (eds.), *Agnotolology: The Making and Unmaking of Ignorance*, 1–33, Stanford, CA: Stanford University Press.

Roberts, J. (2013), "Organizational Ignorance: Towards a Managerial Perspective on the Unknown," *Management Learning*, 44 (3): 215–36.

Roberts, J. (2018), "Luxury and Ignorance: From 'Savoir Faire' to the Unknown," *Luxury: History, Culture, Consumption*, 5 (1): 21–41.

Roberts, J. (2019), "Is Contemporary Luxury Morally Acceptable? A Question for the Super-rich," *Cultural Politics*, 15 (1): 48–63.

Roberts, J. and Armitage, J. (2008), "The Ignorance Economy," *Prometheus*, 26 (4): 335–54.

Samuel, H. and Allen, N. (2016), "Karl Lagerfeld: Kim Kardashian 'cannot display wealth then be surprised' when she is robbed", *The Telegraph*, 4th October. Available at: https://www.telegraph.co.uk/news/2016/10/04/karl-lagerfeld-kim-kardashian-cannot-display-wealth-then-be-surp/ (accessed 07.04.2019).

Slawson, N. (2018), "Mossack Fonseca Law Firm to Shut Down after Panama Papers Tax Scandal," *The Guardian*, March 14. Available at: https://www.theguardian.com/world/2018/mar/14/mossack-fonseca-shut-down-panama-papers (accessed May 7, 2018).

Smithson, M. (1989), *Ignorance and Uncertainty: Emerging Paradigms*, New York: Springer.

Thompson, D. (2008), *The $12 Million Stuffed Shark: The Curious Economics of Contemporary Art*, London: Aurum Press.

UNESCO (2016), Intergovernmental Committee for Promoting the Return of Cultural Property to Its Countries of Origin or Its Restitution on Case of Illicit Appropriation, Twentieth Session UNESCO Headquarters, Room II, September 29–30, 2016, ICPRCP /16/20.COM/12 Paris, July 2016 Available at: http://www.unesco.org/new/fileadmin/MULTIMEDIA/HQ/CLT/pdf/2_FC_free_port_working_document_Final_EN_revclean.pdf (accessed July 30, 2018).

Veblen, T. (1899), *The Theory of the Leisure Class: An Economic Study in the Evolution of Institutions*, London: Macmillan.

Wealth-X (2016), *Billionaire Census Highlights*, Wealth-X. Available at: http://www.mediapool.bg/files/252/Billionaire_Census_2015-2016_HIGHLIGHTS.pdf (accessed April 16, 2017).

Willsher, K. (2016), "Kim Kardashian robbed at gunpoint by men disguised as police in Paris", *The Guardian*, 3rd October. Available at: https://www.theguardian.com/lifeand style/2016/oct/03/kim-kardashian-west-held-at-gunpoint-fake-policemen-paris-hotel-kanye-concert (accessed 07.04.2019).

Wingfield, Brian (2010), "Security Concerns of the Super-Rich," *Forbes*, October 20. Available at: https://www.forbes.com/sites/brianwingfield/2010/10/20/security-concerns-of-the-super-rich/#4a0a258a4a70 (accessed May 7, 2018).

Of space and time in California wine

Ian Malcolm Taplin

Wine is a product that has been a dietary staple for millennia, a beverage that enhances a meal and provides conviviality among friends. For some cultures, it was viewed as an integral part of life, fulfilling gastronomic needs and providing a pleasurable counterpoint to an otherwise harsh life. When the Romans entered what is now France, they derided the local population for their beer drinking customs which they viewed as savage and uncivilized and encouraged, in the not so subtle ways that conquering armies do, the consumption of wine (Phillips 2016).

But while simultaneously being an everyday beverage, wine has also acquired an aura of sophistication when special blends were associated with celebratory events. There is anecdotal evidence that in Roman times wine had acquired a luxury status, since the best wine was often served at banquets. The fact that it was used for rituals, ceremonies, and elaborate formal functions suggests that in some instances it was more than a mere complement to food. Thus constituted, it acquired an elevated status—that something special for significant occasion or for someone who is important and deems the beverage an appropriate signifier of their position. Conferring such an attribute endowed wine with an importance that far exceeds its simple functionality. For those who saw something more in it, consuming it suggested sophistication and elegance, or at least the financial means to procure it in the first place. The further consumption occurred from production, inevitably the more valuable (and expensive) the wine became. Wine was thus a normal drink as well as something that transcends the everyday. For some, it remained a commodity; for others, however, it was a differentiated product to be enjoyed by the few or on special occasions.

It is sometimes easy to forget that wine is also an agricultural product that is firmly rooted in a geographic space, a region-specific identity that confers a cultural form to those who harvest the grapes and convert them into a quaffable beverage. In the regions where grapes were easy to grow (often the least fertile soils unsuitable for other forms of agriculture), producers (whom the French termed *vignerons*) were recognized for their skills in producing wines with certain characteristics. From that came regional identity that connoted specificity, quality, and eventually price. This marks the beginning of a sense of place that is associated with where certain wines are made and from which the spatial dimension becomes paramount.

The ubiquity of wine throughout much of Europe over the centuries endowed it with cultural and commercial significance. As an agricultural product it nonetheless transcended the essentialism of most food stuffs, providing pleasure to consumers and a sociocultural cornerstone that was often a focal point for communal life. Economically, it sustained rural communities, providing employment, and it became an important item in early trade between countries. For example, following the 1152 marriage of Eleanor of Aquitaine to Henry II, England assumed oversight over much of southwestern France, and in the subsequent centuries wine was exported from the Bordeaux region to England. Because the wine was light in color, with low levels of alcohol it acquired the moniker of claret (*clairet*) among the English—a name that persists to the present day even if the wine is very different now. Thus popularized, wine became a staple in the taverns in England and for the wealthy at their meals. The wine had to be consumed fairly soon after production, so the spatial/time relationship was quite compressed. It was in one such tavern that a Bordeaux wine attained early fame. A Bordeaux merchant by the name of Jean de Pontac established a winery he named *Château Haut Brion* in 1533. A century later, his descendant Arnaud III de Pontac marketed his wine in London using the place-name where it was produced. This wine, called Ho Bryan (*sic*), was favored by Samuel Pepys in 1663 who commented on it when visiting a London tavern. The *London Gazette* of 1707 further identified Lafitt (*Lafitte Rothschild*), Margouz (*Chateaux Margaux*), and La Tour as wines that commanded price premiums based upon their quality (Faith 1996: 26). Thus began the practice of wineries marketing their wines through specific place identity (rather than as products blended by merchants) that subsequently became the château system that we are familiar with today (Lawther 2010: 9).

It is difficult to ascertain the quality of these wines other than by relying upon the local accounts noted above. However, the first documented systematic attention to quality in wine can be found earlier among the Benedictine and Cistercian monks in medieval Europe, particularly in France where vineyards were flourishing. Founded in 1098, the Cistercians turned viticulture into a commercial venture, and the Benedictines soon followed suit (Chapuis and

Charters 2014). Needing wine for eucharistic masses, as a complement to meals, and as a beverage in their food and drink hospitality obligations, their commitment to producing quality came from wine's high symbolic value in masses—the presumption being that only the best should be served. Their scrupulous attention to detail and willingness to defer immediate returns on their investment enabled them to focus upon quality rather than quantity.

Subsequent improvements in winemaking techniques and vineyard management during the seventeenth and eighteenth centuries led many French producers (especially in the Bordeaux region) to produce wines that were richer (fuller bodied), darker, and more tannic. The latter proved indispensable to aging wine, thus permitting longer periods between production and consumption. This provided opportunities for wine to be shipped further afield and not spoil, thus augmenting the possibility of cellaring wine for the discerning wealthy who were prepared to pay an upfront price premium for quality wine that could be drunk in the years to come.

It was also becoming apparent that there were significant variations in the quality of wine, in part a function of winemaking techniques as well as location-specific factors such as soil, terrain, and microclimate. Together, these factors became known as *terroir*—the uniqueness of place that bestows crucial characteristics to wine and which has traditionally been associated with French wines. Wines from certain regions and properties were recognized for their distinctiveness and informal classifications developed to rank the better quality wines. The wines that were typically richer and more robust were often accorded higher status and priced accordingly. When the French developed a formal classification in 1855, perhaps not surprisingly price was used as a principal criterion in determining quality and subsequently rankings.

Napoleon III had requested a classification of the best Bordeaux wines to be displayed at the *1855 Exposition Universelle de Paris*. Local brokers were consulted, and wines were ranked according to the château's reputation and trading price since these variables were deemed the accepted measure of quality. The classification, which remains in place today, formalized what experts were noting about certain wine estates, and it created a hierarchy in which the top wines (from first to fifth growths [*crus*]) acquired considerable status. Subsequent classifications occurred in Burgundy, achieving similar results for those wineries designated the top status. Such formalization of quality marks the beginning of market differentiation where an elite group of wineries acquire status and enter the pantheon of luxury goods. Their prestige derives from the specific locational characteristics of the vineyard (real space and place), but for the discerning connoisseur who buys the wine and lays it down, that person derives satisfaction in the knowledge of ownership and the anticipation of deferred gratification. In this sense, he/she is imagining what it will be like in the future while enjoying the satisfaction that comes from such anticipation—sentiments in keeping with the third realm aspects discussed elsewhere in this volume.

Building upon quality improvements, if we fast forward to the twentieth and twenty-first centuries, one notes the growth of an iconic segment of very expensive, limited availability, high quality wines from various regions in the world. Such iconic wines currently account for 1 percent of wine produced but have a reputation that far exceeds their limited production.

Wine's changing role as a beverage of choice to a marketable commodity reflects not just altered habits of consumer behavior but a more purposive attempt to produce and subsequently categorize a product that transcends it original function. This is the cultural space of luxury in which fine wines are positioning themselves. While the vast majority of wines are drunk within twenty-four hours of purchase, a small segment of the market is designed to improve with age. For example, wines from some Bordeaux producers were traditionally heavily tannic, making immediate consumption difficult but allowing the wine to dramatically improve in the bottle as it aged. Such tannins were a product of growing conditions and harvesting techniques, and while harvest vintages varied considerably in quality (and yield), they were seen as features that connoted future quality and age worthiness. This time dimension has been particularly important for top producers (the so-called classified growths) with older vintage securing premium prices.

A combination of improved viticultural knowledge, scientific/technological innovations in winemaking, and a greater understanding of the importance of place (soil types, etc.) meant that quality wine could be more consistently made providing the right combination of factors were present. Some of this was resource driven, as in nineteenth-century Bordeaux where wealthy businessmen, financiers, and merchants acquired vineyards and lavished cash to improve operations. In the New World regions such as Australia and California, it lay in identifying appropriate land for vineyard sites and then investing in what were essentially new and unproven markets. The collective result of these endeavors has been the growing importance of a category of very expensive, limited availability, and difficult to obtain wines that are associated with specific regions. But who buys these expensive wines?

Some purchasers of expensive wines undoubtedly fit the category of wine lovers with extensive financial resources who buy wine to eventually drink. They enjoy wine, appreciate fine quality wine, have discerning palates, and above all have the money to buy what they like. Others, somewhat pejoratively referred to as "stamp collectors" (Taplin 2015: 97), can be seen as collectors whose wine purchases are a mark of their status to be displayed in expensive, easily viewable wine cellars. Presumably they enjoy drinking wine, but their satisfaction comes from the imagined luxury that their product confers. This is the visible manifestation of their cultural aspirations as well as the enological demonstration of their actual refinement. It is both a reality and a desire. For some of them, wine provides immediate status benefits with the possibility of longer term financial gains should they wish to sell their collection. Such high price and presumably high quality wine confers an aura of sophistication upon the owner, who might also consider it as a marketable asset that improves both financially and quality wise with age. In such instances, wine goes from a beverage of varying quality and price points that is typically drunk with food or as an aperitif, to an item to be treasured in an almost reverential way.

In wine, we thus see a product whose initial function has changed over time and in some instances acquired venerable status as a luxury product. That is not always surprising since many objects assume different functional status as they age—for example, old tables become collectible antiques after acquiring a certain patina. In a contemporary age of mass production, individual craftsmanship is venerated, hence the presumption that a handmade product is an expression of uniqueness rather than serving a mere utilitarian function. And what might have been an inexpensive item designed for everyday use 100 years ago now becomes a collector's item, even if its function remains the same. The greater the lapse in time, the more intrinsic value is attributed to the object. Similarly, the further the distance from its initial inception, the more unique it can become. Not surprisingly, some mass-produced objects have attempted to capture the aura of antiquity, designed to evoke an elevated status by simple reference to a past distinguished age. As McNeil and Riello (2016) argue, Josiah Wedgwood was the master of using classical vocabulary as he deployed new production techniques to manufacture tea sets and decorative items. By giving them classical names and emphasizing that they were produced in a factory called Etruria, they were designed to suggest a traditional elegance and luxury. In doing this he was the consummate marketing genius of the eighteenth century, providing the "luxury" of antiquity for the rising middle classes and enabling mass-produced objects to resonate with sophistication that has continued over the centuries. He manufactured a sense of time and historical imagery by invoking the past to endow a product that was designed to be essentially timeless—a product for the ages.

While recognizing that what constitutes luxury varies through time and space as well as being culturally and socioeconomically context specific (Armitage and Roberts 2016), it is interesting to examine the trajectory that certain goods take as they acquire such esteemed status. How did certain wines assume iconic status when the majority are considered a mere commodity? While Old World producers saw their status gradually improve over the centuries, how have some New World producers been able to attain high status in a short period of time? How much of these changes can be explained by the emergence of individuals (enophiles) whose wealth propels them to the sort of status-seeking behavior that we associated with luxury goods purchases, of which wine is now another category? And finally, does such action suggest a subtle link between the real and imaginary spaces of luxury? Wine is a product where the anticipation of future pleasures constitutes as important a hedonistic indulgence as the actual ultimate imbibing.

To address these questions, I examine the evolution of Napa Valley, California, from an agricultural backwater dominated by orchards in the nineteenth century to the pre-eminent site of luxury wines in the United States by the twenty-first century. It is a fairly short history compared to Old World regions, but one that resonates with purposeful behavior on the part of key innovators, many with resources that permitted the requisite experimentation, who were determined to make a quality product. This is even more surprising given that wine was not a popular beverage among Americans in the nineteenth and first part of the twentieth centuries (it was often viewed pejoratively as an immigrant drink) and for several decades suffered Prohibition that stifled what had been early signs of market growth. The dramatic growth of wine consumption in the country since the 1970s is the background to the emergence of specialist producers who were determined to realize the potential of a region like Napa Valley. A subset of wineries is now making a wine that is revered for its elegance, distinctiveness, high price, and limited availability—in other words, a luxury good.

Early history of Californian wine

The California wine industry had been established in the late eighteenth century by missionaries but did not grow significantly until the latter part of the nineteenth century. A combination of population growth in the state (through extensive immigration following the Gold Rush in 1849) and experimentation by newcomers with grape-growing experience brought both supply and demand changes to the embryonic wine industry. The rich soils and abundant sunshine in the northern parts of the state led to big harvests but varying quality especially since many growers were paid by the ton. The problem was that nobody really knew what grapes grew best. This began to change when Hungarian immigrant Agostan Haraszthy came to California in 1849 and experimented with a large number of grape varietals before deciding upon European ones (*vinifera*) instead of native and "Mission" grapes. He bought 560 acres north of the town of Sonoma and planted 14,000 imported vines in what was to become the 160-acre Buena Vista winery (Pinney 1989). His wine was deemed of sufficient quality that he was asked to write about his success by the state Agricultural Society (California State Agricultural Society 1858). He is seen as the originator of the fine wine movement in California since he was the first to adopt a more scientific and technical approach to winemaking—a departure from the trial and error approach of others in the state.

Alongside individuals such as Haraszthy, institutional attempts to address shortcomings in industry practices—particularly adulteration of wines— eventually led to the formation of the California Wine Growers Association in 1862. Comprising some of the larger wineries, this group effectively became the lobbying arm of growers who protested imports of wine and taxes on their products (Pinney 1989). Eventually the group morphed into the California Wine Association in 1894 and formally adopted policies that encouraged modernization, planting better quality vines, and a more scientific approach to winemaking (Taplin 2015). It encouraged more systematic and technical knowledge-driven techniques, and growers were subsequently rewarded with higher prices for better quality grapes (rather than a large quantity). While many growers initially resisted the imposition of these practices, they eventually adopted them when they realized that better viticulture led to better quality wine and subsequently an enhanced reputation for the region.

Sonoma and Napa counties eventually emerged as sites where some of the best wine was made, which further attracted the arrival of newcomers with grape-growing experience (and financial resources) to establish wineries. For example, a German immigrant called Charles Krug bought 540 acres in the northern part of Napa Valley in 1860, and despite numerous setbacks (including bankruptcies) by the time of his death in 1892, he was recognized as the pioneer who first established the credibility of Napa wines (Sullivan 2008; Taplin 2015: 86). In addition to being a dynamic entrepreneur who was in the forefront of establishing Napa's credibility as a wine-producing region, he was one of the first to articulate the collective interests of growers at the state level. During his ten-year presidency of the newly formed St. Helena Winegrowers Association, he stridently advocated the growing importance of the region's ability to make fine wine—thus establishing the legitimacy of the incipient industry (Taplin 2015: 86).

Interest in Napa as opposed to Sonoma County for producing excellent wines had also occurred following the writings and speeches of a UC Berkeley professor of agriculture, Eugene Hilgard. Earlier he had correctly identified phylloxera infestations in California that had destroyed many vineyards and was forceful in arguing for replanting with *vinifera* that was crossed with American hybrids to protect against this disease. He pushed for better quality management in both vineyard and winemaking practices, arguing that this was how Napa could differentiate itself from other regions with inferior quality wine. In doing this, he was the first person to recognize the power of branding and how one could use this to further elevate the growing reputation of fine wine. His views were vindicated when eleven of the twenty-one medals won by California producers at the 1889 Paris Exposition came from Napa. This also led to the acknowledgment that Napa had a distinctive "terroir" (soil, microclimate, and elusive sense of place) that facilitated the creation of fine wine if people were willing and able to use correct techniques.

By the end of the nineteenth century, more immigrants with viticulture experience were arriving, and this complemented the dissemination of increased technical knowledge from local universities in such areas as fermentation, cellar treatment, pruning, and ways of combating diseases such as mildew that continued to plague vines. This combination of experienced individuals and formalized knowledge put the industry on a more solid footing and further contributed to the region's growing status.

Despite this progress, most Americans were not wine drinkers, and this severely limited the market for a product whose quality was nonetheless improving. What limited market did exist was on the East coast, some 2,500 miles distant from where the product was made in California. Furthermore, wine was typically stored and shipped in barrels for bottling at the final destination—a process that often resulted in adulteration and questionable blending practices in the winery. It was also during this time that long-standing moral concerns regarding alcohol consumption were solidifying around the Women's Christian Temperance Union (the "Drys" as they were popularly known) in the late nineteenth century. While hard liquor was deemed the principal problem by this group as many men spent their pay checks on excessive indulgence, wine inevitably fell under the umbrella of demonized drinking and moral decay.

Eventually this movement was able to influence legislators to pass the Eighteenth Amendment to the Constitution, which was ratified in 1919 in the Volstead Act. Thus began Prohibition, which together with the ensuing recession years of the 1930s significantly dented Napa's growth. During the former time period the industry virtually shut down with only a handful of producers supplying wine for religious institutions. Of the 700 wineries in California prior to Prohibition, only 130 existed shortly before repeal in 1933 (Taber 2005). Furthermore, American drinking habits had changed with a growing interest in fortified drinks, which continued for the next few decades. Even established producers such as Inglenook and Beaulieu found it difficult to sell wines, and the secular decline of wineries continued until the 1960s (Taber 2005).

Industry rebirth

The revival of the California wine industry can be dated to the late 1960s when a number of new winemakers arrived, especially in Napa. Some brought experience from making wine elsewhere (including Europe), while others were seeking a lifestyle change although often they lacked viticulture knowledge. In either case they recognized the potential to make great wines in this area and created informal networks to exchange information about how to accomplish this. Intent on sharing with and learning from their peers in a cooperative fashion, they created a network for organizational learning that reinforced the commitment to quality (Taplin 2011). These efforts were complemented by the growth of systematic and codified viticulture and winemaking techniques that were increasingly available from local universities. UC Davis was one of the first to provide a rigorous curriculum in viticulture and enology that was firmly grounded in chemistry. The program offered degrees designed to provide the requisite skill sets and knowledge for successful winemaking with particular attention paid to the prevailing conditions in California. It was an unambiguous science-based curriculum grounded in academic studies that some argued resulted in a formulaic and standardized production method geared toward maximizing climate over soil types (Bonné 2013). It did enable winemakers to identify and mitigate flaws that had hindered consistency in production in the past, but it was also a training suited to California's climate and how best to take advantage of it. In the absence of regulations governing yield and irrigation that often stymied French producers, Napa wineries were increasingly able to consistently make full-bodied, fruit forward wines that stood out in blind tastings with similar varietals. These evolving best practices were further institutionalized following the formation of the Napa Valley Grape Growers Association in 1975, structuring information transfer as well as providing *de facto* governance to protect the embryonic Napa brand (Taplin 2010).

The seminal event that legitimized not only Napa but also California wine in general was the Paris Tasting in 1976. Organized by a Paris-based English wine merchant, Stephen Spurrier, a blind tasting by a panel of judges awarded top scores to several California wines over those from distinguished Bordeaux and Burgundy vineyards. The effect was twofold. Not surprisingly, it angered many traditional enophiles, especially those in France who cherished the natural superiority of their wine. But it also alerted others to the excellent quality of New World wines, in this case those from Napa that had bested several French first growths (Taber 2005).

By essentially demystifying traditional notions of the sense of place, Napa had demonstrated that a combination of tacit knowledge, scientific and technological innovations, *terroir* plus significant capital investments could result in a wine that was equal to if not sometimes better than one made in the Old World according to strict conditions and guidelines. French winemakers had assiduously argued about the importance of place and tradition as being key to the production of excellent wine, simultaneously objectifying authenticity as well as mystically invoking the importance of the "soul" of the wine producer (Guy 2002). Centuries-old practices, governed by strict rules about what could and could not be done in the vineyard, had consolidated the status of the classified growths by essentially limiting market entry by newcomers in France. Now, producers in the New World were capitalizing upon their own unique growing conditions in a less regulated environment and, aided by a rigorous science-based approach, were making quality wines. The irony was that many of the Napa producers had often benchmarked themselves against Bordeaux and now their wines were garnering reputations for consistency that their French competitors often lacked because of vintage variation.

As quality wine production increased, so too did consumption habits by Americans who were beginning to drink premium quality wine ($20 and above). The problem, however, was that many newcomers to wine consumption felt insecure about purchasing expensive wines because their product knowledge was limited. Public awareness outside a small number of true enophiles was limited. Unlike search goods where numerous features of the product can be determined prior to purchase, wine is an experience good. You don't really know what it is like until you have purchased and tasted it. To solve this "confidence" problem and simplify buying, two organizations started providing quasi-objective measures of quality. *Robert Parker's Wine Advocate* created a system in the 1970s based upon the numerical (100 point) standardized grading system used in schools. With his system, he evaluated and scored wine along a number of dimensions, principal of which was quality. Industry magazine *Wine Spectator* adopted a similar system shortly thereafter. In addition, *Wine Advocate* provided extensive tasting notes for customers who subscribed to the magazine, but most people used the numerical scores (out of 100) that *Parker* and *Wine Spectator* published. Wines that were awarded scores of 90–94 were deemed outstanding; those about 95 truly exceptional. Since scoring was predicated on a quasi-scientific metric, it lent significant legitimacy as well as apparent transparency to quality categorization. It also simplified purchasing decisions for people who lacked confidence in spending much money for a supposed quality wine. Many wine shops appended labels to wines on the shelves indicating high scores and in this way eliminated more of the uncertainty surrounding purchasing decisions. More fundamentally, this scoring established a *de facto* ranking of wines not dissimilar to that of the classified growths in France, except in this case it was provided by critics in a seemingly more objective manner.

In vino luxe

The number of wineries in Napa doubled between the late 1970s and the early 1990s with many newcomers establishing wineries using capital derived from successive business ventures elsewhere (Kramer 2004). Napa in particular was increasingly recognized as a place where some great wines were being made; finely crafted to meet the varied palates of American consumers who were beginning to show eagerness to consume wine and try local products. Perfect soils, a long hot growing season, irrigation when necessary, and cool nights were ideal for making robust red wines, and increasingly Napa became associated with Cabernet Sauvignon as its signature wine. Such climatic consistency enabled wineries to avoid the seasonal problems that plagued French and other Old World wine areas. That and formally taught technological innovations in various facets of viticulture and enology enabled many wineries to annually produce a good if not excellent wine. In most cases, the wines were full bodied, a style that came to be associated with Napa. For some, this was the true expression of the Valley—its varying *terroir*; for others, however, it was seen as a manipulated wine often designed to meet the palates of the increasingly important wine critics.

Given the importance of such critics in legitimizing quality wines, it is not surprising that such stylistic actions might occur. In interviews I have conducted with over fifty ultra-premium wineries in Napa, all but a few acknowledged the importance of high scores for sales, pricing, and credibility.

Whatever the case, perhaps most importantly the wines could be drunk soon after purchase. Lacking the high tannins that made Bordeaux wines inaccessible for many years, Napa wines provided an imbibing immediacy should the consumer desire. This further distinguished the area from Old World wines where aging was seen as salutary characteristic of the product—the time element that endows elegance and sophistication with age. Unlike most American wine, which is drunk within twenty-four hours of purchase, ultra-premium wines are still more likely to be laid down/stored for later consumption. Even though this is not enologically necessary, its practice is a mark of cultural significance given the presumption that age confers enhanced quality as well as the ability to enjoy the status of possession and the imagined benefits of final consumption.

By the 1980s, some of those purchasing land for vineyards in Napa were resource-rich individuals whose previous careers could subsidize their passion for making an excellent wine. They were able to make the necessary investments (ideal vineyard land, top winemaker and vineyard manager, etc.) to make a wine that would be comparable to Bordeaux first growths. Their explicit goal was to locate land that would enable them to craft an excellent quality wine. They might hire a renowned consultant winemaker and focus on producing small quantities of wine to reinforce their commitment to quality. Their aim was to identify special (often hillside) sites where single vineyard wines might be made. Since many of these new owners had extensive financial resources, they were able to take a very long-term approach to winemaking and brand development, sometimes not releasing wines in the initial years if they felt it didn't meet their stringent quality expectations. This further enhanced their uncompromising reputation.

Small production inevitably meant limited availability and, given the expense entailed, a probable high price. Their reputations were enhanced when many of their wines received high scores from external critics such as Robert Parker and *The Wine Spectator*. A top score validated the high price, which in and of itself was often perceived as a mark of quality. Because many of these wineries had been inspired by the elegance of Bordeaux wines and used them as benchmarks, they evoked the notion of becoming first growth equivalents. But they also were purposeful in articulating the essence of their own authenticity in the uniqueness, relationship to place, and handcrafted techniques plus a compelling story or narrative that embellishes their status. Such authenticity, as Beverland (2005) argues, is typically crucial to luxury brand development even if the proponents might eschew the implied commercialism in such a narrative. Many of the top wineries eschewed marketing, in part because their growing reputation did not necessitate it and also because they were convinced that the excellence of their product spoke for itself or wine critics spoke for them in a laudatory way. Their wines were exclusive, recognized as an exceptional quality brand, and retained high levels of customer loyalty. Most of the top wines are sold on allocation, with a maximum of three bottles to a case per customer per year. In some instances, the waiting list to get onto the allocation list is measured in years and few people drop off. This easily maintains exclusivity through scarcity and gives those on the list a sense of "belonging to something special" or the secret space of luxury that Roberts discusses in Chapter 9 of this volume.

The 1990s was the period when the so-called cult wines emerged, consolidating Napa's enological credibility and pushing such wines into a small category of ultra-luxury products accessible to a few privileged individuals. Some of the best-known ones are *Harlan Estate* (five 100-point Parker scores between 1994 and 2007); *Colgin Cellars* (nine 100 point scores since 2002); *Schrader Cellars* (nine 100 point scores between 2002 and 2008); and *Abreu Vineyards* (six 100 point scores since 1997). And of course, there is *Screaming Eagle*, founded in 1992, the winery many argue started the cult wine craze, as prices soared from $75 a bottle to $750 in a few years and now selling for over $7,500 a bottle on the open market. In each case receiving high scores not only affirmed the excellence of the wine's intrinsic quality but also contributed significantly to its branded status and the subsequent high price that is charged. Similar to most luxury products, high price is seen as a marker of quality and, when combined with limited availability, affirms the desirability of the wine. Or as one winery owner commented, "if you don't charge a lot you don't get noticed" (Taplin 2016: 8).

The prevailing stylistic features of Napa Cabernet Sauvignons were sufficiently pronounced that it set them apart from most Old World wines. For Parker, such wines combined Bordeaux complexity with Napa ripeness and power. The terroir provided the natural comparative advantage, but as Hira and Swartz (2014) argue social capital and entrepreneurship behind technological leadership have been central to Napa's competitive advantage. This is what fundamentally set the region apart from Old World producers—less formal regulations, an enthusiasm for informed experimentation, and the embrace of technical solutions to perennial viticultural problems. Napa's reputation continues to grow, and stringent efforts have been made to protect the collective Napa brand. Meanwhile, the wine critics have effectively organized the market with their scores and wineries responded accordingly with their pricing strategies. Subsequent newcomers to the industry face limited availability of land and its increasingly high price, plus increased land use regulations that have effectively circumscribed incumbents.

In examining the growth of Napa, we can trace an early interest in wine from a local population lacking in discerning palates followed by a gradual recognition that with the right attention to detail a quality wine was possible if quantity goals were sacrificed. Even in the late nineteenth century, individuals with plentiful financial resources bought land and established wineries, and many of these survived to be reborn after Prohibition. When the industry in the area next took off, it was because of enthusiastic winemakers who were in many respects learning their craft in the valley, trying to determine what grapes grew best and how to efficiently utilize techniques that were available from winemaking programs at local universities. As more money poured into the area in the 1980s and 1990s, largely from individuals with successful previous careers, it led to further improvements in quality and the gradual consolidation of brand Napa. Given the growing start-up costs (high price of land, winery construction, etc.), it was inevitable that a premium price would be charged for the wine. But what is notable is how a small subset of producers focused upon a strategy of producing finely crafted, exceptionally high quality, and inevitably high-priced wines that were internationally recognized and available for the discerning few. In producing such a "status" product, they fall clearly into the luxury category inasmuch as they have created an aura surrounding their brand, often as Kovesi (2016) argues in ways that are reminiscent of that bestowed upon religious objects. They have successfully positioned their wine at the top of an informal hierarchy where price, quality, value, and exclusivity are all intertwined. They have transformed a commonplace utilitarian product into a credible, desirable, and exclusive object that simultaneously fulfills the material aspects of acquisition as well as the anticipatory pleasure of consumption.

Discussion and conclusion

This brief narrative provides several stories. One is how markets evolve as consumer tastes change, institutional settings alter, and production capabilities are transformed following technological innovation. This is also part of continuing structural changes in society, more pronounced inequality, and in the twentieth century more fluid identities. Less fixed statuses provide individuals with a more constant ability to seek to differentiate themselves not just from others but also from their past. This has provided a surge in materialism and at the top end a dramatic increase in demand for luxury goods.

The second theme traces how commodities function differently in time periods as they meet varied demand imperatives. Wine has gone from a simple beverage that provided a pleasurable complement to meals to in certain cases a luxury product whose status confers privilege not just on the producer but also those few fortunate enough to procure it. In this instance, a small group of wineries have capitalized upon improved knowledge about growing techniques, applied considerable resources to perfect their product, and gained enological legitimacy from industry rating experts. In doing this, they have successfully built a brand that has iconic status.

From the above, one can trace the evolution of markets in which scarcity has been the inevitable byproduct of the search for excellence by a committed few and the ability of a privileged group willing to purchase their products. One might in fact argue that rather than an expression of material wealth, possession of cult wines conferred a cultural superiority for the consumer. They are an experience good that can be appreciated by connoisseurs because they privilege an aesthetic dimension that is timeless. But wine also constitutes an imagined luxury for many because it provides an almost visceral anticipation of pleasures the product will give them. One is never completely certain about the eventual consummate action of drinking the wine since it is an experience good whose qualities can never be perfectly ascertained *ex ante*. Taste is always subjective and in the case of wine, perhaps even more so.

Wine continues to be not only a commonplace but also a perplexing, almost transient product. High quality performs a crucial cultural (and socioeconomic) function, as well as signifying the exotic that restricts its availability to all but a select few. For most people, it is a product that is consumed within twenty-four hours of purchase, most probably with a meal at home. For others, however, it assumes a transcendent quality and almost reverential status even before it is consumed. As the other chapters in this book document with different products, wine similarly possesses a spatial dimension (a traded good that travels far from where it is produced) and a time element (aging in bottles deemed to enhance quality as well as convey visually the material properties of possession).

Status and wealth can be ephemeral, inequality timeless and also fraught with uncertainty for those currently exercising the material options of their wealth. Those who purchase fine wines are participating in an evolving marketplace whose values change subtly but nonetheless confer a sense of satisfaction for the owner in knowing that they are part of an exclusive club. How much they seek acknowledgment of such a position varies. But they are occupying a unique space that for centuries has enabled the wealthy to circumscribe their way of life with material acquisitions that provide reassurance and enhanced self-satisfaction.

Acknowledgments

Thanks to Bill Harlan, owner of Harlan Estate, for his useful comments on an earlier version of this chapter plus a long and engaging dinner critically discussing the essential properties of an iconic wine.

References

Armitage, J. and Roberts, J. (2016), "Critical Luxury Studies: Defining the Field," in J. Armitage and J. Roberts (eds.), *Critical Luxury Studies*, 1–21, Edinburgh: Edinburgh University Press.

Beverland, M. B. (2005), "Crafting Brand Authenticity: The Case of Luxury Wines," *Journal of Management Studies*, 42 (5): 1003–29.

Bonné, J. (2013), *The New California Wine*, Berkeley, CA: Ten Speed Press.

California State Agricultural Society. (1858), *Report on Grapes and Wine in California*, Sacramento, California: G. H. Springer.

Chapuis, C. and Charters, S. (2014), "The World of Wine," in S. Charters and J. Gallo (eds.), *Wine Business Management*, 13–23, Paris: Pearson France.

Faith, N. (1996), *The Winemakers of Bordeaux: The Inside Story of the World's Greatest Wines*, London: Prion Books.

Guy, K. M. (2002), *When Champagne Became French: Wine and the Making of a National Identity*, Baltimore: Johns Hopkins University Press.

Hira, A. and Swartz, T. (2014), "What Makes Napa Napa? The Roots of Success in the Wine Industry," *Wine Economics and Policy*, 3 (1): 37–53.

Kovesi, C. (2016), "The Aura of Luxury: Cultivating the Believing Faithful from the Age of Saints to the Age of Luxury Brands," *Luxury: History, Culture and Consumption*, 3 (1–2): 105–22.

Kramer, M. (2004), *New California Wine*, Philadelphia: Running Press.

Lawther, J. (2010), *The Finest Wines of Bordeaux*, Berkeley: University of California Press.

McNeil, P. and Riello, G. (2016), *Luxury: A Rich History*, Oxford: Oxford University Press.

Phillips, R. (2016), *French Wine: A History*, Berkeley: University of California Press.

Pinney, T. (1989), *The History of Wine in America: From the Beginnings to Prohibition*, Berkeley: University of California Press.

Sullivan, C. L. (2008), *Napa Wine: A History*, San Francisco: Wine Appreciation Guild.

Taber, G. (2005), *Judgment of Paris*, New York: Scribner.

Taplin, I. M. (2010), "From Cooperation to Competition: Market Transformation Among Elite Napa Valley Wine Producers," *International Journal of Wine Business Research*, 22 (1): 6–26.

Taplin, I. M. (2011), "Network Structure and Knowledge Transfer in Cluster Evolution: The Transformation of the Napa Valley Wine Region," *International Journal of Organizational Analysis*, 19 (2): 127–45.

Taplin, I. M. (2015), "Bottling Luxury: Napa Valley and the Transformation of an Agricultural Backwater into a World-Class Wine Region," in *Luxury: History, Culture, Consumption*, 2 (1): 97.

Taplin, I. M. (2016), "Crafting an Iconic Wine: The Rise of 'Cult' Napa," *International Journal of Wine Business Research*, 28 (2): 8.

Notes

Chapter 1

1 The super-rich are often referred to as High Net Worth Individuals (HNWIs). Capgemini (2017: 6) divides HNWIs into three wealth bands: "those with US$1 million to US$5 million in investable wealth (millionaires next door); those with US$5 million to US$30 million (mid-tier millionaires) and those with US$30 million or more (ultra-HNWIs)."

2 https://www.rolls-roycemotorcars.com/en-US/ghost-black-badge.html (accessed June 24, 2018).

Chapter 2

1 Heidegger, of course, sought to deepen his questioning of being through later attempts to account for space after the publication of *Being and Time* in essays such as "Building, Dwelling, Thinking" (Heidegger 1971), "The Origin of the Work of Art" (Heidegger 1978), and "Art and Space" (Heidegger 2009). However, in this chapter, first, because I am primarily concerned with Heidegger's conceptions of being, space, and time, and, second, because I am restricted by word length, I shall confine my remarks to those that relate to Heidegger's *Being and Time*.

2 I would like to thank Andrew Boyle at Rolls-Royce Motor Cars for discussing the Rolls-Royce Ghost Black Badge with me, for his insights into its clientele, and for giving me written permission to reproduce Rolls-Royce's press photographs of the Rolls-Royce Ghost Black Badge in this chapter. Rolls-Royce's own description of the Rolls-Royce Ghost Black Badge used in this chapter can be found at: https://www.sytner.co.uk/rolls-royce/new-cars/ghostblackbadge/ (accessed August 10, 2018).

Chapter 4

1 https://www.nycgo.com/boroughs-neighborhoods/brooklyn/gowanus (accessed May 25, 2018).

2 https://www.363bondstreet.com (accessed April 16, 2018).

3 https://www.363bondstreet.com (accessed April 16, 2018).

4 https://www.363bondstreet.com/art/ (accessed April 16, 2018).

5 https://www.flexform.it/en/mood-collection (accessed April 10, 2018).

Chapter 5

1 Luxury as experience—by the 1990s this was to become what David Howes describes as "hyperesthesia" or "the sensual logic of late capitalism," where traditional values of work and restraint have been replaced with those pertaining to self-fulfillment, impulse buying and experience (Howes 2005: 291).

2 According to David Frum, "In 1972 only 20% of women said that pre-marital sex was 'not wrong at all.' Almost twice as many men, 35%, did so" (2000: 191).

3 Obelkevich discusses the British distrust and dislike of central heating as a badge of immorality and wastefulness, and which did not reach most UK homes until 1977. Advertising campaigns promoted central heating with the slogan "You don't have to be selfish to be warm" (Obelkevich 1994: 147).

4 Morton Hunt's *Sexual Behavior in the 1970s* (1974) is a comprehensive survey of the sexual mores and preferences of Americans during the period. His findings indicate that although more men and women engaged in premarital sex and were able to discuss sex more openly, little had changed since earlier sex surveys, for example, the Kinsey Reports (1948, 1953).

Chapter 6

1 "Oscar Arrives," *Sacramento Record-Union*, March 27, 1882 cit. in Hofer and Scharnhorst (2010: 120).

2 "The Apostle of Art," *Chicago Inter-Ocean*, February 11, 1882, cit. in Hofer and Scharnhorst (2010: 111).

3 "Aesthetic: An Interesting Interview with Oscar Wilde," *Dayton Daily Democrat*, May 3, 1882, cit. in Hofer and Scharnhorst (2010: 142).

4 Balinese art was experienced as "expressionist" by the European artists such as Rudolf Bonnet and Walter Spies. Spies helped to craft the famous "kecak" dance (in which an all-male case chant) for Western consumption in the 1930s. For important thinking in this space, see Michel Picard on cultural tourism in Southeast Asia (Picard 1998); Picard and Robert E. Wood (1997); Adrian Vickers on syncretic modernism and the creation of a "Balinese" art in a country that had no word for "art" before Dutch contact (Vickers 1996); on the perils of reading within the space of the racialized and oriental "other," see Eng-Beng Lim (2013).

5 Muller planned to build a large hotel using local materials on a piece of land in Sanur in which Friend had an interest, but the venture failed.

6 John Boyd is a property developer. The penthouse was completed in 2015 as a part of a deal in constructing the office tower.

7 Observations made by sociologist Gianna Moscardo, James Cook University, at World Luxury Destination Conference, Bangkok, March 2018. Moscardo argues that all tourism is unsustainable, particularly in terms of water usage, food and beverage, and housekeeping, and that the design of luxury hotels in the developing world needs to be rethought using mindfulness among other strategies.

Chapter 7

1 The planning history available from Ealing Council underlines this correspondence in space standards. The development was originally designed and approved as student housing, and subsequently reapproved for co-living without any significant changes to floor layouts.

2 This report suggests annual growth in cafés and coffee shops in the UK of 6.3 percent from 2012 to 2017.

Chapter 8

1 A different version of this chapter appeared in the March 2018 issue of *Cultural Politics*.

2 Interestingly, this crafted vision based on a probing horizon or limit of what can be seen suggests an affinity for a skill and aesthetic of observation capacity that anthropologists involved with environmentalism have urged as a contemporary, intensive renewal of artful method in anthropology. I am thinking here of the recent writings of Tim Ingold (2011) and Anna Tsing (2015), the latter of whom, for example, eloquently argues for "noticing." Neither would likely advocate for this heightened capacity for observation/perception (the idealistic core of traditional anthropological field method) in the realm of a discourse about limit, horizon, or enclosure, as I am here, as the key to elite luxury of designed or landscaped emplacement, but I am struck by the similarity of the sensory aesthetic or capacity involved.

3 This importance of the emplaced subject is actually at the deep core of many classic bodies work in ethnography: I think immediately of the anthropological corpus on Australian aborigines, more specifically in recent times, of Steven Feld's studies among the Kaluli and Keith Basso's work among the Cibecue Apache (see Feld and Basso [1996] for a comprehensive statement and collection).

4   While the intent of my 1995 essay was to "normalize" eccentricity, or attribute to it critical insight and value, within elite families of wealth, I actually used the experience and situation of Howard Hughes as a case to explore, although he was and is a type example of extreme eccentricity and not in conditions of luxurious enclosure, in any conventional sense. Still as I read the details of his experience, for which there were then (in the early 1990s) excellent in-depth journalistic accounts, I thought his case demonstrated the arguments about mimetic transactions across the self-imposed horizons or boundings of enclosed worlds that Hughes negotiated for himself in his quarters in Las Vegas. In his weird existence within self-imposed emplacement, he continued to operate in an unseen world of agents, relations, and institutions. I suggested that the mode of communication might have been of the mimetic character that Taussig conceived out of Benjamin's influence and his close reading of ethnographic accounts of alterity and contact. In his own eccentric character, Hughes continued to act in the world through intermediaries, however those events and agents were mimetically represented in the enclosed world that he had defined for himself in luxuriant, minimalist, and obsessive eccentricity. Indeed, in the current storm of scandal regarding the American presidency, I was reminded what the break-in at the Democratic Party Headquarters at the Watergate Hotel, which eventually led to the impeachment of Richard Nixon in 1974, was all about. John Mitchell, Nixon's Attorney General ordered the burglary to find out if and how much the Democrats knew about the illegal $100,000 as a cash campaign contribution given to and accepted by Bebe Rebozo, Nixon's campaign manager, by Howard Hughes!—presumably from within his Las Vegas hermitage. It was later learned that Howard Hughes gave another cash contribution of the same amount and illegal as well to the Democratic campaign.

While Donald Trump's personal eccentricities are far from Howard Hughes's, an analysis of his experience of emplacement in growing up in luxury enclosures and further in creating a life within them and continuous with them (indeed, Trump's signature enterprises are all about building luxury enclosed environments—hotels, golf courses—for others, and always for himself as well) would probably explain a lot (but not explain away a lot!) about his behavioral characteristics subject to public scrutiny that seem odd, boorish, awkward, unsocialized. He is operating outside his usual enclosures, without its limits, horizons, and clearly he is uncomfortable in his skin. He has an untrained eye for the horizons he must live within or relation to now, when he cannot be at Mar a Lago or other Trump properties.

5   To adequately pursue the analysis of a future where current luxury immersion and enclosure would become a capacity of mass consumption, one would need the kind of scenarios of current science fiction writing that imagine a world where regimes of artificial intelligence and human intelligence operate in relation to one another, such as brilliantly conceived in the recent novel of Zachary Mason, *Void Star* (2017). In the meantime, there are many excellent analyses of the current and emerging states of immersive technologies as mass "leisure time" activity (see Lukas 2016).

Chapter 9

1 The super-rich are defined as those classified as High Net Worth Individuals. Capgemini (2017: 6) divides HNWIs into three wealth bands: "those with US$1 million to US$5 million in investable wealth (millionaires next door); those with US$5 million to US$30 million (mid-tier millionaires) and those with US$30 million or more (ultra-HNWIs)."

2 The terms "art" and "fine art" are used interchangeably in this chapter.

3 The information presented on Fine Art Logistics Natural Le Coultre derives from pages of the company's website: https://www.falnlc.lu/luxembourg/ and https://www.falnlc.lu/network/ (accessed July 27, 2018).

4 Despite the popularity of the Mei Moses Indices as measures of the growing value of art, they have been questioned by art market experts who point to weaknesses such as its lack of transparency and incomplete market coverage (Boucher 2016).

5 See https://www.falnlc.lu/network/ (accessed July 27, 2018).

Contributors

John Armitage is Professor of Media Arts at Winchester School of Art, University of Southampton, UK. He is co-director of the Winchester Luxury Research Group and a member of the editorial board of the academic journal *Luxury: History, Culture, Consumption*. He is the author of *Luxury and Visual Culture* (2019) and the co-editor, with Joanne Roberts, of *Critical Luxury Studies: Art, Design, Media* (2016) and *The Spirit of Luxury*, a special issue of the academic journal *Cultural Politics* (2016). His main research interests are in luxury culture and luxurious forms of consumption, luxury and visuality, luxury and art, photography, cinema, television, and social media. John's books and articles have been translated into Dutch, German, Korean, Mandarin, and Spanish.

Samuel Austin is Lecturer in Architecture at Newcastle University, UK, where he is Degree Programme Director of the BA in Architecture and Editor of *arq: Architectural Research Quarterly*. He completed his doctoral thesis *Travels in Lounge Space: Placing the Contemporary British Motorway Service Area* at Cardiff University in 2012. Past experience includes architectural practice at Mecanoo Architecten, Delft, and at the Design Research Unit, Wales.

Verena Andermatt Conley teaches in the Departments of Comparative Literature and Romance Languages and Literatures at Harvard University, USA. She has written on ecology (*Ecopolitics*, 1997) and ecology of space (*Spatial Ecologies*, 2012). She is currently working on the space of a garden in Algiers and on the care of the possible.

Mark Featherstone is Senior Lecturer in Sociology at Keele University, UK. He is the author of *Tocqueville's Virus: Utopia and Dystopia in Western Social and Political Theory* (2007), *Planet Utopia: Utopia, Dystopia, and the Global Imaginary* (2017), and a range of articles in journals including *Cultural Politics*, *Journal of Cultural Research*, and *Ctheory*.

George E. Marcus is Chancellor's Professor of Anthropology at the University of California, Irvine, and founding Director of the Center for Ethnography. His career has run along the dual tracks of the ethnographic study of traditional and comfortably established elites facing uncertain futures and of the critique and study of the ethnographic form of writing and research itself since the 1980s (e.g., he co-edited with James Clifford the volume *Writing Culture*, 1986). As an ethnographer of elites, he began with a study of the contemporary nobility on their landed estates in the Kingdom of Tonga, followed by research on dynastic fortunes and organizations in the United States (*Lives in Trust*, 1992), and then an interest in art worlds and collaborations between anthropologists and designers (*Ethnography by Design*, forthcoming).

Peter McNeil is Distinguished Professor of Design History at the University of Technology Sydney, Australia, and Academy of Finland Distinguished Professor at Aalto University. His many publications include the award-winning *The Fashion History Reader: Global Perspectives* (2010, with G. Riello), *Fashion: Critical and Primary Sources, Renaissance to the Present Day* (2009), and *Luxury: A Rich History* (2016, with G. Riello). McNeil was Investigator in the *Humanities in the European Research Area* project "Fashioning the Early Modern: Creativity and Innovation in Europe, 1500–1800." *Membre suppléant*, Comité International d'Histoire de l'Art (CIHA), he was Foundation Professor of Fashion Studies at Stockholm University 2008–17. He is a fellow of the Australian Academy of the Humanities and Section Head for "The Arts" therein. His monograph *"Pretty Gentlemen": Macaroni Men and the Eighteenth-Century Fashion World* was published in 2018.

Joanne Roberts is Professor in Arts and Cultural Management and Director of the Winchester Luxury Research Group at Winchester School of Art, University of Southampton, UK. Her research interests include knowledge, innovation, creativity, and luxury. Joanne has published articles in a wide range of international journals, including *Journal of Management Studies*, *Journal of Business Ethics*, and *Research Policy*. She has authored and edited a number of books. Her latest book, co-edited with John Armitage, is *Critical Luxury Studies: Art, Design, Media* (2016). She is also the co-editor, with John Armitage, of *The Spirit of Luxury*, a special issue of the journal *Cultural Politics* (2016). Joanne is a member of the editorial board of the journal *Luxury: History, Culture, Consumption*.

Adam Sharr is Professor of Architecture and Head of the School of Architecture, Planning and Landscape at Newcastle University, UK, Editor-in-Chief of *arq: Architectural Research Quarterly*, Series Editor of "Thinkers for Architects," and Principal of Adam Sharr Architects. His edited book *Reading Architecture and Culture* (2012) examines how architecture mirrors the values of the cultures and individuals which produce it.

Ian Malcolm Taplin is Professor of Sociology, Management, and International Studies at Wake Forest University, USA, and Visiting Professor at Kedge Business School, Bordeaux, France. His current research is in the area of wine with particular focus upon ultra-premium wineries in Napa Valley, California, and Bordeaux. He has also written about emerging wine regions in the United States, particularly North Carolina in his book *The Modern American Wine Industry: Market formation and Growth in North Carolina* (2011). He is currently writing a book on luxury goods that focuses upon fashion, art, and wine.

Jo Turney is an associate professor in fashion and design at Winchester School of Art, University of Southampton, UK. She is the author of *The Culture of Knitting* (2009) and *In Private: The Domestic Interior in the 1970s* (forthcoming) and contributing editor of *Fashion Crimes: Dressing for Deviance* (2018). She is also co-editor, with Alex Franklin, of the journal *Clothing Cultures* and is an editorial board member of *Textile: The Journal of Cloth and Culture*. Her research interests address inter-sectional contemporary fashion, dress, and textile practices, on which she has published widely.

Index

www.ingramcontent.com/pod-product-compliance
Lightning Source LLC
Chambersburg PA
CBHW050436280326
41932CB00013BA/2138